GROWING BONSAI
A PRACTICAL ENCYCLOPEDIA

GROWING BONSAI
A PRACTICAL ENCYCLOPEDIA

The complete guide to a classic art with essential techniques,
step-by-step projects and over 800 photographs

KEN NORMAN

PHOTOGRAPHY BY NEIL SUTHERLAND

LORENZ BOOKS

This book is dedicated to YOSHI,
a lifelong best friend

This edition is published by Lorenz Books

Lorenz Books is an imprint of Anness Publishing Ltd
Hermes House, 88–89 Blackfriars Road
London SE1 8HA
tel. 020 7401 2077; fax 020 7633 9499
www.lorenzbooks.com; www.annesspublishing.com

If you like the images in this book and would like to
investigate using them for publishing, promotions or
advertising, please visit our website
www.practicalpictures.com for more information.

© Anness Publishing Ltd 2005, 2006

UK agent: The Manning Partnership Ltd
6 The Old Dairy, Melcombe Road, Bath BA2 3LR
tel. 01225 478444; fax 01225 478440
sales@manning-partnership.co.uk

UK distributor: Grantham Book Services Ltd
Isaac Newton Way, Alma Park Industrial Estate
Grantham, Lincs NG31 9SD; tel. 01476 541080
fax 01476 541061; orders@gbs.tbs-ltd.co.uk

North American agent/distributor: National Book
Network, 4501 Forbes Boulevard, Suite 200
Lanham, MD 20706
tel. 301 459 3366; fax 301 429 5746
www.nbnbooks.com

Australian agent/distributor: Pan Macmillan
Australia, Level 18, St Martins Tower
31 Market St, Sydney, NSW 2000
tel. 1300 135 113; fax 1300 135 103
customer.service@macmillan.com.au

New Zealand agent/distributor: David Bateman Ltd
30 Tarndale Grove, Off Bush Road, Albany
Auckland; tel. (09) 415 7664; fax (09) 415 8892

Publisher **Joanna Lorenz**
Editorial Director **Judith Simons**
Executive Editor **Caroline Davison**
Designer **Lisa Tai**
Editorial Reader **Rosanna Fairhead**
Production **Wendy Lawson**

10 9 8 7 6 5 4 3 2 1

Page 1: *Rhododendron* 'Double Pink'
Page 2: Beech (*Fagus*)
Page 3, from left: Kumquat; Japanese maple (*Acer palmatum*); and European olive (*Olea europaea*)
Page 4, from top: Chinese juniper (*Juniperus chinensis*); European beech (*Fagus sylvatica*); Japanese maple (*Acer palmatum*); Sacred bamboo (*Nandina domestica*); *Acer palmatum* 'Kiyohime'
Page 5, from top: Group display; *Fagus crenata*; *Cotoneaster horizontalis*; *Cotoneaster* × *suecicus* 'Coral Beauty'

Contents

INTRODUCTION	6
What is Bonsai?	8
The History of Bonsai	10
Inspirational Trees	14
Suitable Trees and Shrubs	16
Bonsai Sizes	20
Bonsai Proportions and Aesthetics	22
Buying Bonsai	24
BONSAI GALLERY	26
BONSAI TECHNIQUES	52
Tools and Equipment	54
Collecting Plants from the Garden	58
Propagating from Seed	60
Propagating from Cuttings	62
Propagating by Grafting	64
Propagating by Air Layering	66
Soils for Bonsai	70
Pruning Techniques	72
Pinching Out and Defoliating	76
Shaping by Pruning	78
Shaping by Wiring	80
Creating Jin	82
Creating Sharimiki	84
Root Pruning and Repotting	86

BONSAI STYLES   90

Formal Upright   92
Informal Upright   94
Slanting   98
Semi-cascade   100
Cascade   102
Twin Trunk   104
Triple Trunk   106
Group or Forest   110
Windswept   114
Raft   116
Root-in-Rock Planting   120
Root-over-Rock Planting   122
Literati   126
Driftwood   128
Twisted Trunk   132
Exposed Root   134
Clump   136
Broom   140

INDOOR BONSAI   142

Aralia elegantissima   144
Crassula arborescens   146
Ficus benjamina 'Wiandii'   148
Myrtus communis   150
Sageretia theezans   152

DISPLAYING BONSAI   154

Pots and Containers   156
Display Stands   160
Slabs and Rocks   162
Accessories   164
Accent Planting   166
Suiseki   168
Indoor Displays   170
Outdoor Displays   176
Bonsai Shows   182

THE BONSAI YEAR   184

Spring   186
Summer   190
Autumn   194
Winter   198

BONSAI DIRECTORY   202

CARE AND MAINTENANCE   224

Environmental Conditions   226
Watering   228
Feeding   230
General Maintenance   232
Pests and Diseases   236
Calendar of Care   240

Glossary   244
Suppliers   248
Bonsai Collections   250
Organizations   251
Index   252
Plant Hardiness Zones   256
Acknowledgements   256

INTRODUCTION

To get started in the fascinating art of bonsai, you will need some gardening knowledge, some common sense, some practical ideas, a little bit of artistic feeling and the will to succeed. You may already grow container plants or trees that need some control of their growth combined with regular repotting, so you will probably, albeit unknowingly, have already mastered some of the basic techniques required for bonsai culture.

If you have purchased a ready-grown bonsai from a bonsai nursery, garden centre or supermarket, and experienced mixed success in keeping the tree healthy (or even looking like a tree), this book will give you the practical skills to achieve satisfactory results and improve your understanding of the art and culture of bonsai.

Left: *Cascade-style Chinese elm (*Ulmus parvifolia*) displayed on an elegant Chinese stand in a domestic situation.*

What is Bonsai?

The Japanese word "bonsai" basically means a plant, tree, or group of trees or plants growing in a container (from *bon* "basin" and *sai* "to plant"). Bonsai is all about growing miniature trees in the form of full-size mature trees, mostly using the same species and varieties from which the full-size trees are grown. Bonsai is a living art form that can provide hours, weeks, months or even a lifetime of studying and understanding trees. You can learn about bonsai from a number of different sources, whether from an experienced bonsai artist or consultant or from books such as this. It is a very good idea to combine various ways of learning about bonsai techniques, so that the wide range of traditional, as well as modern, ideas can contribute to your whole bonsai experience.

Above: Acer palmatum *'Ukon', styled into a beautiful twin-trunk bonsai and typical of a mature Japanese maple, but in miniature.*

SEARCHING FOR INSPIRATION

The detailed study of trees, whether they are full-size or miniature, can be very therapeutic and can lead to a thorough understanding of their growth patterns and potential. Indeed, a serious examination of the natural development and structure of full-size trees growing in the wild and in the garden can open up a new understanding of the design concepts that are used for the development of bonsai. As you progress in your bonsai career, this study can lead to an even greater enthusiasm for looking more closely at this most rewarding art form.

WHERE TO START

Many people often misunderstand bonsai, thinking that it just means growing a small plant, somewhere in the region of 25cm (10in) tall, or even smaller, in a bonsai pot. Bonsai can, in fact, be almost any size, ranging from as small as 2.5cm (1in) high to probably so large that it would need to be carried by two or more very strong people. There is a tendency to grow small- to medium-sized trees when you first begin to grow bonsai, but if this hobby develops into an all-consuming obsession, you will probably move on to growing larger and larger trees. There is a much greater scope to develop ideas when growing large trees, but it is very important not to become too ambitious too soon in the process. Instead, move forward slowly and in logical steps, proceeding with caution, so that you absorb all of the very varied techniques employed in bonsai culture. Taking time to become

Left: *Japanese maples* (Acer palmatum) *are some of the most popular plants from which bonsai specimens are created.*

TYPICAL BONSAI FEATURES

This is a typical bonsai, showing the key elements that make up a good specimen, including the spacing between branches and the basic branch structure.

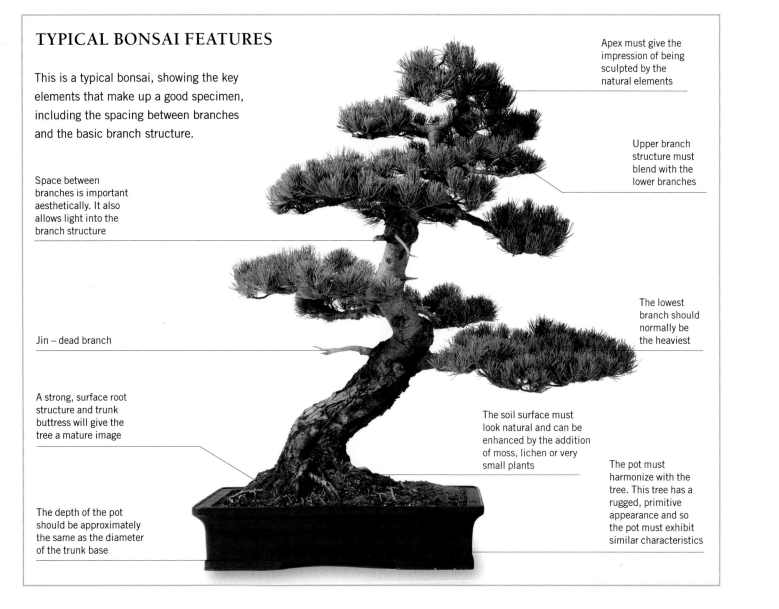

Apex must give the impression of being sculpted by the natural elements

Upper branch structure must blend with the lower branches

Space between branches is important aesthetically. It also allows light into the branch structure

The lowest branch should normally be the heaviest

Jin – dead branch

A strong, surface root structure and trunk buttress will give the tree a mature image

The soil surface must look natural and can be enhanced by the addition of moss, lichen or very small plants

The pot must harmonize with the tree. This tree has a rugged, primitive appearance and so the pot must exhibit similar characteristics

The depth of the pot should be approximately the same as the diameter of the trunk base

familiar with these techniques will mean that they will remain with you as reference for all your future projects.

The art of growing a bonsai comes from the ability to choose a tree, shrub or plant that has the potential of developing into a bonsai and then growing it on, employing mostly general horticultural techniques coupled with common sense and a touch of artistic expression. Many horticultural techniques are often refined for bonsai growing, so that the tree blends with its pot or container to give a feeling of being a mature tree, but in miniature form.

The actual tree is only one part of the complete picture that we are setting out to create, the others being the pot, the appearance of the soil surface and – most importantly of all – the shape and

style of the tree. The tree, container and the soil surface must all complement each other in terms of size, shape, colour and texture.

Acquiring a ready-grown bonsai is how most people enter the fascinating world of bonsai as a hobby, and for many it then develops into an obsession. There are many bonsai clubs or societies in existence worldwide, and becoming a member of such a group will enable you to achieve much more than you could by working alone. Established members of such societies will encourage any beginners to proceed in a balanced, methodical manner.

Right: *A 44-year-old Japanese larch (*Larix kaempferi*) grown from seed and measuring only 30cm (12in) in height.*

The History of Bonsai

Almost certainly, the very first examples of *penjing* (which is the Chinese version of bonsai) and bonsai were made from trees and plants that had been collected from the wild mountainous areas of China and Japan. Indigenous, naturally stunted trees were arranged and planted in ceramic pots and containers and kept in or around the collectors' homes, tended carefully and eventually regarded as natural works of art. These trees and plants would have been formed by nature's elements, often into contorted and extremely interesting shapes. Men would have risked their lives to collect very old, gnarled trees from high mountain areas, such as sheer rock faces, and other types of inhospitable terrain, in order to acquire the very best material for study and display.

Above: *Late 19th-century Japanese woodblock print of a* Chrysanthemum *bonsai in the twin-trunk style.*

EARLY ORIGINS

Penjing appears to cover a very wide range of different styles that includes rock plantings and tray landscapes. When literally translated, *penjing* means roughly the same as bonsai: that is, a plant which is grown in a container. This fascinating art form is believed to have originated in China some 1,500–2,000 years ago. In Japan, there are records of the cultivation of bonsai that go as far back as 1,200 years, many of which include simple descriptions and drawings of bonsai, leading up to more recent woodblock prints and screens. These show how Japanese interiors looked in the past and clearly feature bonsai plants.

During the Chin dynasty (221–206BC), China and Japan started to make social and spiritual contact with each other when Buddhism was introduced into both countries via Korea. It would appear that many of the Buddhist priests encouraged the ceremonial use of potted plants as a part of their religious rituals.

Just as with cars, cameras and computers (among many other technical products), the people of Japan seem to excel in recognizing the potential of an idea and then developing it into a serious piece of engineering. This precision and attention to detail also applies to art forms such as bonsai. They develop, improve and mass-produce the product until it is perfected. Bonsai may be regarded as one of these products, one which the Japanese have developed into a recognized art form.

Left: *A late 19th-century Japanese lacquer screen depicting a Japanese winter scene with Mount Fuji in the distance. The pine shown is typical of those used to influence bonsai styling.*

LATER DEVELOPMENTS

A very early piece of Japanese documentation is a scroll dating back to 1195. This is entitled the *Saigyo Momogatari Emaki*. A priest named Saigyo apparently used a potted plant as an important symbol of his status, and this scroll depicts an example of this type of plant. There are other early mentions of bonsai in Japan shown in the Kasuga Shrine records of the

Kamakura period (1192–1333) and in Heian period scrolls dating back to AD794–1191. These show scenes of household activities, including the displaying of potted plants and bonsai in and around the home. There are also drawings originating from the same time which give absolute evidence that bonsai were being created and cultivated throughout this period in Japan. This, of course, tells us that the

Above: *This is the central panel of an antique Japanese triptych woodblock print by Kunisada II which dates from the 1860s. The delightful print shows Prince Genji, probably in a teahouse. This panel of the triptych includes two women, with a bonsai specimen clearly displayed in a tokonoma behind them.*

art and culture of bonsai growing existed in Japan as far back as 1,300 years ago.

$\triangleright$

The popularity of bonsai increased in the late nineteenth century, and the introduction of much improved techniques enabled many growers to produce commercial quantities of these miniature trees. Bonsai arrived in London in 1901 via the Japan Society of London, and was mentioned in *Cassell's Encyclopedia of Gardening* as early as 1905.

Windsor Castle appeared to have a collection of bonsai in 1907, and the first bonsai went on exhibition in London in 1909. Bonsai were shown at exhibitions in several major cities, including Paris, and caused great excitement and interest wherever and whenever they were seen.

THE WORLD OF BONSAI TODAY

For more than 50 years, these exciting miniature trees have become very popular around the world, and it would be extremely difficult to find a country where there is no interest in the art and culture of bonsai.

This international interest has meant that there are now many bonsai societies operating locally, nationally and internationally. These societies work together to advance bonsai culture worldwide. Consequently, there are many excellent nurseries

that specialize in growing bonsai plants, as well as operating as wholesale and retail suppliers.

Most of the world's growers and suppliers operate in Japan, China and Korea, and many are still small, family-run businesses, sometimes working in small growing areas. These growers often specialize in single-species production and then only for part of the bonsai-growing process.

Some growers will start their plants from seed, while others prefer to produce plants from cuttings or by grafting. Some still collect plant material from any source that makes available suitable varieties for bonsai.

Above: *Original antique Japanese triptych woodblock print by the artist and printmaker 'Gekko' c.1897 depicting a Japanese plant nursery displaying 'Morning Glory' plants arranged on timber benches. On the left of the print there are two rock landscapes.*

Each bonsai grower handles one part of the production process and then sells their product on to another nursery for the next stage and so on, until the bonsai trees suitable for sale have been completed. These trees, which come in lots of different sizes, are then sold around the world as a wholesale product or to individual purchasers who may already have large collections.

Left: *This is an ivory Netsuke of a seated man tending a bonsai. These are very unusual but are historically important artifacts.*

Right: *Late 19th-century Japanese woodblock print of a* Chrysanthemum *bonsai in the cascade style.*

Inspirational Trees

Old trees develop some of the most beautiful shapes and forms that can be seen, both in the countryside and in mature and very old parks and gardens. Some of the most spectacular natural tree forms can be seen in rugged mountainous districts of the world, where they have been subjected to the ravages of time and weather. These old trees are looked upon in the bonsai world as inspirational trees, as it is through the study of these natural forms that the bonsai grower, designer and artist can produce bonsai of high quality. Every last detail of mature trees growing naturally is important because it is the study of these details that will make or break your progress into the real and sometimes compulsive world of bonsai. It should never be forgotten that all bonsai, however large or small, must resemble full-size natural trees.

Above: *Scots pine* (Pinus sylvestris) *collected from the wild and undergoing initial training as a literati-style bonsai.*

Most people do not notice trees in their natural habitat, but once you become interested in trees in general, or develop a more refined interest in trees such as bonsai, you will find that trees in their natural forms become noticeable. Mature trees of all species almost always grow into spectacular shapes, as can be seen upon closer inspection. Some species, such as pines, develop very gnarled trunks and thick, plate-like bark, while others retain very smooth bark growing into very elegant or gentle styles, whatever their size.

Very large, mature, full-size trees can often be seen to have hundreds of branches making up a very complex structure. When cultivating and developing a bonsai that is perhaps only one twentieth or even one fiftieth of the height of a full-size tree, it becomes clear that the smaller the tree, the fewer branches are needed (maybe only nine or ten) in order to impart the same impression of size but in a very

Above: *A Himalayan cedar* (Cedrus deodara). *The drooping branches are often emulated when growing similar species as bonsai.*

Above: Fagus sylvatica *'Laciniata' planted in 1955, here growing naturally in a style of bonsai known as broom. The tree is multi-branched from low down on the trunk, with a very fine, twiggy structure that radiates outwards from the trunk.*

Above: *Douglas fir (* Pseudotsuga menziesii*), giant redwood (* Sequoiadendron giganteum*) and a Japanese red cedar (*Cryptomeria japonica*), all inspirational for bonsai growers.*

much smaller form. Therefore, the intricate examination of full-size trees will play a very meaningful part in the bonsai learning process.

Bonsai, although produced by the human hand, must always look like mature trees. The species or variety is of little importance when the tree's structure is studied in terms of its artistic or aesthetic form. Mature trees can vary so much in shape and size that it is almost impossible to classify them into any sort of groupings, but this has been done in bonsai.

Right: *Old Scots pines (*Pinus sylvestris*), in a natural literati style. These trees are sparsely branched with a weathered canopy at the apex.*

Suitable Trees and Shrubs

Pine, juniper, larch and cedar are some of the most popular coniferous trees that are turned into bonsai, and there are, of course, many more species from which to choose. It should be remembered that larch is a deciduous conifer and will therefore lose its foliage (needles) in the winter. There is also a wide variety of deciduous trees to choose from, including maple, elm, beech, hawthorn, hornbeam, Judas tree, pomegranate, crab apple, wisteria and many more. The last three also bear flowers and fruit, and it should be noted that flowers and fruit produced will always be their natural size even when a tree is grown and trained as bonsai. Virtually any tree or shrub can be grown as a bonsai as long as it is able to produce suitably small foliage, flowers and fruit when it has undergone bonsai training and is mature.

Above: *Close-up of the trunk and buttress of a 55-year-old Japanese maple (Acer palmatum) showing the excellent roots and trunk flare.*

When deciding which type of plant material to use to grow and develop into a bonsai, a visit to a good garden centre or plant nursery will probably be the best place to start. Any establishment of this type should stock a wide variety of suitable species and varieties suitable for both beginners and more experienced growers. (To help you, a detailed list of the large range of plants available is provided in the plant directory section on pp.202–223.)

If you are not sure what type of tree to choose or how to differentiate between certain specimens, follow the golden rule of looking for a plant that exhibits a woody trunk structure with a reasonably chunky appearance. This will give you a head start when shaping your tree, as you will have something with a semi-mature appearance right from the start.

If you want a flowering bonsai, some of the most spectacular examples can be grown using rhododendrons and azaleas, of which there is a wide variety available.

INDOORS OR OUTDOORS?

Whether these subsequently become known as indoor or outdoor plants depends on the area of the world in which they are going to be grown. If, for instance, you wish to grow a tropical species as a bonsai in a temperate climate, you will need to keep it indoors for at least part of the year. Similarly, trees from temperate regions may need to be kept indoors if grown in a tropical or sub-tropical area.

Left: *A typical small needle juniper (Juniperus rigida) which is available from many bonsai nurseries and normally imported from Japan.*

PLANTS SUITABLE FOR OUTDOOR BONSAI

You can use a range of different plants for developing into beautiful bonsai specimens. The ones pictured below are just a selection of trees that you might already have growing in your garden. These can be collected and then trained into a wealth of different bonsai styles.

Cryptomeria japonica

Cotoneaster

Juniperus chinensis

Juniperus davurica

Juniperus procumbens

Juniperus squamata

the most popular are the many varieties of *Ficus* or fig, the most common of these being *F. benjamina* and *F. microphylla*. Other species frequently used are *Crassula arborescens, Nandina domestica, Serissa foetida, Punica granatum*, as well as *Sageretia theezans, Aralia elegantissima, Myrtus communis*, fuchsias, gardenias and many more. Trees grown indoors may need more frequent checking of the climatic conditions. Make sure the soil is always kept moist. Spray the foliage regularly to maintain a fairly high humidity and keep the leaves healthy.

Whether you are growing or buying plants for indoor or outdoor bonsai, they must always be healthy, and insect- and disease-free. By achieving this, you will give your bonsai a good start and it will be much easier to work with during repotting, root pruning, shaping and general maintainance.

When purchasing from nurseries or garden centres, always check for any sort of problem and reject plants if you find anything that looks suspicious in terms of leaf problems, such as spots, holes or infestations by insects, or root problems such as being too wet or generally loose in the pot.

This book generally deals with trees that are hardy when kept outdoors in a temperate climate. In any event, bonsai should not be subjected to deep-freezing – below -4°C (25°F) – which is why in cold winter regions they need the protection of a cold greenhouse or frame. When trees are referred to as indoor trees in this book, it means that they must be kept in a more controlled environment, such as in a house or greenhouse. These so-called indoor trees usually need extra warmth and humidity to maintain a healthy growth pattern. They may also be kept outside during the summer when, and if, the climate comes close

to the original conditions in which the plant would be grown. Suitable material for indoor bonsai can be bought at almost any garden centre or supermarket. Tropical or sub-tropical plants that are used as houseplants can often be turned into bonsai. These plants are normally those that have a wealth of green leaves as their dominant feature, but you should always check the trunk to consider whether it would look good when transformed into a tree-like form. You will have to use your imagination to decide if your choice will be suitable as a bonsai. Species used for indoor bonsai vary considerably, and some of

BONSAI SUITABLE FOR GROWING INDOORS

Bird plum cherry (*Sageretia theezans*)
Bougainvillea
Dwarf myrtle (*Myrtus communis*)
Finger aralia (*Aralia elegantissima*)
Fuchsia
Indian laurel (*Ficus microcarpa*)
Money tree (*Crassula arborescens*)
Pomegranate (*Punica granatum*)
Sacred bamboo (*Nandina domestica*)
Tree of a thousand stars (*Serissa foetida*)
Weeping fig (*Ficus benjamina*)

PLANTS SUITABLE FOR INDOOR BONSAI

There is a wealth of exciting plants that can be grown and kept indoors. Those shown here are some of the most popular plants from the list on page 18. Any of them will make a decorative feature in the home, but it is important to ensure that the environmental conditions in the room in which you keep your bonsai are correct for each plant.

Ficus benjamina 'Wiandii'

Aralia elegantissima

Crassula arborescens

Myrtus communis

Sageretia theezans

Bonsai Sizes

A bonsai can be virtually any size as long as it is a potted plant that takes on the appearance of a full-size, mature specimen tree as would be seen growing anywhere in the wild or in a parkland situation. Basically, if it can be carried it could probably be referred to as a bonsai even if it takes several people to actually do the carrying. At all times the pot and tree should complement each other, so much so that whatever their size they always take on an air of extreme maturity and elegance. It could be said that the smaller the bonsai the easier it is to look after; however it is most likely to be the opposite because very small trees are in reality quite difficult to style and maintain. This is because there is so little material in a small plant with which to work.

Sizes of bonsai can range in height from no more than 2.5cm (1in) up to about 1.2m (4ft), although in reality there is no prescribed limit. They are generally classified under three categories, but in some cases there could be seen to be four, which is how they are described here.

Below: *Three bonsai, from left to right:* Mame *elm,* shohin *juniper and* chumono *hornbeam. The three different sizes are clearly shown here.*

The very smallest size is known as *mame* (pronounced "ma-mey"). These tiny trees, which can vary in size from just a few centimetres up to about 15cm (6in) in height, create a fascinating image but are not easy to shape and care for because of their small size. Obtaining true tree-like images at this size can be very difficult, but a compensatory factor is that their diminutive size makes them easy to move around.

Above: Mame *English elm (*Ulmus procera*), only 15cm (6in) high, with a very mature trunk and branch structure.*

The next size is now commonly known as *shohin* (pronounced "sho-hin"), and can be 15–30cm (6–12in) high. Being larger than *mame* means that more detail can be incorporated into the design, and so a more tree-like form can be achieved. Once again this size of bonsai can be easily moved

about. This can prove especially useful if you are intending to move your display or exhibit it at bonsai shows.

From about 30cm (12in) upwards in size to about 1m (40in) the trees are known as *chumono* bonsai. These can generally be carried by most people unaided. Some, especially those that include a piece of rock, may need to be carried by two people. These larger trees are relatively easy to look after, as the watering situation may not be so critical as for *mame* or *shohin* trees, whose smaller pots mean that they require more frequent watering.

The final grouping includes trees up to 1.5m (5ft) or more. Although trained as bonsai, these are normally displayed as patio plants in much larger pots to suit the size of the tree. Once in place, they are moved only very occasionally.

Trees that are trained in the same way as bonsai but grown in the ground are not generally classified as bonsai.

Above: *A medium-sized, clump-style bonsai Japanese maple (Acer palmatum), showing good balance between the pot, root structure, trunks and canopy.*

Left: *An excellent example of two extremes of bonsai size, showing how maturity can be achieved from as little as 15cm (6in) to 90cm (36in) tall.*

Bonsai Proportions and Aesthetics

The words "proportions" and "aesthetics" are probably two of the most important words to bear in mind when growing, designing and styling plants into bonsai. The relationship between the overall height, width and depth of a bonsai is extremely important just as the relationship between the density of foliage and thickness and taper of the trunk must be complementary. The thickness of the base of the trunk compared with the size and shape of the pot is equally crucial, and when all these elements are combined and related to each other a truly magnificent bonsai can be the result. Features such as the position of the first branch and whether it is on the left or right of the trunk can make or break the final appearance of your bonsai, so careful consideration of all these aspects is of the utmost importance.

Above: *Acer palmatum 'Deshojo' buttress, showing the excellent trunk flair and surface root structure.*

Traditionally, bonsai are usually seen as beautiful, graceful and pleasing-to-the-eye artistic creations, but some examples can appear to be rather contorted or artificial for some people's tastes. It must be appreciated that bonsai could just be considered to be an illusion of grandeur, because nowadays these trees are almost totally human-controlled creations throughout the entire production process. It should be understood right from the beginning that there is no real finished product with a bonsai. Bonsai are, of course, living works of art, and by their very nature they do not stand still, but are always evolving and need to be cared for correctly for their entire lifespan. If these important points are not fully understood and observed, then any bonsai can lose its shape completely within a very short period of time.

Throughout the process of growing a bonsai, there are some rules about design and aesthetics that should be constantly borne in mind. These very basic rules, which relate to the relationship between the trunk structure and branch positioning, are for guidance only and can be varied to suit each individual tree. This flexible approach will ensure that the best design for that particular specimen can be achieved.

Above: *Buttress of a Japanese white pine bonsai showing the surface root structure, taper and angle of the lower trunk.*

Above: *Detail of a European larch bonsai showing superb bark texture and a dead branch stub known in bonsai terms as a "jin".*

Above: *This is the same tree as the one on the left, but showing a larger part of the trunk with three jins and how they are spaced.*

Above: *This is a Japanese black pine (*Pinus thunbergii*) showing the early stages of styling into a slanting bonsai and the basic branch* *structure in relation to the trunk. The young bonsai specimen has also been wired to shape the basic branch structure.*

KEY FEATURES OF BONSAI

- The height of the first branch up from the base of the trunk should be approximately one-third of the total height of the tree.

- The width of the trunk should be roughly the same as the depth of the chosen pot or container.

- The overall shape of the branch structure should generally be an irregular triangle, with all three sides of different lengths and the bottom side being slightly off the horizontal.

- Branches should alternate in their position going up the trunk, with the first being on the left or right, the second on the opposite side to the first and the third at the back of the tree. This layout should be followed right up to the top of the tree, so that when viewed from the top, the branches radiate out in a regular pattern. At no time should two branches be immediately above or covering each other.

Above: *Trunk and buttress detail of an* Acer palmatum *'Deshojo', showing the relationship between the trunk and the main branches.*

Above: *Trunk and buttress detail of a* Chamaecyparis pisifera *bonsai. The trunk and root structure is very realistic.*

Above: *Buttress detail of a European larch (*Larix decidua*). This clearly shows the strong tree roots as they enter the soil.*

Buying Bonsai

Bonsai can be very expensive, as it can take many years of dedicated work to produce a good-quality tree, but you need not spend vast sums of money to acquire your first tree. Realistically, you could be throwing money down the drain if you buy a very expensive tree before you have the knowledge to look after it, so it is always better to begin with an inexpensive tree from which you can learn as you go along. Begin with something that is relatively easy to look after, such as Japanese maple for outdoor use or a Chinese elm for indoors. Acquire some plants specifically for use as learning material on which you can practise pruning, wiring and repotting techniques, and remember that you will have failures in the early days. Do not be too hasty to desert a project, as plant development can be slower than expected.

Above: *A crab apple (*Malus cerasifera*) bonsai entered by a member in the Bonsai Kai Members' Competition at an RHS flower show.*

A so-called "finished bonsai" can easily be purchased from a garden centre, nursery or supermarket, but if you are looking for a better-quality first tree, you should visit a good bonsai nursery or shop. Here, you should be able to obtain expert advice on the type and size of tree that would be most suitable for your particular situation, as well as guidance on care.

The first thing to check is that the store or nursery looks good, is clean and tidy, and has good, healthy plants for sale. If you are buying from a bonsai centre, be sure to ask as many questions about the trees as possible, as bonsai growers are always pleased to share their extensive knowledge with you, whereas if you go to a garden centre or supermarket there is usually no advice available at all.

The tree that you buy should be firm in its pot. If it is not, then it has either been recently repotted or has very little root system, and it should be left alone. Check the soil to see that it is a good, open, free-draining mix and is not waterlogged. If the tree has wire on its trunk or branches, check that it is not cutting into the bark. If it is, this shows that the wire has been left on the tree for too long.

Thoroughly check the condition of your intended purchase, as it could be too late once you have taken it home.

Left: *Typical display benches at a bonsai retail outlet, showing a wide range of bonsai of various sizes, styles, species and varieties.*

Above: *A varied collection of both indoor and outdoor bonsai shown in an indoor environment. The outdoor varieties can only be kept inside for about one day.*

Right: *An exhibit of bonsai/penjing landscapes at an RHS Spring Show in London, showing a variety of styles and designs.*

EASY BONSAI PLANTS

Beech *(Fagus)*
Chinese elm *(Ulmus parvifolia)*
Cotoneaster
Fig *(Ficus)*
Japanese maple *(Acer palmatum)*
Juniper *(Juniperus)*
Larch *(Larix)*

BONSAI GALLERY

Bonsai are seen at their best only when displayed correctly, which is normally against a plain background, usually white, off-white, or any similar natural shade. In this section, a slightly different approach has been taken, which incorporates a variety of different background colours and textures. A range of different types of stand, including various styles and textures of matting, have also been incorporated to give as wide a range of appearances as possible. Each illustration has its own caption, which includes the botanical and common name, style, size and approximate age of each tree as well as the type of pot and its maker. Also included is a short biography of each tree from its origin, through its known or possible history and a final description as it is seen in this chapter.

Left: *A very old – approximately 145 years – Japanese white pine (*Pinus parviflora*), with a well-balanced and refined branch structure.*

INFORMAL UPRIGHT

Chamaecyparis pisifera
Sawara cypress

◁ Imported from Japan in 1990, this bonsai has been refined since then using some minor wiring and shoot pinching. The original pot was replaced by the one shown in 1998.

Height 62cm (25in)

Pot English (Derek Aspinall)

Approximate age 90 years

INFORMAL UPRIGHT

Fagus sylvatica
Common or European beech

◁ This plant, shown here with summer foliage, was collected as a very small seedling, approximately 53 years ago, and grown as a bonsai by the collector for 50 years before being handed on to Ann and Ken Norman.

Height 70cm (28in)

Pot English (Joey Connolly)

Approximate age 55 years

TWIN TRUNK

Acer palmatum 'Ukon'
Japanese maple

▷ This bonsai was imported from Japan in 1990 and the original pot replaced by a more suitable design in 1997.

Height 83cm (33in)

Pot English (Denis O'Neil)

Approximate age 45 years

INFORMAL UPRIGHT

Pinus sylvestris
Scots pine

▷ The Scots pine is common throughout Europe. This particular example was collected from the wild in England in 1988. It was reduced in height by two-thirds, with the section above the two lowest branches resulting from a repositioned small side branch.

Height 68cm (27in)
Pot English (Gordon Duffett)
Approximate age 65 years

INFORMAL UPRIGHT

Ulmus procera
English elm

◁ Collected from beside a footpath as a sucker, this is now a very beautiful, small bonsai tree.

Height 16cm (6¼in)
Pot Japanese
Approximate age 20 years

CLUMP

Acer palmatum
Japanese maple

▷ This bonsai was imported from Japan in 1990, and the diameter of the trunk base of the tree has almost doubled since that date. It was possibly started as shown in the clump section or as a multiple grafted trunk.

Height 80cm (32in)
Pot English (Bryan Albright)
Approximate age 55 years

INFORMAL UPRIGHT

Acer palmatum 'Nomura'
Japanese maple

◁ Purchased from a Japanese supplier in 1987 and transferred into its current pot in 1997, this is a very difficult tree to maintain because of its large leaves and long internodal growth.
Height 65cm (26in)
Pot English (Gordon Duffett)
Approximate age 50 years

DRIFTWOOD

Larix kaempferi
Japanese larch

▷ The living part of this tree which is attached to the rear of the driftwood gives a realistic impression of a very old, naturally formed tree.
Height 52cm (21in)
Pot English slate
Approximate age 25 years

FORMAL UPRIGHT

Fagus crenata
Japanese beech

▷ This tree was imported from Japan and has developed well as a result of constant pinching out of shoots during late spring and early summer. Bronze autumn leaves remain in place throughout the winter.
Height 83cm (33in)
Pot Japanese
Approximate age 40 years

SAIKEI

Nandina domestica
Sacred or Heavenly bamboo

◁ This is a simple design made up of a relatively young specimen planted into a piece of Japanese *ibigawa* rock with a planting hollow. The rock is volcanic, is very hard and has interesting textures.

Height 45cm (18in)
Pot Japanese *ibigawa* rock
Approximate age 6 years

ROCK LANDSCAPE

Ulmus parvifolia
Chinese elm

▷ This rock formation is constructed of several small pieces of rock that are cemented to the pot for stability. The elm is planted artistically within the rock arrangement.

Height 45cm (18in)
Pot Chinese crackle glaze
Approximate age 20 years

ROOT-ON-ROCK

Picea mariana 'Nana'
Black spruce

△ The two spruce trees are attached with copper wire to shallow hollows on the sides of this very heavy piece of quartz.

Height 33cm (13in)
Pot Japanese
Approximate age 32 years

INFORMAL UPRIGHT

Pinus parviflora
Japanese white pine

◁ This tree originally had a second heavy low branch opposite the lowest right-hand branch. It has been removed and "jinned" to give a better balance to the tree. Compare this with the image of the same tree taken in 1995, on page 9.

Height 75cm (30in)

Pot English (Derek Aspinall)

Approximate age 80 years

ROOT-OVER-ROCK

Acer palmatum 'Deshojo'
Japanese maple

◁ This is an unusual composition using a Japanese maple whose roots have been trained over an interesting piece of Japanese volcanic rock.

Height 58cm (23in)

Pot English (Derek Aspinall)

Approximate age 39 years

SLANTING

Rhododendron obtusum
'Amoenum'
Kirishima azalea
◁ Collected as a very large garden
plant in 1992 when it was
approximately 62 years old, this plant
was transformed into a very beautiful
bonsai in only 13 years.
Height 85cm (34in)
Pot English (Derek Aspinall)
Approximate age 75 years

GROUP OR FOREST

Cryptomeria japonica
Japanese red cedar

△ These trees were imported in 1989
and arranged as a group at the FOBBS
National Bonsai Convention hosted
by the Sussex Bonsai group.

Height 50cm (20in)
Pot English (Petra Engelke-Tomlinson)
Approximate age 20–35 years

GROUP OR FOREST

Carpinus laxiflora
Japanese hornbeam
◁ Many trees with slim trunks planted close together can make a very lifelike natural forest. It is realistic to have a suggestion of a footpath running roughly through the centre of the group.
Height 80cm (32in)
Pot English (Derek Aspinall)
Approximate age 31 years

INFORMAL UPRIGHT

Acer palmatum
Japanese maple
▷ An interesting surface root structure gives this tree a very powerful appearance. The pot glaze is designed to blend with the shape of the roots.
Height 70cm (28in)
Pot English (Bryan Albright)
Approximate age 55 years

INFORMAL UPRIGHT

Pinus thunbergii
Japanese black pine
◁ The relatively heavy nature of this pot and the squat appearance of the tree beautifully complement the powerful root structure.
Height 33cm (13in)
Pot Japanese
Approximate age 33 years

CLUMP

Acer palmatum 'Kiyohime'
Japanese maple

△ The trunk base has trebled in diameter and the branch structure improved beyond recognition over the past 25 years.

Height 40cm (16in)
Pot English (Derek Aspinall)
Approximate age 46 years

BROOM

Zelkova serrata
Japanese grey bark elm
▷ A very good example of the broom style, showing that a simple, shallow pot is ideal for this style of bonsai.
Height 52cm (21in)
Pot English (Yew Tree Potters)
Approximate age 45 years

ROOT-OVER-ROCK

Acer buergerianum
Three-lobed or Trident maple
◁ In this composition, the rock blends beautifully with the container, but the appearance of the roots could be improved using grafting techniques.
Height 68cm (27in)
Pot English (Gordon Duffett)
Approximate age 36 years

INFORMAL UPRIGHT

Pinus parviflora
Japanese white pine
◁ This is a very interesting, well-balanced bonsai that has a very refined branch structure and a subtle jin about half way up the trunk.
Height 95cm (38in)
Pot Japanese
Approximate age 145 years

INFORMAL UPRIGHT

Acer buergerianum
Three-lobed or Trident maple
◁ A thick, heavy trunk with well-defined branches gives this bonsai a very mature feeling. It would be advisable to defoliate this specimen in late spring.
Height 68cm (27in)
Pot Japanese
Approximate age 36 years

INFORMAL UPRIGHT

Rhododendron indicum 'Komei'
Satsuki azalea
▷ A beautiful Satsuki azalea which was imported from Japan. It produces multi-coloured, deep pink through to white flowers in the spring.
Height 90cm (36in)
Pot Japanese
Approximate age 40 years

GROUP OR FOREST

Zelkova serrata
Japanese grey bark elm
◁ This picture was taken in the autumn of 1992, six months after the group was first constructed using seven trees. The overall length of the display was then 80cm (32in).
Height 65cm (26in)
Pot English (by Ken Potter)
Approximate age 32 years

BROOM

Olea europaea
European olive
◁ A very young, small bonsai that is within easy reach of most beginners to the art form. Styled from a plant which is freely available from most plant centres, this tree will produce delicate creamy white flowers, followed by green fruits that will eventually become black olives.
Height 30cm (12in)
Pot Japanese
Approximate age 8 years

INFORMAL UPRIGHT

Acer buergerianum
Trident maple

▷ This tree has a massive trunk that initially was quite uninteresting. It is now undergoing a transformation by hollowing out parts of the trunk to give the tree more character and a more aged appearance.

Height 68cm (27in)

Pot English (Gordon Duffett)

Approximate age 45 years

INFORMAL UPRIGHT

Rhododendron indicum 'Komei'
Satsuki azalea

▷ A beautiful Satsuki azalea which was imported from Japan. In the spring, this azalea produces multi-coloured, deep pink through to white flowers.

Height 90cm (36in)

Pot Japanese

Approximate age 40 years

CLUMP

Acer palmatum
Japanese maple

▷ An unusual Japanese maple, styled into a clump, with a well-defined branch structure and foliage which turns rich red in the autumn.

Height 58cm (23in)

Pot English (Bryan Albright)

Approximate age 35 years

INFORMAL UPRIGHT

Malus cerasifera
Nagasaki crab apple

◁ This small, well-proportioned bonsai crab apple has small flowers and very small, cherry-like red fruits in the autumn.

Height 35cm (14in)

Pot Japanese

Approximate age 20 years

ROOT-OVER-ROCK

Acer buergerianum
Three-lobed or Trident maple

▷ This is a superb example of a style of bonsai that has very mature roots clinging tightly to a very interestingly shaped piece of rock.

Height 68cm (27in)

Pot Japanese

Approximate age 36 years

INFORMAL UPRIGHT

Acer palmatum 'Deshojo'
Japanese maple

△ The brilliant carmine-red spring foliage of this maple fades to red/green in the summer and changes to brilliant deep red in the autumn.

Height 70cm (28in)
Pot English (Derek Aspinall)
Approximate age 50 years

BROOM

Acer palmatum
Japanese maple

▷ This is an interesting broom-style Japanese maple with an unusual buttress formation that is sometimes seen in plants that were originally grown in pots.

Height 47cm (19in)

Pot Japanese

Approximate age 55 years

GROUP OR FOREST: 23 TREES

Zelkova serrata
Japanese grey bark elm

▽ The very mature trees in this group vary considerably in height, but work well together on this very well-proportioned two-piece slab.

Height 70cm (28in)

Pot English (Brian Albright)

Approximate age 25–45 years

INFORMAL UPRIGHT

Acer palmatum 'Deshojo'
Japanese maple

▷ The good buttress and structure of this bonsai blend perfectly with the well-chosen pot. The proportions of the height relative to the width, as well as the branch placement, pot size, colour and shape, work very well.

Height 80cm (32in)

Pot English (Derek Aspinall)

Approximate age 55 years

INFORMAL UPRIGHT

Larix kaempferi
Japanese larch

▽ This is an example of a small tree, grown from seed, and painstakingly developed into an excellent small bonsai that exudes great maturity.

Height 30cm (12in)

Pot English (Bryan Albright)

Approximate age 44 years

SEMI-CASCADE

Ulmus parvifolia
Chinese elm

▷ This is an interesting variation of the cascade style planted in a Chinese pot and displayed on a tall stand that was imported from Taiwan. This tree has good aerial roots that lead into a very rugged, thick trunk that gently curves down and away from the pot. The branches are well arranged and terminate in densely foliated pads that require close shoot pinching throughout the growing season from spring to late summer.

Height 40cm (16in)
Pot Chinese
Approximate age 25 years

LITERATI

Larix decidua
European larch

◁ Grown from seed that was sown 28 years ago, this tree spent 12 years growing in the ground to develop its excellent trunk formation before being lifted and trained into a bonsai. It was initially envisaged as a formal upright but when it was discovered that the trunk was not straight, some of the lower branches were removed and turned into jins that clearly give the tree a lot more character.

Height 60cm (24in)
Pot English (Susan Threadgold)
Approximate age 28 years

BONSAI TECHNIQUES

There is a range of techniques that are essential for the successful development of any plant into a bonsai. These techniques include work at the very beginning when the plant is propagated right through to the final minute details that are required to achieve a mature, but miniature, representation of a full-size tree. Along the way, you will need a variety of tools and pieces of equipment that will enable you to achieve a satisfying result. Everyday tools, such as scissors and chopsticks, will be very useful and inexpensive parts of your toolkit, but, inevitably, you will want to acquire some better-quality tools as your experience grows. Under no circumstances should you try to reach your goal too quickly as the result may not be as good as you would expect. Take your time and plan your work very carefully before you embark on complex procedures. Stick to the simple methods and techniques first and slowly graduate to more complicated designs.

Left: *Several bonsai techniques, such as tight shoot and branch pruning, as well as trunk carving and hollowing, have been applied to this trident maple* (Acer buergerianum).

Tools and Equipment

There is a wide range of specialist bonsai tools designed for specific purposes when pruning bonsai, but a few very basic gardening tools will suffice at the beginning of your bonsai career. These tools, which will enable most pruning jobs to be carried out with minimum expense, are a pair of scissors and secateurs (pruners). As you become more experienced, however, you will find that specialist Japanese tools will start to appeal to you more. Given the ability and experience, it is possible to make some tools inexpensively or even purchase general everyday tools that will suffice for the beginner. However you begin, you may well find it useful to keep your bonsai tools separate from any other gardening tools, as well as keeping them in a special tool container.

Above: *This shows the correct use of branch or side cutters, with the cutting edges held horizontally to the trunk.*

TOOLS FOR PRUNING

For small-scale pruning, involving trimming shoots and leaves, the most useful tool is a pair of pointed scissors. Normal secateurs can be used for pruning branches, but they will leave a short stub. This will not only appear unsightly, but will also leave a wound that may never heal correctly. To carry out a much better, cleaner job, therefore, you should purchase some bonsai side or branch cutters. Using these cutters will enable you to make a clean concave cut close to the trunk, which results in a more rapid healing of the wound and so gives a much cleaner appearance to the tree. These cutters have a single curve to the cutting edges.

Possibly the next most useful tool to buy for your collection is a pair of "wen" or "knob cutters". These are mostly used to remove a branch or a branch stub close to the trunk. They have concave cutting edges in both directions, resulting in a small concave hollow that will heal much more quickly. By leaving such a hollow, you will help the callusing bark to "roll" into the hollow and leave only a slight trace of the pruning cut.

TOOLS FOR WIRING

Wiring is an important part of the shaping process and requires different tools for the job. The wiring process is dealt with in detail later on, but the tools and equipment required are described here. The three main items normally used during the process of wiring a bonsai are wire cutters, pliers and the wire itself.

Wire cutters are available in several sizes, normally small, medium and large, but they can be very expensive if you buy the genuine Japanese article. You can, however, execute just as good a job with a standard pair of electrician's wire cutters, which can be purchased at a much lower price. The Japanese wire cutters are superior

Left: *Wire can be used to shape your bonsai as well as pruning. Here, the wire is being placed in a trunk and branch junction.*

Right: *You can prune the roots of your bonsai plants with vine pruners or with ordinary household scissors.*

Above: *You will need to use wiring techniques when styling some bonsai plants. If this is the case, it can be easier to have a special dispenser containing wires of different gauges.*

Above: *When potting up or repotting your bonsai, you will need a good-quality container, as well as a suitable soil for the bonsai. Here, akadama is being used.*

because they have longer handles in proportion to the cutting blades, which makes the process of cutting through thicker wires much easier than with the electrician's version. They also enable you to cut the wire close to the trunk or branch of the tree without damaging the bark.

A good pair of pliers can also be a very useful part of the wiring toolkit. Normally these would be the Japanese variety, called jinning pliers, which double up here for holding and bending thicker gauges of wire. These specialist pliers are normally used for the forming of jin (areas of removed bark, revealing heartwood below), but they can also be a very valuable asset as a general-purpose bonsai item to add to your bonsai toolkit. Jinning pliers may also be needed for repotting, as is shown in more detail later on. Once again, a more economical alternative to the Japanese pliers would be a standard pair of engineer's pliers.

Traditionally, annealed copper wire, which needs to be heated to soften (or anneal) each time it is reused, can be used in the styling process. The special appeal of copper is that it oxidizes quickly and soon blends with the bark of a tree to become inconspicuous. In recent years, however, anodized aluminium wire has become more popular because it is easy to use and can be reused without being heated. Nowadays, only more experienced growers use copper.

The wire is available in many gauges, from 1mm (1/25in) up to 6mm (1/4in) in diameter, and in rolls weighing 500g–1kg (1lb 4oz–2lb 4oz). The gauge of wire used must be thick enough to enable the branch or trunk to be held in place after it has been bent into shape. If you use a wire that is too thin to do the job properly, you will simply have to replace it.

SPECIALIST TOOLS

Other special tools are available and you will doubtless add them to your collection as you gain experience. Make sure you keep your tools sharp for good cuts and also clean, so that the chances of introducing disease into a wound are kept to a minimum. You can also purchase a specialist turntable on which you can place your bonsai while you work.

Right: *You may find it easier to work on a specialist turntable when styling and caring for your bonsai.*

RANGE OF TOOLS

A large variety of specialist equipment is available for bonsai, but, just a few basic tools are all that is required to get started. You will find that all you need to begin are a large and small pair of scissors, secateurs (pruners), wire cutters, old chopsticks and an old household fork. These tools will do most jobs, but, as you gain experience, you will need to buy some specialist Japanese tools. These will make a much better job of all the tasks that need to be performed when training and styling a bonsai. You will probably invest in these tools over a period of time. The essential ones include a sharp pair of pointed scissors and a pair of heavy-duty scissors for pruning roots. Branch cutters and knob cutters may well be your next purchase. The other tools shown here are useful, but not essential to begin with. Tools should be sharp for making clean cuts, and free of dirt, so that the possibility of introducing disease into pruning cuts is reduced.

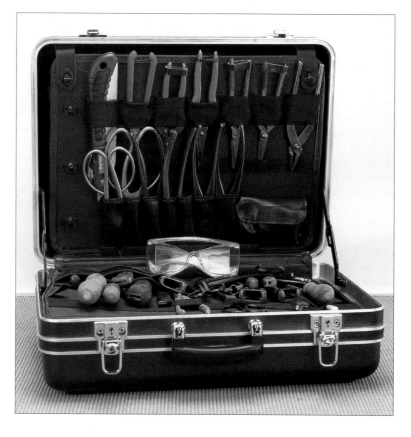

Right: *A comprehensive bonsai tool kit that includes all the tools required for bonsai culture.*

Small bonsai tool kit

Long-nosed pliers

General-purpose scissors

Square-nosed pliers

Vine pruners

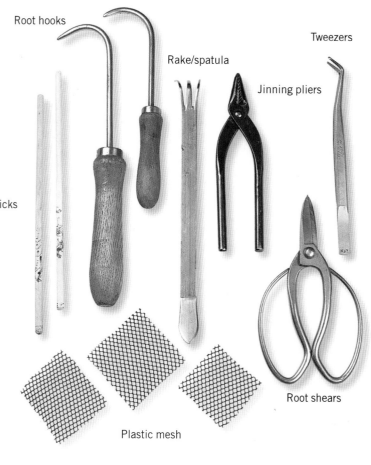

Root hooks

Rake/spatula

Tweezers

Jinning pliers

Chopsticks

Plastic mesh

Root shears

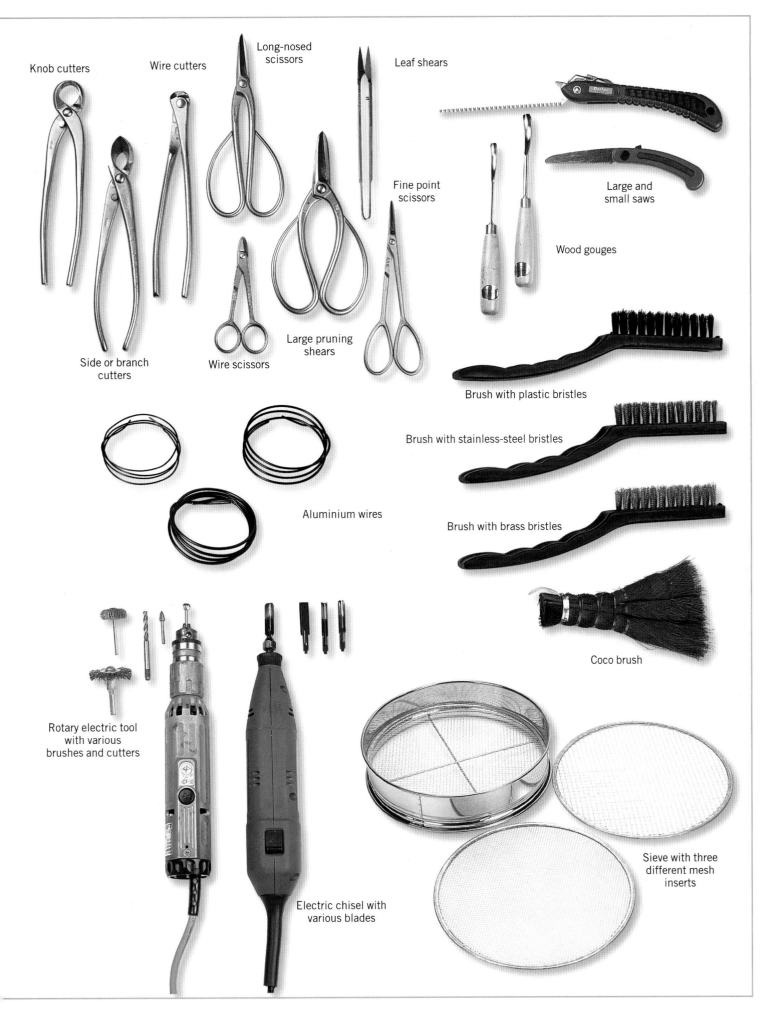

Knob cutters

Wire cutters

Long-nosed scissors

Leaf shears

Fine point scissors

Large and small saws

Wood gouges

Side or branch cutters

Wire scissors

Large pruning shears

Brush with plastic bristles

Brush with stainless-steel bristles

Aluminium wires

Brush with brass bristles

Coco brush

Rotary electric tool with various brushes and cutters

Electric chisel with various blades

Sieve with three different mesh inserts

Collecting Plants from the Garden

Plants that have been growing vigorously for many years, whether in your own garden or in an area of countryside nearby, can produce some of the best-quality bonsai, as they will almost certainly have thick, mature trunks, including well-developed root structures. It is therefore always worth checking trees and shrubs in your own garden, and those of family and friends, for suitable candidates. If you see an ideal specimen growing wild somewhere, you will need to seek authorization before digging it up. You will often find a plant that is no longer needed in its current place in a garden that would be ideal for training into a bonsai. Check it out thoroughly to ascertain if it is possible to remove and make sure that it is dug up in early spring to be sure of the maximum chance of survival.

Above: *This Satsuki azalea, a garden plant for about 50 years before being trained as a bonsai, shows the all-important mature trunk.*

It may require more than one season to prepare an old plant for removal from the ground. As a mature plant, it will have a substantial root system spreading several yards, and these roots cannot simply be severed and the plant removed in one operation. Cut through the roots with a sharp spade in spring by plunging the spade into the soil to its full depth. Complete a circle around the plant with the spade, about 30–45cm (12–18in) from the trunk base, and then undercut to sever any long taproots. Leave the plant for another season to allow it to develop a new, compact root structure, and remove it from the ground in the following spring just before any new growth begins. Before digging up the plant, carry out some basic pruning in order to aid the development of the basic structure.

When you have dug up the tree or shrub, plant it in a training container, using a gritty, open soil to encourage good root growth. Any type of container can be used for this initial growing period. You can make your own from timber pallets or even

LIFTING AND STORING A GARDEN PLANT

1 This is a good example of some suitable plant material for styling into a bonsai specimen, growing in the open ground. The tree can be prepared in advance by digging around the roots with a sharp spade during the season before lifting.

2 Remove the plant from the ground using a spade, cutting the roots as necessary with the spade or secateurs (pruners), but leaving a good fibrous root system. Having lifted the tree, prepare the roots by knocking away excess soil with the spade or a rake, and pruning any large roots so that it will fit into its training box.

3 This is the prepared training box. You will need to put a layer of coarse grit over the bottom of the box, followed by a layer of very gritty soil. You will also need to pass some wires through the holes in the bottom of the box, leaving sufficient length for "tying in".

4 Place the tree in the box, work the roots into the soil, and tie in by twisting the ends of the wire together until the tree is firmly held. Having filled up the box with more soil and watered well, the tree can now develop a new compact root system. Whatever container you use, it must have good holes in the base to allow free drainage of water.

1 This Satsuki azalea, *Rhododendron indicum*, was removed from the open ground two years prior to this shot and then pruned, leaving only the roots and trunk. This shows two years of new growth.

2 Once the plant has been removed from its pot, remove most of the unwanted shoots.

3 There is an old branch stub that will need to be removed. Remove the unwanted stub, as well as some more small shoots. Wire the branches ready for shaping.

4 The potential bonsai has now been shaped and repotted in to a temporary pot.

5 Following twelve weeks of re-growth, a considerable amount of new growth has appeared which can again be shaped and pruned.

6 Select and remove any internal adventitious shoots, using a sharp pair of cutters.

7 Prune the tips of minor shoots in order to promote new, dense inner growth for the new season.

8 The finished bonsai following completion of the styling work. The young bonsai will take many years to reach maturity.

plastic washing bowls, storage boxes or anything that will contain your plant. Large drainage holes in the base of your container are very important in order to allow excess water to drain away freely. Always tie the plant into the container so that it is held firmly; this will allow the new roots to develop unchecked.

The Satsuki azalea shown in the sequence above was collected from a large plantation of unwanted material.

It had been previously cut back while in the ground, but required further work to turn it into a plant with some bonsai potential. Azaleas and rhododendrons grown in these situations make excellent material, as they will have a compact, fibrous root system and are easy to dig up and repot with minimal risk to the plant.

In addition to single plants, you should also look out for old hedges being removed by your neighbours,

and offer to relieve them of the best-looking plants; you may even be looking at a whole row of possible bonsai material. Check the plants closely to see if they have a compact habit. As a hedge, they will have been clipped for many years and would be ideal plants from which to start some new bonsai. Some species that are worth looking out for are azalea, beech, field maple, hedging honeysuckle, juniper and privet.

Propagating from Seed

Growing from seed is a time-consuming way to produce any plant, let alone a bonsai, but it does have one benefit: it is the only way that you will be able to quote the exact age of your trees, which is always one of the first questions you will be asked about them. The seeds of some tree varieties, especially Japanese maples, can produce variable results. Leaf shape, size and colour can vary enormously, and this variety can, in many cases, enhance your collection of trees with a large range of interesting leaf shapes and colours. Only very basic equipment, such as pots, seed trays, chopsticks and some suitable soil, is required for the initial seed-sowing process. It is not a time-consuming exercise, but needs to be carried out correctly to obtain maximum chance of germination taking place.

Above: *The European larch (*Larix decidua*) can be propagated from seed and grown on in plastic flowerpots.*

PREPARING SEED

When growing bonsai, it is best to choose seeds that grow into plants with naturally small leaves, needles, flowers and fruit. Make sure that any seeds you purchase or collect are fresh. Seeds with a shell or case may need to be cracked or chipped in order to aid germination. To crack them, gently squeeze the hard-shelled seeds with pliers until the seed coat cracks, which will then allow moisture to reach the kernel and so aid germination. To chip them, use a very sharp knife to cut a small chip from the seed coat for the same purpose.

An alternative method for aiding germination is to stratify seeds. To do this, you will need to mix them with a small amount of moist peat or sand, put this mixture in a covered container, and place the container in the salad compartment of a refrigerator for three to four weeks before sowing. This is a more natural way to break the dormancy of the seeds and speed up the germination process. The action of stratification normally takes place naturally when seeds either remain on trees or fall to the ground during winter. As they over-winter, the seeds will be repeatedly frozen or chilled, and the dormancy will be broken naturally.

SOWING SEED

Almost fill a seed tray or pot with some seed compost (soil mix) and gently flatten it, but do not compress it. With fairly large seeds you will need to place them carefully at regular intervals over the surface of the compost and finally

Left: *Seven Japanese larch (*Larix kaempferi*) of various ages grown from seed and arranged as a small forest in a shallow pot.*

PROPAGATING FROM SEED

1 Fill a seed tray almost to the brim with soil and lay the seeds on the surface, spacing them out evenly.

2 Cover the seeds with a layer of soil which is approximately the same thickness as the seeds you are sowing.

3 Press the surface down lightly to firm the seeds in place.

4 Spray with water that has had a fungicide added; this helps to prevent the seeds from rotting and also the "damping off" of the seedlings when they appear.

5 If the seeds are from hardy trees, the completed tray should be covered and placed outdoors; if they are from tropical or indoor varieties, they will need to be kept indoors in a warm place.

cover them with a layer of compost no deeper than the size of the seeds. Firm this top layer gently before watering from a watering can with a fine rose head. Following watering, it is a good idea to spray with a fungicide to guard against fungal attack.

Cover the tray of seeds to retain some humidity and warmth, and place in an unheated greenhouse until the seeds start to germinate. At this point, you can place them outdoors and remove the cover after a week or two so that the new plants can advance naturally.

Keep a close watch on your new young plants, because they are vulnerable to attack from a large variety of creatures, including slugs, snails and a wide range of insects.

Left: *Several one-year-old English oak (Quercus robur) seedlings growing in a seed tray and ready for transplanting into individual larger pots. These will enable the plants to develop freely for a few years before being styled.*

Propagating from Cuttings

Since growing plants from seed is a slow process, you might prefer to speed up your journey into the world of bonsai by propagating from cuttings. Plants produced from cuttings will have exactly the same characteristics as the parent plant from which the cuttings originated. The process entails cutting small parts from the parent plant of your choice and inserting them into some potting compost (soil mix) that is specially formulated for growing cuttings. For this technique you will need some flowerpots or seed trays, some suitable soil, a chopstick, possibly a sharp knife, a pair of scissors and tweezers, as well as some rooting powder, although this last item is not always required. The soil should have a good, free-draining, granular structure in order to encourage young root growth.

Above: *A four-year-old Chinese juniper (Juniperus chinensis) cutting propagated by the method described on these pages.*

Softwood and hardwood are the two types of material normally used when propagating woody plants for bonsai. Softwood, or semi-ripe, cuttings are taken in late spring or early summer, and hardwood cuttings in the autumn.

PROPAGATING BROAD-LEAF TREES

For broad-leaf trees, take a cutting with several nodes and remove the lowest leaves, as well as the growing tip. If the leaves are large, remove about two-thirds of each leaf using a pair of sharp scissors. This will reduce the rate at which the cutting will lose water through transpiration from its leaves by approximately two-thirds, so increasing its chances of survival.

PROPAGATING CONIFERS

For conifers, take heel cuttings by pulling down on shoots until they become detached. (The "heel" refers to the small amount of hardwood material from the branch that will come off with the shoot.) The amount of foliage should be reduced, as with broad-leaf cuttings, but not removed, as most cuttings will die without any foliage.

Fill a seed tray or flowerpot with some cuttings compost (soil mix), which is generally a more gritty mixture than that used for seeds. Make a small hole for each cutting using a chopstick or something similar and insert the cuttings into the compost to about one-third of their length and firm in by hand. When the tray or pot is complete, water as for seed sowing and spray with a fungicide as a precaution against fungal attack. Cover the tray to retain humidity and place in a cool shady spot.

Instead of using commercially available cuttings compost, you could use a Japanese potting soil called akadama. This is ideal for encouraging root production.

Left: *This* Acer palmatum *was grown from a cutting and is approximately ten years old. It is very difficult to raise Japanese maple cultivars from cuttings, as they do not freely produce roots.*

TAKING *JUNIPERUS* CUTTINGS

1 Remove the heel cutting – here from a Chinese juniper (*Juniperus chinensis*) – by pulling it down and away from the main stem.

2 After the cutting has been removed, you will be able to see the "heel" at the end of the cutting.

3 You can put several cuttings in each pot. Here, a heel cutting is being taken from a *Juniperus procumbens* 'Nana' shoot.

4 Make a suitable hole in the soil (this is akadama) using a chopstick.

5 Place each cutting into a hole in the soil and firm in using the chopstick.

6 Three different cuttings have been planted in this pot: *Juniperus chinensis*, *J. procumbens* 'Nana' and *Chaenomeles japonica*. All three are heel cuttings.

TAKING BROAD-LEAF AND CONIFER CUTTINGS

1 For broad-leaf trees, take a cutting that has several nodes and cut off the lowest leaves and the growing tip. Remove half of each leaf on the cutting to reduce water loss.

2 For conifers, take a heel cutting by pulling down on the shoot until it breaks free. Remove any excess long strands of bark that remain on the heel of the cutting.

3 Having filled a tray with very sandy soil, make a small hole with a chopstick for each of the cuttings.

4 Insert the cuttings into the soil for about one-third of their length. Spray with a mix of water and fungicide.

5 Cover the tray to retain humidity and place outdoors in a shady place.

Propagating by Grafting

A graft is the name applied to a union made between two plants and also between two parts of the same plant. Grafting can occur naturally, such as when branches rubbing together over a period of time eventually produce wounds, and then calluses, before fusing together to form a graft. It can also be created artificially by making a wound with a knife into two parts of similar plant material, pressing the two together – making sure that the cambium layers come into contact – and binding them with raffia or other suitable material until the graft has formed. Grafting techniques are not commonly used by amateur bonsai growers but, as they can produce almost instant results in terms of adding a new branch or root, for example, they can be an invaluable asset.

Above: *The small round mark in the centre of the old wound is the cut-off end of a thread graft on an* Acer palmatum.

There are several types of graft used in horticulture that can easily be used to add branches or roots where they are required to improve the form of bonsai. The most common forms of graft used in bonsai work are root, thread and inarch grafting. Several other graft forms do exist, but these are normally used to produce plant material by propagating nurseries, and are not generally used by bonsai growers.

ROOT GRAFTING

This commonly used form of grafting in bonsai enables the grower to add roots to the base of the trunk. This improves the appearance of the root system and ultimately of the trunk buttress.

Root grafting consists of making a union between the main tree and a small plant of the same species, fixing them together securely and sealing the join to exclude water from the union. This will enable the union to bond together more quickly. The seal may be removed after about one season's growth, by which time the callus should have completely taken over.

THREAD GRAFTING

This is a relatively easy method of replacing or adding a new branch to a tree and is achieved normally by growing a long individual shoot on the plant needing the new branch. This can then be stripped of any side shoots and foliage before being passed

through a hole that has been drilled at the required place on the trunk of the tree. This is then sealed at both entry and exit points and allowed to grow and graft on to the main trunk.

INARCH GRAFTING

This technique is used to introduce a new branch into the trunk of a tree. Similar starting procedures are needed for this as for thread grafting, but the shoot is laid into a cut in the bark and tied in place with grafting tape or raffia. Any grafting technique will be described in detail in specialist books.

Left: *The right-hand branch of this* Acer palmatum *has been attached by a method of propagation known as thread grafting.*

Right: *The trunk base of a grafted Japanese maple. The lower part is the stock plant that will be* Acer palmatum, *while the upper section is the grafted scion of a Japanese maple cultivar.*

ROOT GRAFTING ON TO AN *ACER BUERGERIANUM*

1 Close-up of trunk base of a root-over-rock *Acer buergerianum* that needs an extra root grafted into place.

2 The main tree and donor tree side by side. The lower trunk of the donor tree will become the new root on the main tree.

3 Using a small saw, cut a suitably sized piece of root from the main tree.

4 Carefully remove the cut-out piece of soil and root.

5 Place a small amount of new soil into the bottom of the hole.

6 Using wen or knob cutters, cut a hollow into the side of the knobbly, unsightly root of the main tree.

7 Tidy the cut using a very sharp wood-working gouge. Remember to take great care when using extremely sharp tools.

8 Place the donor tree into the hole and mark on its trunk where it touches the main trunk.

9 Remove the donor tree from the hole and remove a piece of bark, using the gouge, so that the two areas of cambium on the donor and recipient tree match.

10 The points on each tree that will be in contact with each other are shown here. Remember that the cambium of each piece must come into contact with the other.

11 Place the donor tree back into the hole and press its trunk on to the main tree so that the cambium areas come into contact. Secure the donor tree to the main tree.

12 Apply wound sealer over the screw head and around the contact area between the trees. The sealer has been applied and the area topped up with soil.

13 The completed grafting procedure, showing the donor tree with its upper growth still in place. This will eventually be removed when the graft has successfully completed in about three months.

Propagating by Air Layering

This is a relatively straightforward method of propagation by which a plant is encouraged to produce roots from its trunk or from one or more of its branches. Some plants layer themselves naturally and produce roots when their branches droop and come into contact with the ground; this is known as ground layering. However, the most commonly used layering method for producing plants for styling into bonsai is air layering, which generates roots at any point above the level of the soil on woody plants. For bonsai purposes, this technique is mostly used to produce an annular root system around the trunk because, overall, annular roots give a better, and more realistic, impression than the odd individual root protruding from one side of the trunk base.

Most woody plants can be layered, and, if you find propagating a plant from seeds or cuttings difficult, it is worth trying to propagate by air layering instead.

With a sharp knife, make two cuts, about 2cm (¾in) apart, around the trunk, through the bark and to the heartwood. Using the tip of the knife, prise the bark from the trunk as a complete band, exposing the heartwood beneath. Place about two handfuls of wet sphagnum moss around the exposed area of the trunk, making sure that it comes well above

and below the exposed area. You can use your hands in order to squeeze out any excess water.

You should also aim to improve the stimulation of the roots by dusting the exposed ends of the cambium layer of the tree with some rooting powder or liquid.

Cover the sphagnum moss with a strip of plain polythene (plastic sheet) or even some bubble wrap, tying it close to the trunk with string or wire. The strip of polythene or bubble wrap should be tied both above and below the sphagnum moss in order to

Above: *Damp sphagnum moss which is now ready for covering a bare stem when air layering. Soak in water and squeeze out any excess water by hand.*

create a ball-like structure. The ties should be airtight to keep any moisture loss from the layered area to a minimum.

This operation can be carried out from early spring to midsummer, so that the layer has plenty of time to achieve good root development. This will be removed in late summer when the newly rooted plant will be severed from the parent plant. To do this, remove the polythene or bubble wrap and expose the area of removed bark. (Do not attempt to remove all the moss because you will be in danger of removing the delicate roots as well.) Carefully cut off just below the new root system. The new roots will be fragile at this stage, so take great care when potting this part of the plant into its new container. Use a good open soil mixture when potting and protect the delicate roots from frost over the first winter.

Left: *This layering only has roots on the lower side of the cut, so it is acceptable to remove the moss from where there are no roots.*

AIR LAYERING A *JUNIPERUS CHINENSIS*

1 This shows the area on the trunk of a *Juniperus chinensis* to be air layered.

2 Cut a ring through and around the bark using a sharp knife.

3 Make a similar second cut about 2.5cm (1in) below the first.

4 After making a vertical cut between the two ring cuts, remove the ring of bark using the tip of the knife.

5 The ring of bark is completely removed, so that the two areas of bark are separated.

6 Take a large handful of damp sphagnum moss and wrap it around the bare part of the trunk so that it extends about 5cm (2in) on either side of the cuts.

7 Squeeze the sphagnum moss tightly around the stem using your hand.

8 The moss will stay in place if it is wet and tightly compressed.

9 Wrap a suitable length of bubble wrap around the moss so that the wrap extends beyond the moss both on the top and on the bottom.

10 Secure the bubble wrap with two lengths of wire or string.

11 The preparation of the air-layering process is complete and it will now require two or three months for sufficient roots to develop so that the newly air-layered plant can be removed from the parent plant.

REMOVING AND POTTING ON A LAYERED PLANT

Once an air layering has taken and produced sufficient roots, it must be removed from the parent plant as soon as possible. This can be carried out at any time of the year but preferably in midsummer so that the newly severed plant has a reasonable time in which to settle in to its new container and produce new roots before the winter. The new roots will be very tender so winter protection will be required.

You will need to plant your newly air-layered plant in a suitable training pot. The roots will be very delicate at this stage and, for this reason, they must be treated with the utmost care. Do not attempt to remove too much sphagnum moss because the newly formed roots will break away very easily. This will leave the air-layered plant with very little upon which it can survive.

AIR LAYERING AND REPOTTING AN *ACER PALMATUM*

1 This is a large *Acer palmatum* with air layering in progress. The wrapped area is covered with black polythene (plastic sheet).

2 A close-up of the wrapped air layering, showing how it has been tied in to create a ball shape.

3 Remove the black polythene wrapping in order to expose the sphagnum moss beneath.

4 Here, the new young roots can clearly be seen emerging from the surface of the sphagnum moss.

5 Using a sharp saw, cut through the base of the branch close to the main trunk of the parent plant.

6 The branch has been removed. Here, you can see the cut end and where it was cut from the trunk of the parent tree.

7 Part of the parent tree, showing the gap left, two-thirds of the way up on the left side of the trunk, by the removal of the branch.

8 The air layering only has roots on the lower side of the cut, so it is acceptable to remove the moss from where there are no roots. Leave the rest of the moss in place because the roots are very delicate and could be damaged if there is any attempt to remove it.

9 The air layering will need to be planted in an inexpensive training pot.

10 After inserting "tying-in" wires and adding some soil to the bottom of the pot, insert a piece of foam to prevent the wire from cutting into the bark.

11 Using a pair of pliers, twist the wire tightly over the foam until the plant is totally secure in the pot.

12 A wire support is added to prevent the trunk from resting on the side of the pot.

13 Top up the pot with akadama because this is an ideal growimg medium for promoting good root growth.

14 Finished planting displayed on a round Chinese stand. This tree will need some winter protection and has the potential to become a very good cascade bonsai.

Left: *With the tree finally potted, all the leaves have been removed – a process usually known as defoliation – in order to help the tree to concentrate on the important task of producing a new root system. Within six weeks of this process taking place, a new set of leaves will begin to appear that will be slightly smaller than those that have been removed.*

Soils for Bonsai

Bonsai can be grown in almost any type of soil, but if you wish to keep them in the best of health at all times, then they must be grown in the correct soil or potting mix. Soil for bonsai may consist of just one ingredient or a mixture of two or more different ingredients, all of which must be of a good quality in order to maintain the health and vigour of your tree for many years to come. All soils will also need to be dry to aid the mixing and potting processes. If the soil is wet, you will find that it can be very difficult to work into and around the root system of any tree when you are repotting, for example. If the soil is dry, however, it will flow freely in and around the roots of the tree. This will ensure that the roots are all in good contact with the soil at all times.

The soil's function is to hold sufficient nutrients, water and air to provide a regular supply of these three vital components to the roots of your bonsai tree. If the soil stores too much water around the roots, it will encourage the roots to decay. It is therefore very important that the texture of the soil is open and free-draining to allow excess water to drain away. In fact, free-draining soil is one of the most important elements in the successful culture of bonsai. Any soil mixture must be open and incorporate as many air spaces as possible around the granules of soil, because it is these spaces that allow the root system to breathe.

Above: *Sift all soils to remove the finest particles that could "clog up" the root structure of bonsai. Remove only fine dust and retain small granules for top dressing.*

The soil is also partly responsible for securing the tree into the pot and it needs to be firm enough to achieve this. The action of tying the tree into the pot with wire, using the holes in the base of the pot, is a standard bonsai procedure that will stop the tree moving around in the pot and therefore aid the formation of a good root system.

SOIL TYPES

A general-purpose soil mix can be one part sphagnum moss peat to one part loam to two parts coarse sharp grit. These ingredients can be bought from a garden centre or DIY store.

Coarse grit with angular particles measuring 3–6mm (⅛–¼in) will be ideal, but do not use grit that has very sharp edges, as it can cause severe damage to roots during repotting. There are many varieties of grit available, as well as other suitable substitute materials, and these can be added to the soil mix as you become more experienced in growing bonsai. A commercially prepared soil mix can

Right: *This tree has been potted in medium-grade akadama, with a top dressing of fine granules that look much better from an aesthetic point of view.*

be used to replace loam, but bear in mind that this mix already contains loam, grit and nutrients.

It is also important to make sure that the components of your soil mix are completely dry when you combine them, and pass them through a sieve in order to obtain particles measuring 3–6mm (⅛–¼in). Particles that are smaller than this will congest the air spaces in the soil and so will be detrimental to the development of the root system of your tree.

Other soils, which are imported from Japan, are available from good bonsai suppliers. While these soils are probably more suited to the experienced grower, they do provide excellent growing conditions for bonsai, as well as many other types of potted plants. Three varieties of soil for bonsai are obtainable: akadama, kanuma and kiryu. Akadama is a general-purpose clay granule soil and is suitable for most bonsai; kanuma is highly recommended for ericaceous

(acid soil) plants such as azaleas; and kiryu is good for pines (*Pinus*) and junipers (*Juniperus*), but is not always available to the average bonsai grower. These soils can be more expensive than normal ingredients, but they can be mixed with peat and grit to help keep the costs down.

It is not normal to mix fertilizers with any soil when you are potting, but they can be added as necessary at regular intervals throughout the growing season.

GROWING MEDIUMS

Various types of soil can be used for bonsai culture. They can be used on their own or mixed in different proportions to suit individual plants or growing conditions. Many bonsai growers develop their own special recipes but they will be mostly based on the materials described in this section.

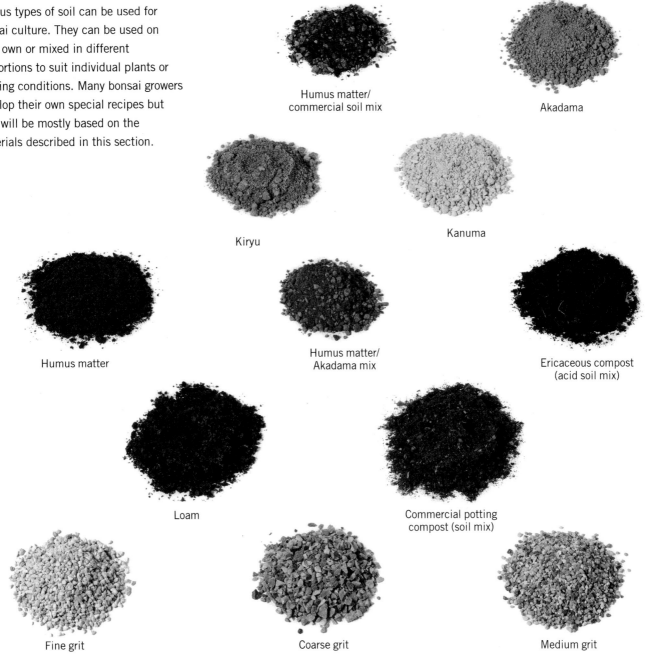

Humus matter/ commercial soil mix

Akadama

Kiryu

Kanuma

Humus matter

Humus matter/ Akadama mix

Ericaceous compost (acid soil mix)

Loam

Commercial potting compost (soil mix)

Fine grit

Coarse grit

Medium grit

Pruning Techniques

All bonsai require some branches to be removed or pruned and other structural alterations to be made during their life. This may be necessary to improve the design or appearance of a tree or to style a tree during the initial training stages. Removing a branch, or part of a branch, is a straightforward process, but care should be taken to make a clean cut that will heal and leave little or no scar. Various purpose-made tools are available that allow bonsai growers to carry out pruning operations that will successfully achieve the required result. Gardening or household tools, such as secateurs (pruners) and scissors, are satisfactory for beginners, and require less financial outlay. As the various pruning techniques become familiar, you will find that proper tools will be a beneficial addition to your tool kit.

Above: *The difference between the scale-like adult foliage of the Chinese juniper (*Juniperus chinensis*) and the needle-like juvenile foliage is clear. Hard pruning will result in a proliferation of juvenile foliage.*

BASIC PRUNING TECHNIQUES

Using the correct type of cutters for the task in hand is vital. Also ensure that any cutters are clean and sharp. This will give good pruning cuts and reduce the risk of any infection to the tree or plant. Make the cut as close to the trunk as possible, placing the cutting edges at 90 degrees to the trunk. Using cutters with the edges vertical or parallel to the trunk can cause severe damage .

You can protect the wound left by the pruning process with a sealer specifically formulated for bonsai. Sealing the wound protects the cut bark edge, preventing it from drying out and accelerating the healing process. New

buds may appear around the pruned area. If too many appear, rub them off, leaving only those that may be in a useful position as future branches. You will need to feed the tree after pruning.

In all cases, care should be taken to ensure that flower-bearing growth is not pruned away before it blooms.

PRUNING DECIDUOUS TREES

Basic pruning of deciduous trees can be done using a pair of scissors. When removing a branch, cut as close to the trunk as possible. If you have a pair of concave branch cutters, you will be able to prune even closer to the trunk. If you are left with a small stub after

Left: *For beginners to bonsai, secateurs (pruners) will be adequate as a pruning tool.*

USING BRANCH CUTTERS

1 This is the correct use of branch or side cutters, with the cutting edges held horizontal to the trunk.

2 After removing the branch, it can be seen that the cut end is convex and the wound on the trunk is concave.

3 This is the incorrect use of branch cutters, with the cutting edges held vertical to the trunk. This usually results in a vertical split on the trunk that will slow down the healing process.

USING VINE PRUNERS

1 Removing a very long shoot on a Japanese hornbeam (*Carpinus laxiflora*) with vine pruners.

2 The long shoot has been removed and the cut end can be clearly seen.

3 Three shorter shoots also need to be pruned to correct the balance of the foliage.

4 One of the shorter shoots being removed with vine pruners.

5 Appearance of the foliage following the removal of all three shoots.

6 Backed by white paper, the foliage following pruning can be clearly seen.

pruning, this can be removed using a different tool called a knob cutter, which leaves a small hollow that also aids the healing process.

When pruning maples, particularly Japanese maples (*Acer palmatum*), do not cut back the shoots close to a bud as the branch or shoot will probably die back beyond that point. Leave about 12mm (½in) of shoot to allow for this die-back, as this can be tidied up later.

PRUNING CONIFERS

Most of the techniques used when pruning deciduous trees also apply to conifers, but there are one or two extra points that need to be considered. When removing a branch from a conifer, always leave a substantial length of the branch intact. This can be used to enhance the tree by creating a jin. A jin is where the bark is stripped from the stub, exposing the heartwood which

dries out to leave a natural-looking dead branch. This is often seen on full-size conifers in the wild.

When pruning conifer branches, you must always leave some foliage on the end of the branch so that there is something to draw the sap. This is not the case with deciduous trees because they will regenerate new shoots without you having to leave any foliage in place.

REMOVING UNWANTED SHOOTS

1 This rather long shoot on an *Acer palmatum* 'Deshojo' does not fit in with the tree shape and is spoiling the outline of the bonsai specimen.

2 Remove the shoot with a pair of vine pruners or even an ordinary pair of household scissors.

3 Following the removal of the offending shoot from the bonsai, this is how the outline of the bonsai looks.

▷

PRUNING OUT SHOOTS AND NEEDLES

You will need to maintain the shape of your bonsai by pinching or cutting out the growing tips during the spring and summer. Broad-leaf trees generally produce shoots with pairs of leaves or single leaves on alternating sides of the branch. Conifers vary widely in the appearance of their tip growth, but the pruning technique is similar for each. Spruce (*Picea*) and some junipers (*Juniperus*) form small bunches of needles that can be removed using your fingers. Each week, remove the largest shoots, but make sure there is always some fresh growth remaining.

On maples and some other broad-leaf trees, you can remove all the leaves in late spring when they are fully developed. This encourages the tree to produce a second, smaller set of leaves, but should only be carried out once every two years, and then only if the tree is healthy. Always use clean sharp scissors for any pruning operation.

ANNUAL PRUNING

Every year your trees will produce an abundance of shoots from their leaf axils, which, if left in place, would eventually dominate the appearance of your bonsai.

For trees in training, you may be able to leave some of these shoots in place if you need to thicken the adjacent trunk or branch, but, in mature trees, remove them as soon as possible. You will need to cut back unwanted growth in the dormant season to allow the tree to develop the required shape. Prune out branches that are too thick for the design. The tree may look a little bald, but during the next season each bud will produce a new branch and leaves. Trim back any long shoots to a dormant bud and, where possible, to a bud pointing in the required direction of growth.

PRUNING DECIDUOUS TREES (*ACER BUERGERIANUM*)

1 An *Acer buergerianum* with extended shoots that require some radical pruning.

2 The tree has been wired and the branches positioned prior to pruning the shoots.

3 Prune the long shoots or branches to a suitable length.

4 Using wire cutters, cut any wiring back to suit the new branch or shoot length.

5 Bend the end of the wire back on itself in order to retain the end of the branch.

6 Following the restyling process, the tree has been transformed.

PRUNING CONIFERS (*CRYPTOMERIA JAPONICA*)

1 A *Cryptomeria japonica* group that requires some shoot pruning.

2 Close-up of foliage, showing the bright green young shoots that need pinching out.

3 Trim the long shoots using scissors, with the blades following the angle of the needles.

4 Close pruning is required on *Cryptomeria japonica* to encourage compact growth. Here, three branches have been completed.

5 Compare the pruned branches with those that are awaiting the pruning process.

6 The tree on the left shows how the trees in this group were initially trained.

SHOOT PINCHING ON *CRYPTOMERIA JAPONICA*

1 Hold the tip of the shoot between your thumb and first finger. Gently pull the shoot tip until it breaks free.

2 The same procedure can be carried out using a pair of tweezers. Pull gently to free the tip of the shoot.

3 If the shoots do not break using your fingers, use scissors. The scissor angle must follow the needle angle to avoid damaging the needles that are to remain.

4 The top of a *Cryptomeria japonica* following shoot pinching and showing the new buds beginning to grow.

PINCHING OUT "CANDLES"

1 Hold the "candle" to be removed with a pair of tweezers.

2 Snap the "candle" free by gently twisting the tweezers to one side.

3 The removed "candle" can be clearly seen in this shot.

Pinching Out and Defoliating

As bonsai trees develop, they produce a plentiful supply of new growth each year. However, during the main period of growth, which in both northern and southern hemispheres comes in mid-spring to late summer, the actual growth rate of some trees can be very high, so you will need to monitor their size and shape closely to stop them becoming too large. Both pinching out (removing shoots) and defoliating (removing all the leaves) encourage your trees to produce a tighter, more twiggy growth pattern, but note that defoliating applies only to deciduous trees: defoliating an evergreen conifer would kill it. The reason for any type of shoot and/or leaf pruning is to force the tree to produce more buds and thus more compact foliage, which will improve the appearance of any bonsai.

Above: *This* Acer palmatum *'Ukon' has been defoliated, leaving only the petioles to die back naturally. A full set of new leaves will be produced within six to twelve weeks.*

PINCHING OUT

Deciduous, or broad-leaf, trees need to have their shoots pinched out at the growing tips regularly during the spring and summer months. This encourages them to produce back budding – new buds within the branch structure which have been encouraged to grow by pruning the tip growth – and hence a more compact growth pattern.

Generally, broad-leaf trees will produce shoots consisting of pairs of leaves or single leaves on alternate sides of the shoot. Allow the shoots to grow several pairs of leaves before pinching them out, using your fingers or some scissors, to one pair of leaves.

DEFOLIATING

To improve the density of growth and assist with the size reduction of leaves, it is possible to remove all the leaves on a deciduous tree. This is generally known as defoliating, and its purpose is to deceive the tree into thinking it is winter. This process should be carried out only when the first set of leaves has matured, normally in late spring or early summer, and then only if the tree is in good health. If you have been following the correct watering, feeding and general care techniques for bonsai, your trees should be healthy enough for defoliating to take place. Complete defoliation of any deciduous tree should be carried out only every other

year so that your trees do not become unduly stressed. Some trees can be defoliated several times a year, but these are usually the very vigorous growers such as some varieties of maple.

The defoliation process entails removing all the leaves, leaving just the petiole, or leaf stalk, in each case. (The petioles are left in place to drop naturally, so that any goodness within them can drain back and feed the dormant buds at their base.) You will be left with a tree that looks rather

DEFOLIATING

1 Remove the leaf, leaving a complete petiole in place to die back naturally.

2 Petioles left on the plant die back and prompt dormant buds to break.

3 The remaining petioles following leaf pruning can be clearly seen.

COMPLETE DEFOLIATION

1 Commercial-style *Acer palmatum* 'Deshojo' that requires defoliation.

2 The defoliated tree, showing some petioles remaining on the plant and some that have fallen.

3 After about three weeks, the petioles will begin to fall from the tree.

4 Smaller, new leaves will soon begin to grow.

PARTIAL DEFOLIATION

1 Partial defoliation means that some old leaves are retained, allowing some smaller new leaves to develop.

2 Common beech (*Fagus sylvatica*) group that has been partially defoliated, giving a realistic impression of full-size trees.

"spiky", but the petioles will die back and fall away over the next three to four weeks. After a further three to four weeks, new shoots will begin to appear at the point where the fallen petioles were attached. As the new shoots grow, they will in turn need to be pinched back to one pair of leaves in order to maintain an even distribution of foliage.

Defoliation should result in the following crop of leaves being approximately two-thirds of the size of the first set.

Left: *Two small Acer palmatum 'Deshojo' bonsai, with the left-hand tree shown following defoliation and the right-hand tree before defoliation.*

Shaping by Pruning

Some deciduous trees grow at an alarming speed during the four- to five-month growing season, and can easily grow completely out of shape in a very short space of time. Conifers are normally very much slower growers and are therefore not so likely to be in need of drastic pruning at any time of the year. There are, however, always exceptions to any rule, so keep a close watch on all your bonsai trees in order to make sure that they do not grow out of hand, and be prepared to start pruning to re-establish their shape. It is generally obvious which shoots need pruning because they will have extended well beyond the original form or outline of the tree. It is normally just a matter of cutting off the excess shoots until the outline of the tree has been restored.

Above: *This is a close-up of the long shoots at the apex of the literati-style Japanese larch (*Larix kaempferi*).*

The normal process of shaping a bonsai specimen is carried out using pointed scissors or branch cutters. Shaping of your bonsai tree has to be carried out at the right place, in the right way and at the right time of year. A good-quality pair of bonsai scissors, and possibly a similar quality pair of branch cutters, would be a great advantage when you are pruning any bonsai into shape. If you do not wish to spend a lot of money on tools, however, you could manage with a normal pair of kitchen or general-purpose scissors, though these must be clean and have sharp cutting edges.

Using scissors, cut each extended shoot back to the contour of the original pad-shaped foliage structure. Cut the shoots back so that only one or two needles or leaves remain, or even farther if you think it will benefit the overall shape of the tree. Continue this process of removing shoots until the whole tree has been tidied up and presents a pleasing profile once again.

Following each pruning cut, you may wish to seal the wound with a special bonsai wound sealer or a

PRUNING A FORMAL UPRIGHT LITERATI

1 This upright literati Japanese larch (*Larix kaempferi*) will benefit from shaping by pruning.

2 Using a pair of sharp scissors, carefully cut out the long shoots on the apex without cutting through any individual needles.

3 Remove one shoot at a time until all the excess shoots have been removed and a smooth outline is achieved.

4 Once you have pruned away excess shoots, the tree will start to look more mature.

1 This twin-trunk Japanese larch (*Larix kaempferi*) requires some minor pruning to improve its shape.

2 This shows the typical branch structure and good branch ramification of this type of bonsai style.

3 Individual needles may need to be removed in order to tidy up the overall appearance of the bonsai.

4 Gently pull out any downward-facing needles, using your finger and thumb.

5 The needles should come away by hand without too much effort.

6 After the minor shaping by pruning, the overall appearance of the bonsai has been greatly improved.

general-purpose sealer, which can be purchased from most good garden centres or bonsai specialists. Generally, this will be needed only on larger cuts, and it is not normally necessary if you are just trimming small shoots using a pair of scissors.

The two trees shown on these two pages have been trained as bonsai specimens for at least fifteen years, but they have been allowed to grow a little bit too much. The bonsai trees are both in good condition, but, in both cases, several shoots have been allowed to grow out of all proportion with the trunk and branch structure. This imbalance needs to be remedied through pruning.

When bonsai trees have developed into a mature shape over a number of years, they continue to produce plenty of growth every year. Maintaining these mature shapes requires constant pinching out of the growing tips during the spring and summer. In these two examples, neither of these operations has been carried out and therefore the time has come to rectify the situation. As a bonsai grower, you may often find yourself with this type of scenario and will have trees that have been allowed to grow too much between prunings.

Shaping by Wiring

Shaping with wires is probably the most used, and certainly one of the most important, techniques in bonsai training, because it enables the bonsai grower to place trunks, branches and shoots accurately in the required position. This approach gives the bonsai artist total control over the design and shape of a tree, which, when complete, should resemble a full-size mature tree but in miniature form. Although this is a relatively straightforward technique, wiring can take a considerable amount of persistence and practice to master. It would be a good idea to practise applying some wire to branches of varying degrees of thickness – perhaps on plants growing in your garden – before trying to work on a serious bonsai styling project.

Above: *A completely wired* Cedrus atlantica *'Glauca', following the repositioning of all branches to achieve the required design.*

It is also advisable to practise handling various gauges of wire in order to get an idea of the flexibility of the different sizes and how easy or difficult they are to bend or manipulate.

CHECKING FOR FLEXIBILITY

Before applying any wire, check the flexibility of the branches because some plants are more brittle than others. Maples (*Acer*), for example, can be very brittle and could break easily, whereas junipers (*Juniperus*) and pines (*Pinus*) are much more flexible and therefore not so vulnerable to breakage.

You will find that young branches are generally more flexible than mature branches. Indeed, very old branches can be rather thick and stubborn, and may need the use of other techniques, such as wrapping with raffia, to aid the bending process.

APPLYING THE WIRE

You should begin by doing a trial run on a flexible branch that is not vital to the tree's final appearance. Use a piece of wire about half the thickness and about one and a half times the length of the branch to be wired, making sure that there is sufficient length of wire

for you to hold throughout the wiring process. Place the wire on the branch, holding it in place with one hand, and wind it around and along the branch with the other. The wire should run cleanly along the branch, at an angle of about 45 degrees to it, and should not be too tight or too loose. If it is too tight, then it is better to unwind it and start again.

Check the wired branch at regular intervals during the following year in order to make sure that the bark is not growing up and around the wire, giving the impression that it is cutting into the branch. If you see signs of "cutting in", it is very important to remove the wire immediately or the tree could be permanently damaged.

The branch should stay in place when the wire is removed, but, if it springs back out of position, then you will need to rewire it and leave it for a further period until the process is complete.

Left: *This is a newly planted and designed raft-style bonsai showing the wiring needed for the initial styling.*

1 Push the wire into the soil in order to anchor the wire end.

2 Make the first turn of wire around the trunk.

3 This is the second turn of the wire.

4 Continue twisting the wire around the trunk right to the top.

5 If the trunk is particularly thick, it may need a second wire laid in parallel to the first.

6 The double-wiring process is now complete.

7 With the wire in place, the trunk can now be carefully bent into the required shape.

8 Place the wire in the trunk and branch junction when you are wiring a branch.

9 The wire is placed on one branch and taken on to the trunk for a good anchorage of the wire.

10 Next, run the wire on to the second branch.

11 Take the wire along the length of both branches.

12 Keep applying the wire until you reach the end of each branch.

13 Secure each wire by looping the end of the wire back on itself, as shown.

14 The finished wiring on two branches, which are now ready for bending into place.

15 Fully wired and shaped branch of a mature *Pinus parviflora*.

Creating Jin

In bonsai, jin refers to a dead branch that has lost its bark. In the wild, dead branches are exposed to elements, such as rain and wind, and are eventually bleached by the sun until they turn silvery-white. This occurs naturally on many varieties of conifer, especially junipers and pines. Although jins do not appear on many deciduous trees, they are often seen on oaks. Jin plays a very important part in the final appearance of a bonsai because it creates that small, but often significant, detail that tells the story of an earlier part in the life of a mature tree. A bonsai tree can have as many jins as the grower thinks is necessary, but the total number should not overpower the living part of the tree in any way. Jins do not normally appear on the back of a bonsai, as they would not be seen when viewing the tree from the front.

Above: *You can break the jin back using side cutters to give a natural "weathered" or "torn'" effect that blends with the size of the tree.*

The reason for creating jins by artificial means on bonsai is to create a feeling of substantial age. If this is carried out correctly, the effect can be dramatic. When pruning a branch on a conifer, always leave a stump several inches long, so that it can be converted into a jin. The best time to create a jin is during the summer when sap movement is at its greatest, as this makes the removal of the bark easier. When you have made the jin, you should leave it to dry in the sun before applying a coat of lime/sulphur, which will bleach and preserve the wood. This should be reapplied once or twice a year during the summer to maintain the weather resistance of the jin. The jin can then be refined by carving and smoothing with fine sandpaper until a truly natural effect is achieved. Ensure that the jin is always in proportion to the other branches that have foliage.

Above: *An equal-sized branch on the left of this tree has been turned into a jin to improve the balance of the bonsai.*

Right: *The jin on the left-hand side of this trunk reflects the appearance of the branches on the opposite side.*

HOW TO CREATE A JIN

1 A Chinese juniper (*Juniperus chinensis*) on which it would be suitable to create a jin on the lower left branch.

2 Close-up of the branch that is going to be turned into a jin.

3 To create the Jin, all foliage on the branch will need to be removed using branch cutters and scissors.

4 Cut through the bark at the base of the branch with a sharp knife, making sure that the cut goes all round and penetrates through to the heartwood.

5 Using the tip of the knife, cut into the bark through to the heartwood from the trunk to the branch tip.

6 Squeeze and twist the bark with jin pliers, or any other suitable type of plier, to free the bark from the heartwood and remove all bark from the branch.

7 With the bark removed, the jin is beginning to take shape and look like a naturally occurring formation.

8 The branch can be split and torn back using branch cutters and pliers. This will give a more ragged, natural look to the finished jin.

9 The same process from a different angle shows how the natural look is achieved.

10 Close-up of the completed jin, showing how a naturally weathered look can be obtained using simple tools and just a few minutes of creative work.

Right: The front of the tree, showing how the jin appears relative to the whole tree.

Creating Sharimiki

Sharimiki can be regarded as a bonsai technique that complements jin. It gives a tree an even greater appearance of age when used in conjunction with jin. A sharimiki is where a tree may have been struck by lightning and the bark on part of the trunk has been stripped off. This is commonly seen on pines and junipers, and often connects one jin with another, creating an even more dramatic effect. The technique is relatively straightforward and can be carried out using a few basic tools such as a gardening knife and a pair of electrician's pliers, but when you become more familiar with the technique, good-quality specialist tools will undoubtedly make the job easier to execute. Do not be afraid to experiment because this is the best way to learn what will and will not work.

In bonsai, sharimiki or shari are created by stripping the bark away from part of the trunk. This should be carried out with great care because the tree depends on its bark in order to survive. You should also ensure that you always leave enough bark on the trunk to enable the tree to support the branches that remain as removing the bark can weaken the structure.

Above: *Stripping the bark from the trunk to reveal the heartwood which will become the sharimiki feature on the bonsai trunk.*

The best time to create sharimiki is in the summer when the sap flow is at its greatest, thus allowing the bark to be stripped more easily.

Remember that you are trying to produce an artificial feature that would have normally been created by natural elements such as wind or a lightning strike. Think about how natural forces would have created this damage to the tree and which direction a branch would have fallen or how lightning actually strikes a tree.

Study trees in the wild that have undergone such traumatic events, and relate your observations to your work with your bonsai. When the work is complete, and the newly exposed heartwood has dried, you will need to treat the areas with a lime/sulphur solution to bleach and preserve the exposed wood. This initially gives a yellow appearance that soon fades to white and then to a natural grey.

Left: *A shari or sharimiki in the early stages of the styling process of a mountain pine (*Pinus mugo*).*

HOW TO CREATE A SHARIMIKI

1 The Chinese juniper (*Juniperus chinensis*) before styling has begun.

2 Mark the position of the proposed sharimiki on the trunk with a felt-tipped pen.

3 Cut into the bark through to the heartwood with a knife and peel away the bark from the trunk using the tip of the knife.

4 The area of trunk that is stripped of bark, the sharimiki, is linked to a newly created jin as well as any other old jins.

5 The stripped heartwood will have some fine hair-like elements on the surface. These can be burnt off with a small flame.

6 Any discrepancies on the jin or sharimiki can be dealt with in a similar way.

7 The whole tree begins to take on a much more mature appearance now that the jin and sharimiki are complete.

8 The newly formed jin and sharimiki can be toned down to look even more mature by slightly colouring the surface with charcoal or something similar.

Right: *The completed and textured sharimiki should blend well with the overall appearance of the bonsai tree.*

Root Pruning and Repotting

Maintaining a young and healthy root structure on a bonsai is the basis of producing a thriving and free-growing tree. What takes place in and around the root structure, and in the surrounding soil, is quite complex, as the roots are responsible for providing the tree with almost all necessary nutrients and water, without which it most certainly would not survive. Regular changes of soil, along with regular pruning of the roots, will produce a young, vigorous and fibrous root system, which should be largely free of disease and insect infestations. Root pruning is probably one of the most important and critical parts of the art and culture of bonsai, and one that has often been shrouded in mystery. The age, species and variety of the tree will dictate the frequency of the root-pruning operation.

Above: *A four-year-old cutting that is ready for some root pruning before being repotted into a new training container.*

ROOT PRUNING

Pruning of the roots followed by repotting with fresh soil encourages young feeder roots to multiply and develop. This eventually leads to healthy growth in the upper part of the tree.

The active root system should always be the youngest part of the tree, and root pruning should be carried out as soon as possible in early spring just before any buds begin to swell and break. Pruning the roots in spring means that any new roots will begin to form as soon as the temperature and weather conditions are suitable for growth to commence. It is not advisable to prune the roots of your bonsai in the autumn, as the freshly pruned roots may simply remain static throughout the winter. This could easily lead to the roots rotting rather than beginning to grow.

The first step is to remove the tree from its existing pot. If this proves difficult, use a knife to cut around the soil on the inside of the pot to release the tree. Once you have removed the tree from its pot, use a rake, root hook, chopstick or any other suitable implement to untangle and comb out the roots to remove the soil from most of the root-ball (roots) so that any long roots can hang down freely. A single root hook is ideal for untangling thicker, more complicated mature roots, while a fine rake would be more suited for combing out finer roots.

Using sharp clean scissors, trim the roots on all sides of the root-ball as well as from the underside, so that you are left with a flat circular pad of roots. You should aim for a neat and tidy appearance, while at the same time leaving sufficient fibrous roots to support the tree when it is finally repotted. When all the roots have been pruned satisfactorily, repot the tree.

Left: *The roots of a mature Japanese white pine (*Pinus parviflora*), showing the mycorrhiza, a beneficial symbiotic fungus.*

USEFUL TOOLS FOR ROOT PRUNING

- a pair of long-nosed scissors for trimming fine roots
- a pair of heavy-duty scissors for cutting heavier and larger roots
- a small folding saw for dealing with even larger roots
- a root hook (which has a single steel or brass, heavy-duty hook attached to a handle) for separating out a tangled and congested root system

---

If you are planning major pruning of the roots and top growth at the same time, you should ensure you take a balanced approach to the exercise. In other words, if you need to cut away half of the roots, you may also need to remove half or more of the foliage. This allows the tree to balance its root and top growth activity, and recovery following the repotting process will be much more rapid than if the tree were left unbalanced.

ROOT PRUNING A *JUNIPERUS CHINENSIS*

1 This Chinese juniper (*Juniperus chinensis*), taken from a cutting, has been grown in a flowerpot for four years.

2 Remove the plant from the pot and untangle the roots using a rake.

3 The roots can grow very long and will need to be shortened. Cut the roots short, using a pair of sharp scissors.

4 A good dense set of roots should be left on the cutting. The cutting is now ready to pot on into its training pot.

PREPARING POTS

All pots and containers should be clean and dry. If you are reusing old pots, it is important to clean them with a stiff brush using water to which a small amount of washing-up liquid has been added. This helps to dislodge stubborn dirt, but you will need to rinse the pots thoroughly afterwards.

Cover the drainage holes in the bottom of the pots with a piece of plastic mesh of the type that is usually sold as greenhouse shading material. This prevents soil from falling through the holes, as well as stopping most pests from entering the soil. This type of mesh is ideal because it is very thin and takes up a minimal amount of space in the bottom of the pot. If the traditional method of covering the holes with pieces of broken terracotta pot is used, a substantial amount of space will be taken up, especially in a shallow pot.

Hold the plastic mesh in place with what is loosely described as a wire "butterfly". Taking a short length of wire, bend it carefully into a loop at each end and subsequently bend the two ends up at right angles to produce a "butterfly". Pass the two ends through the holes, with the looped part under the bottom of the pot, and through the square of mesh. Bend the wire ends over to secure the mesh over the holes. This is necessary because when the tree is placed in the pot you will need to move it around to settle it in place, which could disturb the mesh from its position over the holes.

In most cases, bonsai trees will need to be anchored into their pots using a reasonably substantial gauge of wire. So, pass a longer length of wire along the bottom of the pot, thread the ends up through the holes and pull up tight. This tying-in wire will secure the tree within the pot at the repotting stage.

PREPARING A POT FOR POTTING OR REPOTTING

1 Twist a short length of wire into the shape of a butterfly.

2 Place a piece of plastic mesh over each hole. Push the free ends of the "butterfly" through the mesh and drainage hole, bending them back beneath the pot to secure the mesh.

3 Large pots may have special holes in the base for securing the tree with wire. If the pot does not have these holes, pass the wire through the drainage holes.

POTTING AND REPOTTING

Whether you are planting a new tree in a pot or repotting a tree from a smaller pot to a larger one, make sure that the tree is placed correctly and held securely. You also need to use the right type and amount of soil to firm it in place. Repotting often follows on from root pruning and, in such cases, take extra care over watering and feeding.

Prepare the pot as described, then cover the mesh with a layer of coarse grit or akadama. This acts as a drainage course for the soil and root system.

If the pot is rectangular or oval, position the tree so that it is slightly to the rear and to one side of the centre lines of the pot. If it is round, square, multi-sided or any other regular shape, place the tree in the centre.

A very useful tip is to place a small mound of soil in the centre of the pot so that the tree will have plenty of soil under its root-ball (roots). Spread out the roots and rotate the tree carefully both clockwise and anti-clockwise while pushing it down into the pot. This will ensure that the central roots make good contact with the soil.

Bring the two ends of the wire together, cross them over each other, and use pliers to twist the two ends, pulling at the same time, until the tree is firmly secured within the pot.

Add soil until the pot is full, working around the roots with a chopstick. The soil, if completely dry, should filter down among the roots. Never use wet or damp soil, as it will not be possible to achieve good soil-to-roots contact. Carefully brush away any excess soil, so that the soil finishes just below the rim of the pot. Water well with a fine rose on a watering can or submerge the pot in water until the soil is soaked.

Remember that if major pruning of root and top growth is also carried out, you need to retain a balanced structure. So, if you cut away half of the roots, you may need to remove half or more of the foliage. This helps the tree balance root and top growth activity.

Following repotting, keep the soil just moist. Do not apply fertilizer to a root-pruned and repotted bonsai as the nutrients will burn the freshly cut roots. Wait a few weeks before starting any sort of feeding programme.

REPOTTING A BONSAI

1 Use a sharp knife to cut around the edge of the pot and release the tree root.

2 Carefully lift the bonsai – here an *Acer palmatum* 'Ukon' – from the pot.

3 Rake the root-ball (roots) to remove the old soil.

4 The raked root-ball washed clean using a hose and showing the fibrous root structure.

5 The shallow form of the root structure can be clearly seen.

6 A close-up of the fibrous root formation and large surface roots.

7 This long root will need to be removed from the root-ball.

8 Trim the root system using a pair of scissors.

9 Prepare the pot with drainage mesh and "tying-in" wires.

10 Spread a layer of medium akadama over the bottom of pot.

11 Add more soil to create a mound in the centre of the pot.

12 Place the tree slightly off centre in the pot.

13 Work the tree down into the soil with a circular, backward-and-forward motion, using both hands.

14 The soil will push up through the gaps between the roots.

15 Thread the ends of the wire through the roots and then twist them together.

16 Use a pair of pliers to pull the wire taut.

17 Twist the two ends of the wire together, pulling at the same time.

18 Cut off the excess wire with wire cutters.

19 Push the twisted end of wire down into the soil.

20 Fill in around the roots with more soil. If the soil is dry, it will flow down between the roots.

21 Work the soil into the roots until all the gaps are filled.

22 Tidy the surface with a brush and water the soil thoroughly.

23 Completed repot, showing the ideal, off-centre positioning of the tree. The pot should be the same depth as the diameter of the trunk base.

BONSAI STYLES

Styles of bonsai range from single-trunk designs through multiple-trunk to group and forest plantings. The style you decide upon will, to some extent, depend on the plant specimen you have chosen. Indeed, each tree will suggest a particular style, and you should follow that natural suggestion to obtain the best result.

One of the most important points to remember is that all styles of bonsai are based on the way trees grow in the wild. A natural-looking design is therefore the real test of a good bonsai, rather than how well it fits into any particular bonsai category. By observing full-size trees, you can soon start to appreciate how trees grow and into which styles your bonsai may fit.

When styling any tree, the first feature to look for is a good surface-root system. This will give the base of the trunk a more mature look. Rake the soil away from the trunk, exposing the roots to enhance the look of the trunk-to-soil junction.

All bonsai have a best angle, which is usually referred to as the front of the tree, but ideally every bonsai should look good from all angles.

Left: *Pruning a Chinese juniper* (Juniperus chinensis) *using bonsai scissors. Care must be taken to cut only the shoots and not the foliage.*

Formal Upright – *CHOKKAN*

The name of this style is self-explanatory, being upright, straight and very rigid and formal in appearance, a shape that occurs frequently in nature when a tree is growing in ideal conditions. This means that there are no severe or adverse weather conditions and a constant source of suitable nutrients, as well as a good sustainable supply of water. In this bonsai style, the trunk of the tree should ideally have a very even taper from soil level right up to the apex. This straightness and taper create a very elegant and statuesque design which is not apparent in any other style of bonsai. Although these trees can have a symmetrical appearance, this is not so in every case, as a certain amount of asymmetry will give a much more pleasing and natural look.

Above: This Cedrus libani subsp. atlantica 'Glauca' is typical of the plant material that is available from garden centres or nurseries and is approximately 1.2m (4ft) high.

The tree's final shape should be well balanced and centred on the formal, vertical emphasis of the trunk. The branches will be mostly horizontal, which will help to accentuate the formal appearance of the trunk.

Suitable plants for styling as formal upright bonsai include many coniferous species such as pine (*Pinus*), larch (*Larix*), spruce (*Picea*) and juniper (*Juniperus*). Trees that normally develop an informal habit, such as fruiting and flowering varieties, are not very suitable for this style.

If the trunk is not completely straight, apply a piece of wire of suitable thickness and manipulate the trunk until it is straight when viewed from the front. Viewed from the side, the trunk should be angled very slightly to the rear as it rises from the soil, and again very slightly to the front in the upper part of the tree, giving the overall appearance of being vertical.

Assess which branches are best suited for the design. Choose a thick branch as the lowest one and then cut out any insignificant shoots, leaving enough branches to complete the design. Apply wire to the branch, then, after running the wire around the trunk once or twice, wind it along the next branch up the trunk. Continue to wire the rest of the branches and arrange them so that they all complement each other. Finally, trim back the tips of the branches to give a balanced tree.

You will need
- Branch cutters
- Vine pruners
- Wire cutters
- Pliers
- Rake
- Pot
- Mesh
- Wire
- Soil
- Scoop
- Chopstick

CREATING YOUR FORMAL UPRIGHT BONSAI

1 Remove the top of the plant, leaving the thickest part of the trunk, which will give the future bonsai more "character".

2 Using a pair of branch cutters at an angle, remove the top of the plant to leave a tapered top to the trunk.

3 Following the removal of the top of the plant, it can be seen that the plant is beginning to show much better proportions as a future bonsai.

4 After the removal of one right-hand branch, a second similar branch is reduced in length, by approximately one-half, using side cutters.

5 This view shows how different the plant looks at this stage when compared with the first step of the sequence.

6 There are now too many minor branches still in place which will need pruning out using side or branch cutters.

7 One small branch has been removed, but there are still three more that must be cut off to give the plant a more open feeling.

8 There is still a long branch high up on the trunk that needs to be removed in order to give a better overall appearance to the tree.

9 This picture shows the plant after pruning, wiring and basic shaping has been completed, prior to being repotted into a suitable bonsai pot.

Right: *This is the completed tree, planted in a suitable pot and now ready for many years as a bonsai.*

Informal Upright – *MOYOGI*

This style is probably the most commonly seen style both in the natural environment and in bonsai. In the wild, an informal upright tree will have a trunk that bends and curves, and has changes of direction due to competition from other trees or buildings situated close by. These changes could be linked to the prevailing weather conditions surrounding the tree through the seasons. This is probably one of the easiest of bonsai styles to create, which makes it ideal for beginners. Many trees grow naturally with slightly bending or informal trunks, and you will find that working with these natural curves can create a pleasant bonsai design. Remember that any branches should appear to grow from the outside of a trunk curve in order to give a natural look to the finished tree.

Above: *A* Pinus sylvestris *'Jeremy' plant should be easily obtainable from a conifer nursery or garden centre.*

The trunk of an informal upright bonsai should be upright, but not absolutely straight, standing somewhere between the vertical and an angle of 15 degrees to the vertical. It should flow gently from one side to the other with a graceful, fluid form.

Examine the base of the trunk closely before carrying out any work. Carefully study the tree and try to decide on a preferred best side or front. It may be that it would be better viewed from a totally different angle to the one from which it has been seen in its original pot. Any curvature in the lower trunk as it rises from the soil should go in the rearward direction, as any forward bulge tends to look ugly. The trunk may then undulate from side to side and from front to back, finally finishing with the apex just forward of the trunk base. The branch structure is then designed around this informality, with branches coming from irregular points on the trunk and alternating from side to side and around the back. The front of the trunk should not have any branches pointing straight at the viewer unless they are small and near the top of the tree, where they become part of the crown. The informality of this design means that it is possible to style an informal upright bonsai using only pruning techniques and no wire at all.

CREATING YOUR INFORMAL UPRIGHT BONSAI

You will need
- Rake
- Scissors
- Branch cutters
- Tweezers
- Wire cutters
- Pliers
- Wound sealer
- Pot
- Mesh
- Wire
- Soil
- Scoop
- Chopstick

1 Use a rake to clear excess soil from the top of the root-ball until the roots can be seen growing from the lower trunk.

2 Loose surface roots exposed by the raking process can now be identified and the "flair" of the trunk base can now be clearly seen.

3 Remove loose roots with sharp scissors, leaving a soil surface that shows a clean trunk base and some thicker surface roots which will become features in the future.

4 Using branch cutters, remove the central upward-pointing branch in order to open up the structure of the tree.

5 This is the central shoot following removal with a pair of branch cutters.

6 All excess branches should be eliminated until a basic tree shape begins to emerge.

7 Using a pair of tweezers, pull out the old, dark, stiff needles on the trunk and main branches, leaving only those on the shoot ends.

8 You can also remove the needles by gently pulling them out with your fingers.

9 The amount of needles remaining can be clearly seen and the tree is now ready for shaping by wiring and tip pruning.

10 Apply the wire, as described in the section on wiring techniques.

11 The tree is now fully wired and ready for careful manipulation into shape using gentle bending so that you do not break any of the branches.

12 The wire can be applied to two branches and anchored to the trunk between the two branches.

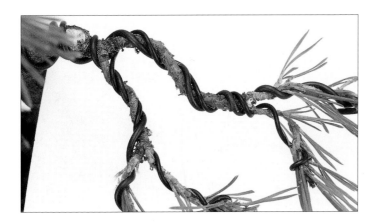

13 This detail of the lower right branch clearly shows how the branch has been bent into a zigzag shape which will eventually enhance the appearance of the tree by giving it greater maturity.

14 The shaping is finished and the tree is now ready to be planted into a suitable bonsai container.

Right: *A Japanese white pine (*Prunus parviflora*), after many years of bonsai training.*

Slanting - *SHAKAN*

This bonsai style is based on a tree growing in the wild that has been exposed to strong winds and very stormy weather, so that it has blown over at an angle slanting away from the prevailing wind. The natural reaction of the tree after this has happened is to redirect its branch growth to suit the new growing angle of the trunk. Most species of tree can be grown in this style and examples in nature can be seen on cliff tops and in mountainous areas where there is a prevailing wind that pushes the tree over to one side. When this becomes more pronounced, it generally falls into the windswept category, but it is difficult to draw a distinction between these two styles.

The slanting style of bonsai should have its trunk leaning to one side, usually by about 45 degrees from the vertical, although it can be as much as 60 degrees. The trunk need not necessarily be straight – it can have some movement in its shape – but the apex should always take on the same angle as the one formed where the trunk rises from the soil.

Following the slant of the trunk, the roots will normally be extended on the side away from the slant, while those on the side under the slant will be compressed. This gives the impression of the roots stabilizing what would otherwise be an unstable-looking design.

The basic steps described previously to ascertain the trunk angle and root structure should be followed so that the angle of the trunk looks as natural as possible. The position of the branches must relate to the trunk so that a mature shape is obtained. Should a branch need to be placed in a drooping position, ensure the junction with the trunk bends down as soon as it leaves the trunk to achieve a natural effect.

Above: *This is a hybrid* Rhododendron *that is commercially available from any good supplier of this type of material and measures 65cm (26in) from the top of the pot to the apex.*

When you are styling a bonsai from scratch, make sure that all of the branches are properly positioned, including the smallest twigs. The degree of attention to this type of detail in the early stages of styling can make or break the appearance of the end product. A suitable type of pot can be seen in the final picture.

CREATING YOUR SLANTING BONSAI

You will need
- Stiff brush
- Branch cutters
- Wound sealer
- Scissors
- Wire cutters
- Pliers
- Rake
- Pot
- Mesh
- Wire
- Soil
- Scoop
- Chopstick

1 The moss that has grown on the lower part of the trunk of the *Rhododendron* should be removed using a stiff brush, so that the plant has a completely clean trunk. The soil of bonsai trees is always just moist and this provides the ideal conditions in which moss will grow. The lower parts of the trunks can quickly become covered in moss, which should be removed regularly.

2 The lower part of the tree trunk has now been completely cleared of unwanted moss and the beautiful texture and colour of the bark can be clearly seen.

3 There are two branches growing from the same point on the trunk, one of which must be removed in order to improve the tree's structure. Using branch or side cutters, remove the branch with a clean cut close to the main trunk.

4 Following the removal of the excess branches and some thinning out of the twigs and foliage in the upper part of the plant, the shape is now much improved. This tree has a long way to go before it becomes properly shaped with an aged-looking branch structure. Several years of shoot pinching, refinement, repotting and correct feeding will produce an excellent flowering bonsai.

Right: *The tree is planted in a temporary pot because it is not known, at this stage, exactly what colour, shape or design of pot should be chosen. When the bonsai specimen is finally developed, it may need a slightly different glazed or semi-glazed pot for display purposes.*

Semi-cascade – *HAN-KENGAI*

This style reflects the effect of extreme growing conditions on a tree. It is designed to give the appearance of a very old tree growing from the side of a quarry or rock face, or perhaps on a riverbank, where all the tree's efforts have gone into growing towards the light. Although the trunk line may initially have been upright, in natural conditions it could have been bent over into a nearly horizontal position by falling rocks, stones or soil. Ideal material for training as semi-cascade bonsai are prostrate-growing plants, such as cotoneaster and juniper, which can be bought from plant nurseries.

Semi-cascade is the name that is usually given when a bonsai leans over to one side or the other from 45 to 60 degrees from the vertical, even as low as just below the horizontal or the rim of the pot. Some people think that it should not go below the rim, while others think that going just below this point often gives a better and more appealing appearance.

Most types of tree can be grown in the semi-cascade style, except for those that normally have a very powerful vertical growth habit which

will overcome the forces of nature. It is important to note that if a tree leans so far that it droops over the edge of the pot and down the side, it should then be classed as cascade-style bonsai.

Just as with the slanting style, there needs to be some root exposure in order to give the feeling of a stabilizing structure at the base of the trunk. Following the initial steps for the formal upright and informal upright bonsai styles that we have already described, assess the structure of the

Above: *The widely available creeping juniper, Juniperus horizontalis 'Green Carpet', is ideal material from which a semi-cascade bonsai can be developed.*

roots, as well as the line of the trunk. Work with the natural flow of the tree, if possible accentuating any of those natural features.

A suitable container would be square, hexagonal or any other regular shape, and it should be of a medium depth so that it is in balance with the tree.

CREATING YOUR SEMI-CASCADE BONSAI

You will need
- Branch cutters
- Wound sealer
- Scissors
- Rake
- Pot
- Mesh
- Wire
- Wire cutters
- Pliers
- Soil
- Scoop
- Chopstick

1 Remove the plant from the original plastic pot and remove any adventitious foliage to expose a clean trunk base. This will provide a better insight into the styling possibilities of this particular plant.

2 Remove the left-hand branch, using a pair of branch or side cutters in order to obtain a clean concave cut.

3 The plant is now ready to be planted into a bonsai container, following the removal of all the excess twigs and foliage.

4 After repotting into a suitable container, the tree is now in the early stages of becoming a fully styled bonsai specimen.

Below: *The finished styling exercise is shown here displayed on a flat slab of sandstone. This shows the basic shape following initial styling. With regular shoot pinching, the foliage area will bulk up over the next few growing seasons.*

Cascade – *KENGAI*

Once again, this style of bonsai represents a tree that has been growing in very difficult circumstances, such as out of the side of a rock face or somewhere similar. In fact, this style is intended to represent a tree in the wild that has been subjected to heavy winter snowfall, rock falls, avalanches and, indeed, its own weight, all of which would cause it to lean and fall vertically from wherever it is rooted. This particular design can be obtained by repositioning various parts of the trunk line and branches, so that a cascading and mature outline is achieved.

In this style, the trunk line will fall well below the horizontal, with its trunk tip resting level with the bottom of the pot or even lower. Just as with the semi-cascade style, the trunk line generally begins by growing almost vertically from soil level before cascading over and down the side of the pot.

This style is not easy to produce and would normally be considered an advanced project if one wished to achieve a satisfying result. A suitable plant to use would be one that has a long, flexible trunk that can be easily

manipulated with wire into an interesting cascade design. Such a plant need not already be cascading at the time of acquisition – it can be vertical or any other shape – but it is essential that the trunk is long and flexible.

All the usual initial procedures should be followed, such as looking at the base of the trunk and the formation of the roots, before deciding on the best way forward. Be careful when applying wire and with the subsequent bending because there is a

Above: *This is a typical, young* Cotoneaster horizontalis *that, due to a flexibility, is highly suited for styling as a cascade bonsai.*

risk of breaking the trunk. Should this happen, however, you could always use the tree for a totally different style.

Cascade bonsai require relatively deep pots to show off the cascading characteristics that you have designed. The pot shape should be regular but can, in some circumstances, also be natural and primitive in appearance to match the rugged look of the tree.

CREATING YOUR CASCADE BONSAI

You will need
- Branch cutters
- Scissors
- Wire cutters
- Pliers
- Wire
- Rake
- Pot
- Mesh
- Soil
- Scoop
- Chopstick

1 When working on a cascade bonsai, it may be helpful to work with the plant positioned on its display stand or post. The first part of the trunk should be cleared of growth, so remove any unwanted material in this area.

2 Begin wiring the trunk by pushing the end of the wire deep into the soil for anchorage.

3 Carefully wind the wire around the trunk to the length that is required, as described in the wiring section, and cut the wire ends cleanly when the process is complete.

4 If the trunk is extra thick, a second run of wire may be needed which can be applied alongside the first. This gives twice the bending power of one run of wire.

5 Using both hands, and your thumbs as levering points, carefully shape the trunk until a full cascading effect is achieved.

6 Continue the process further along the trunk until the whole of the trunk has been shaped satisfactorily.

7 Remove the excess growth, once you have decided on the final length of the trunk.

8 Here, the leading shoot is being removed in order to balance the length of the trunk.

9 Following the full wiring of the trunk and side branches, the tree is now ready to be placed in a decorative bonsai pot.

Right: *The styling is now complete and the bonsai has been potted in a Chinese pot and displayed on a late 19th-century plant stand. A tall stand enables the tree to be seen in the correct perspective.*

Twin Trunk – *SOKAN*

The twin-trunk style is a very popular arrangement of two trees. This occurs naturally when a tree grows with two trunks from ground level. A twin trunk such as this may be the result of seeds germinating close together. As the two plants grow, they combine by natural grafting into one joined at the base. A bonsai twin-trunk tree can be created either by planting two or more trees very closely together or by starting with a plant that already has two or more trunks. If you are starting with a plant that has more than two trunks, then clearly any other trunks will need to be removed. The choice of which trunks to remove depends upon the shape and position of all the trunks on the plant. You will need to select the best pair of trunks in terms of their relationship with each other to achieve a balanced final appearance.

Above: *'Ginny Gee' is a* Rhododendron racemosum *hybrid and is ideal for bonsai by virtue of its small leaves and flowers.*

The simplest way to begin is to buy a twin-stemmed plant from a nursery and convert it into bonsai following the steps shown here. If, however, you have two trees from which to work, tie them tightly at the base with raffia or grafting tape so that they graft together at this point as they grow. Avoid tying with wire, as this has no flexibility and can create a rather unsightly union, especially with smooth-bark species. Check the junction regularly during the early part of the process to ensure that it is going according to plan.

If there had been a space between the two plants in the early years of growth, the expansion of the trunk girths would have been so large that a natural twin-trunk specimen would be the end result.

Always use two plants of the same variety, so that the leaf shape and colour are the same. Also ensure that the two plants have different-sized trunks: the main trunk should be taller with a larger girth than the other trunk. If the two trunks are identical in girth, or almost identical, then the

bonsai will look too regimented. If you want to find a suitable twin-trunk tree in the wild, then remember to look for one with unequal-sized trunks.

When considering the viewing angle of this style, arrange the smaller trunk so that it is alongside the main trunk, but slightly to the rear or to the front of it, as this will give a much better appearance.

CREATING YOUR TWIN TRUNK BONSAI

You will need
- Rake
- Branch cutters
- Scissors
- Pot
- Mesh
- Wire cutters
- Pliers
- Wire
- Soil
- Scoop
- Chopstick

1 After removing the plant from its pot, gently rake away the surface of the soil until the base of the trunk and any surface roots begin to show, and cut out any excess lower shoots until a clear tree image is formed.

Right: *Following pruning and styling, the tree has been planted in a deep rectangular pot and displayed on a simple oak stand. Compared with the off-centre placing on the stand in the picture above, it can be seen that a central placing is best.*

2 Clear away any excess internal shoots and minor branches until the required shape emerges.

3 The finished tree after the pruning and styling process has been completed.

Triple Trunk – *SAMBON-YOSE*

Multiple plantings should consist of three, five, seven and so on as a well-balanced group is difficult to achieve with even numbers except two. Here, we will be looking at the approach to a triple-trunk planting that can often be seen growing naturally in the wild. Any species of tree may be used to create this style of bonsai, but you will discover that it is largely conifers that have this type of growth formation. The plant material that you choose will need to include three plants with trunks of varying thicknesses, as well as of different heights. However, bear in mind that the heights of the trunks can be altered easily by pruning. Trees that have one-sided root systems would also be highly suitable because the bases of the trunks will need to be placed very closely together to create a satisfactory final design.

Above: *Three European larch plants,* Larix decidua, *in plastic flowerpots, which can be purchased from nurseries or garden centres.*

The trees chosen for this grouping are European larch (*Larix decidua*), and have been growing in individual pots for several years. They are about 20 years old and have trunks of varying thickness, which is very important when you are putting a group of this type together.

The traditional approach is to select the tree with the thickest trunk as the main tree which should then be placed towards the front of the grouping, with the subsequent positioning of the other two trees also being extremely important. Each tree must be securely attached to the pot and to the bases of the other two trees in order to encourage them to grow even more closely together as they mature alongside each other.

When cutting the roots back to enable the trees to be placed close together, it must be remembered that sufficient roots need to remain on each tree to enable them to survive the process and to grow on in the future. When the roots have been cleaned of soil, it is also necessary to keep the roots moist to prevent the trees from suffering dehydration. Use a fine atomizing spray to apply a fine mist of water to the roots if they appear to be drying out.

Once the trees are secured and the soil topped up and watered, the branches will need to be wired and manipulated into place to give the trees a mature overall design.

You will need
- Pot
- Mesh
- Wire
- Soil
- Wire cutters
- Branch cutters
- Scissors
- Pliers
- Rake
- Scoop
- Chopstick

CREATING YOUR TRIPLE TRUNK BONSAI

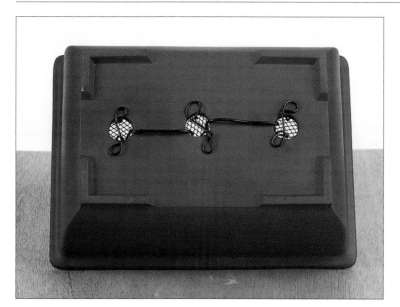

1 Prepare the bottom of the initial training pot with "butterfly" mesh retainers and "tying-in" wire.

2 This is the inside of the training pot showing the drainage mesh and "tying-in" wires in place.

3 Place a layer of coarse akadama over the bottom of the pot in order to improve drainage, followed by some medium akadama which will be the main soil ingredient.

4 Cut away the roots of the two largest plants on one side in preparation for placing them close together.

5 Place the two plants next to each other, with their roots pushed closely together.

6 Using 3mm (⅛in) wire, tie the first tree into the pot by twisting the ends of the wire tightly together with a pair of pliers.

7 Tie the second tree in place, close to the first, so that their bases are almost touching. ▷

8 After cutting the roots to fit, tie in the third tree, making sure that it is very closely positioned alongside the first two.

9 Wire all the trees firmly into the pot, so that they are all very secure because new roots will easily break if the trees are loose in the pot.

10 Here, all three of the trees have been securely wired into place.

11 Top up the soil using a scoop and then work the soil in and around the roots with a chopstick until the pot is completely filled.

12 The three trees are now finally planted and secured in the pot.

13 Prune out any unwanted shoots and branches, thus creating a pleasing shape.

14 After careful wiring and shaping, the triple trunk now looks relatively mature.

Right: *When complete, the group of trees should look like a full-size natural group of trees. Here, the triple-trunk planting has been improved by displaying it on a good-quality mahogany stand.*

Group or Forest – *YOSE-UYE*

This style of bonsai planting is intended to create the appearance of a copse, spinney, small wood or even a large forest, only in miniature. A group or forest can be created using anything from five to fifty or more trees; in fact, you can use as many trees as can be satisfactorily handled. The only stipulation is that there should be an odd number of trees in order to lend a more balanced appearance to the final design. Your aim should be to create a group that gives the viewer the feeling of being within a wooded area, while being aware that it will be viewed from the outside. It may take several plantings to achieve this effect. Most types of plant are suitable, but, by keeping to the same species and variety for each group, you will achieve a more natural appearance.

Above: *A pot of beech plants – here* Fagus sylvatica *'Purpurea' – which are usually supplied for planting a hedge and are normally very inexpensive to purchase.*

Aim for a feeling of authenticity by obtaining a good sense of depth and perspective. Preferably, the group should not include any straight line of three trees or more, and no trunk should be hidden behind another when viewed from the front or side.

Make sure there is good mix of sizes to achieve a natural look. Also, choose one tree that is larger than the rest to act as a focal point. Note that branches may need to be removed from all the trees so they can sit closely together and not become confused with each other.

Starting with the largest tree, remove the lowest branches before positioning it in the prepared pot, just to the right or left of the centre and about halfway back. Place the second largest tree close to the first tree, removing branches as necessary. Then, position the rest of the trees, preferably one at a time, close to each other so that they form a natural-looking group or forest. Place the smaller trees on the outside of the group, but generally not at the front, so that the group appears to have been growing for many years.

Secure the trees into the container as you work, and fill in with soil by working it around the roots with a chopstick. Water thoroughly to settle the soil and trees into the container. Trim any remaining long shoots to give a balanced appearance, then place the completed group outdoors in a shady spot to acclimatize.

CREATING YOUR GROUP OR FOREST BONSAI

You will need
- Scissors
- Branch cutters
- Wire cutters
- Pliers
- Rake
- Pot
- Mesh
- Wire
- Soil
- Scoop
- Chopstick

1 One individual beech plant, showing the slim trunk, which is so suitable for group plantings, and with a good root system.

2 Remove any insignificant roots high on the trunk, thus creating a clean lower trunk.

3 Now, cut off the remainder of the tap root, leaving a cluster of fibrous roots near the required trunk base.

4 Tidy up the remaining roots in order to leave a small, neat set of roots. The roots of all the plants to be used in the group should be treated in the same way.

5 Prepare a shallow pot and add some initial soil. The first two beech plants will be placed to the right of the centre and at about the half-way point from front to back.

6 Plunge the two plants into the soil and then work in some soil around them.

7 The plants may not be very stable at this stage, but when all the plants are in place, they will support each other.

▷

8 Add three more beech plants, making a total of five in all, and again work the roots down into the soil.

9 Using a scoop, add some extra soil around the roots of all five of the plants. It should be noted that the plants are inserted very close to each other. This needs to be done to make the final bonsai group look realistic.

10 When all fifteen plants have been introduced, more soil is added until the pot is full. The plants in this group are roughly arranged in two closely related sub-groups, with all trees set very close together.

11 Use a chopstick to work the soil thoroughly around the roots of the plants, so that there is good contact with the soil throughout the root system.

12 The appearance of the top of the group can be improved by carefully selecting and removing any unsightly shoots that may be too long and look out of place.

13 The final grouping shows the close relationship of all the plants. This positioning is necessary if you are to achieve a natural-looking group or forest.

Right: *When complete, the group will begin to look like a small mature copse. The pot shown is temporary to encourage the trees' root development. Pots for bonsai groups must be shallow, and either oval or rectangular in shape.*

Windswept – *FUKINAGASHII*

On clifftops or mountains, trees grow in many different ways, but mostly in a windswept style caused by constant exposure to the prevailing winds coming from just one direction. Such trees will generally have a slanting trunk, with branches only on the leeward side of the trunk where the forces of nature are less harsh. Many trees in these situations have straight trunks with only the top part curved over away from the direction of the wind. Virtually any plant is suitable for creating a bonsai in the windswept style, although one with a leaning trunk would be easier if you are a beginner.

A straight trunk may be used, but it would have to tilt to give the impression of a wind-battered tree. The main interest of a tree like this is that the branch structure sweeps in one direction, which is the same direction as the one in which the trunk is leaning.

Suitable trees for the windswept style are pines, junipers, or tough deciduous trees such as hawthorn. These varieties are capable not only of surviving in a harsh natural habitat, but also of being manipulated, pruned and wired to form a windswept bonsai.

When selecting a suitable plant, check the root structure to find a plant which has strong roots on one side. This will then become the side that is opposite to the lean of the trunk because, in nature, the roots would develop a stronger structure on that side in order to support the leaning tree.

Remove the branches on what will appear to be the windward side of the trunk, along with any other insignificant branches. Position the remaining branches using the wiring techniques outlined earlier to obtain a

Above: *This* Juniperus chinensis *has been grown as a bonsai for several years and is now suitable for styling as a windswept-style bonsai.*

mature windswept feeling. Once the tree has been prepared, plant it in a suitable pot, tie it in place, top it up with soil and water in well.

Pots for this style of bonsai are generally round and shallow, but may have a rough, primitive finish, reflecting the fact that natural trees of this style would often exist in similarly rough surroundings.

You will need
- Branch cutters
- Scissors
- Wire cutters
- Pliers
- Rake
- Pot
- Mesh
- Wire
- Soil
- Scoop
- Chopstick

CREATING YOUR WINDSWEPT BONSAI

1 When viewed from a lower angle, it can be seen that the branches are all growing in one direction, indicating that a windswept design is possible.

Right: *The bonsai is displayed on a suitable base and against a sympathetic background so that the final design can be fully appreciated. The tree will need several years of work before it is fully developed.*

3 Following the process of wiring and positioning all of the branches, the windswept form is even more accentuated.

2 When the pot is tilted slightly to the rear and left using a suitable block, the potential of the windswept design for this particular specimen becomes even more apparent.

4 The tree has been repotted at a different angle to complete the windswept design.

Raft – *IKADABUKI*

The raft or straight-line style is based upon a natural phenomenon that occurs when a tree is blown over. Although the trunk of the tree lies flat on the ground, it may survive if some of the roots remain attached and viable. Many of the branches will have been broken off when the tree hit the ground, leaving that side of the trunk in contact with the soil. Eventually, roots will emerge from here, while the remaining branches begin to grow into a vertical position. After many years, the original broken roots will have rotted away, and what remains will look like several trees growing together.

When looking for a suitable plant, ideally choose one that has a one-sided branch structure, which will mean less pruning to achieve the raft style. If this is not possible, purchase a tree that has a good set of branches, and remove all the branches on one side of the trunk.

Lay the tree down on the branchless side of the trunk, and use scissors to remove the roots that are now revealed at the base of the upper side of the trunk. Removing half the root system will not harm the tree, as half the branches have already been removed.

In fact, this equal pruning of branches and roots will ensure a balanced regrowth of the plant. If you need to remove more than half the root system for aesthetic purposes, then you should also remove a roughly equal number of branches to balance the plant and so ensure its survival.

Next, select the best remaining branches to be the new set of trunks, removing any that will not suit the shape. You will probably have to wire all the branches and place them in a more suitable, near-vertical, position

Above: *This is a Chinese juniper (*Juniperus chinensis*) that has been previously grown as a bonsai and is ideal for styling as a raft-style bonsai, as can be seen from the fact that the branches are all on one side of the trunk.*

to create a group-like appearance. Finally, select the most suitable secondary branches (removing the rest), position them with wire and trim branch tips where necessary.

The most widely used pots for this style are long, narrow and oval. Thin slabs of slate or rock may also be used.

CREATING YOUR RAFT

You will need
- Rake
- Branch cutters
- Scissors
- Knife
- Wire cutters
- Pliers
- Wire
- Scoop
- Chopstick
- Wound sealer
- Pot
- Mesh
- Soil

1 The congested root system is apparent and needs to be raked, untangled and pruned so that a manageable amount of root remains.

2 Having raked away most of the soil and untangled the roots, cut back the roots until a compact pad of roots remains.

3 It is necessary to remove squares of bark on the lower side of the trunk. When this side of the trunk is beneath the surface of the soil, roots will grow around the edges of the removed squares of bark.

4 Cut into the bark using a sharp knife and then peel away the squares of bark in order to leave exposed areas of the heartwood.

5 Six pieces of bark have been removed. This should result in six areas of root growth on the underside of the trunk following planting in the soil.

6 Begin the shaping process by wiring the trunk and all of the main branches of the tree.

7 In this close-up, it can be seen that some of the wires run from one branch to another. This will ensure that the wire is properly anchored, so that the branches remain in the desired position.

8 The initial wiring is complete and the relationship between the old trunk, which will form the new root system, and the old branches that will be the new trunks, is now becoming clear.

9 A long, shallow pot has been prepared with securing wires and a base layer of soil. The tree is then lowered into position.

10 Press the tree into the surface of the soil using gentle side-to-side movements. Bring the ends of the wires together in pairs.

11 Twist the ends of the wires together with a pair of pliers, pulling at the same time, so that you can be certain that the tree is securely fixed in the pot.

12 Make sure that the pairs of wire ends are twisted and pulled tight because this will enable the new roots to grow without disturbance.

13 Top up the pot with soil using a scoop and work the soil into and around the existing root system, as well as the old trunk that is now below the surface of the soil.

14 Water the completed raft arrangement thoroughly, using a watering can that has been fitted with a fine rose attachment. This will ensure that the soil is not disturbed.

15 This is the completed raft arrangement following the tidying of the surface of the soil and careful watering.

Above: *The smaller branches have now been wired and carefully manipulated into their final position. What was once a rather insignificant-looking plant has been transformed into a root-connected group that is commonly known as a raft.*

Root-in-Rock Planting – *ISHIZUKI*

Throughout the world, there are many places where trees can be seen growing on, over or in rock formations. It will have taken many years for the roots, often exposed over parts of the rock, to have grown into extremely interesting formations. It is these naturally occuring forms, when reproduced for the purposes of bonsai, that can create a very natural and inspirational design. Three variations of rock planting are commonly used in bonsai. These are "root-on-rock", "root-over-rock" and "root-in-rock". The name for each style aptly describes the placing of the roots relative to the piece of rock.

Achieving this style relies upon finding a suitable plant, as well as a matching piece of rock. The roots will be on the surface of the rock and covered with soil and moss; they will not necessarily carry on down to soil level. The roots grow in an artificially created or natural hole or crevice in the rock, which contains all the roots as well as the soil in which they grow.

Start with a piece of tufa (a porous sedimentary limestone that is easy to carve with a chisel or spatula), and make a hollow for the plant's roots.

Choose a small plant with a compact root-ball (roots) that will fit inside the hollow. Place a layer of soil in the cavity, then plant the tree in it, firming it in and topping up with extra soil until the plant is secure. Trim the plant and remove any unwanted branches to give the appearance of a naturally formed composition.

You may need to feed this type of bonsai more often than is normally the case because rain and regular watering will wash away the nutrients quite quickly.

Above: *This piece of tufa already has one hole in a suitable position for growing a cascade-style tree. You will need a couple of plants; here,* Juniperus procumbens *'Nana' has been used. The first plant has had its roots trimmed ready to fit the hole.*

Tufa retains water for some time, but does not waterlog the roots growing in the rock. Stand the tufa in a shallow basin of water so that the water is absorbed slowly. This will help with watering because of the water-retentive quality of tufa.

You will need
- Rock
- Soil
- Branch cutters
- Scissors
- Knife
- Scoop
- Chopstick
- Moss
- Basin

CREATING YOUR ROOT-IN-ROCK BONSAI

1 Using your fingers, carefully press the root-ball of the plant into the hole until it is securely in place. Fill in the cavity with soil.

2 Using a sharp pair of cutters, remove all the branches, except those that are cascading down over the side of the rock.

3 Here, it is clear which branches need to be pruned so that only downward-growing branches remain in place.

4 With the piece of rock standing in its finished position, offer up the second plant to ascertain where the second hole needs to be placed.

5 Tufa is very soft and is easily carved using a spatula or other similar instrument. Make sure that the hole is large enough to receive the roots of the second plant.

6 Gently press the second plant into position, filling in any spaces around the roots of both plants with soil. Place a layer of moss over the soil of both trees in order to complete the natural effect.

7 The completed planting can then be placed in a shallow basin which has been filled with water. As tufa is very porous, it will absorb enough water to suit the needs of the plants.

8 Allow the two plants to settle in for several weeks until the roots begin to grow into the porous tufa. At a later date, the two trees can be wired into shape so that they closely follow the contour of the rock.

Right: *The two trees, having been planted in the tufa, will require several years to reach maturity.*

Root-over-Rock Planting – *SEKIJOJU*

This style can be achieved by choosing a tree that has a long root system and washing away all the soil to expose the roots. If such a tree cannot be found, encourage the roots of your chosen plant to grow by placing it in a very long temporary container, such as a plastic tree guard, until the roots reach the bottom. Then, remove the tree from the tube and spread the roots over a piece of rock with an interesting shape until they fit closely to it. Tie the roots securely to the rock using wire. The preparation of a plant for root-over-rock planting can take several years, as the process of producing the long roots can be very slow, but, once you have achieved your first set of long roots, it is rewarding to know that it really can be done. This will encourage you to try something bigger and better.

Above: *This mountain pine,* Pinus mugo *'Pumilio', underwent extensive wiring and shaping several weeks prior to this exercise and has been allowed enough time to settle in before the next stage of the process.*

Plant the chosen tree – here a *Pinus mugo* 'Pumilio' – in a deep container, covering the whole root-ball (roots), including the rock, with some soil. Over the next few years, the roots will expand and develop a close fit with the rock, appearing to cascade over it. This means that when the rock is eventually exposed, a very interesting root structure should have developed that follows its contours.

This style is probably one of the most difficult of all the bonsai designs to tackle and ultimately perfect

because, while the roots are maturing under the surface of the soil, it is not possible to know what, if anything, is actually happening.

However, you should rest assured that, given sufficient time, the roots of the tree will eventually thicken and become attached, as well as cross over with other roots. The roots will also become naturally grafted to each other while they are submerged beneath the soil. Time is perhaps one of the most important considerations for the successful development of this style.

Patience will also be necessary because it is a serious mistake to uncover the roots too soon. It is crucial that they stay covered with soil if they are to enlarge correctly.

The container for this style should be rugged in appearance to suit the ruggedness of the rock.

CREATING YOUR ROCK-OVER-ROOT PLANTING BONSAI

You will need
- Hook
- Rock
- Wire cutters
- Wire
- Branch cutters
- Scissors
- Pliers
- Rake
- Scoop
- Chopstick
- Pot
- Mesh
- Soil
- Sphagnum moss

1 Following the removal of the lower half of the root-ball (roots), rake out the rest of the roots using a suitable single hook.

2 Rake away the rest of the soil until the roots are free of soil.

3 Wash the roots thoroughly using a low-pressure water jet from a garden hose.

4 You need to wash the roots very thoroughly, so that they can be placed easily and cleanly over the rock.

5 Carefully spread out the roots by hand and then place them over the rock.

6 Press the roots into place so that they straddle as many sides of the rock as possible.

7 Using a length of 3mm (⅛in) wire, tie the tree firmly to the rock and secure by twisting the two ends of the wire together.

8 Wind a longer length of 3mm (⅛in) wire several times around the roots, securing them all in close proximity with the rock, and again twist the ends together.

9 Choose a pot that is large enough to accept the whole rock-and-root system, and place a layer of soil in the bottom.

10 Press the rock, complete with the roots, into the soil, making sure that the top of the rock does not come above the level of the pot rim, and fill in with soil.

11 Add a layer of sphagnum moss to the surface of the soil in order to keep the surface roots moist and soft.

12 Covering the surface of the soil completely with moss is absolutely essential.

13 Following the planting of the whole rock into the pot, the project is now complete, but it will take several years for the roots to grow in close contact with the rock. Eventually, the rock and the roots around it will be exposed.

Right: *The completed tree is finally placed in a temporary pot with the roots and rock below the surface of the soil.*

Literati – *BUNJIN*

This is an unusual style which does not conform to the general rules of bonsai styling. It often appears in nature when a number of trees have grown together over many years, and then some have died or been removed, leaving just a few individual trees. These trees will have grown tall in the stiff competition for available light, and the resulting foliage will be on or near the top of the trees. Examples of this style growing in the wild are often pines. This style of tree can also be seen growing with tall, slim, freestyle-type trunks, with just a few branches positioned quite high up on the tree. The literati style is a very useful one because it can be used to make a bonsai from almost any plant that is tall and gangly, and which does not fit into any other bonsai category.

Above: *This Scots pine* (Pinus sylvestris) *was collected from the wild and grown in a temporary timber training box. It is partially wired and styled, and shown here from its best angle before final styling.*

Trees in the literati style normally have a tall, slim, free-style trunk, often with very little taper, culminating in a small number of branches in the apex of the tree. The trunk is very important: it is almost never straight and should be full of character, with slight twists and turns, although nothing too accentuated.

When you are choosing a tree that is suitable for turning into a literati bonsai, you will need to find one that may have been neglected, damaged, or both, making it unsuitable for any other style. It need not have a particularly good surface root system, as in nature this type of tree tends to grow that way; in fact, they appear to rise straight from the soil with very little visible support. If you intend to start from scratch, making the branches droop severely means that the effect of considerable age can be easily achieved.

Most conifers, but particularly pines (*Pinus*), will make good literati. In fact, it is species or varieties of this genus that seem to adopt the literati shape when growing naturally in the wild.

As this style is tall and slender, suitable pots would be circular, relatively shallow and not too large, as anything too big could overpower the elegant but rugged character of the trees. A rather rough, primitive pot would be suitable for this style, as it would enhance its rugged nature.

You will need
- Branch cutters
- Scissors
- Wire cutters
- Pliers
- Rake
- Pot
- Mesh
- Wire
- Soil
- Scoop
- Chopstick

CREATING YOUR LITERATI BONSAI

1 Close-up of the triple-wiring technique used during the application of the wire.

2 The appearance of the triple-wiring technique after the application of the wire.

3 View of the right-hand side of the partially wired and styled tree.

4 The rear of the partially wired and styled pine showing the extent of branch repositioning.

5 Following the wiring of all the branches, this is now the preferred front of the tree.

6 The left-hand side of the tree after wiring and shaping.

7 Rear view of the tree after final wiring and shaping.

8 Right-hand side of the tree after the final wiring and shaping process. The tree is now beginning to take on the shape of an old mature specimen.

Right: *The finished styled bonsai has been repotted into a drum pot, which is ideally suited to the literati style.*

Driftwood – *SHARIMIKI*

The driftwood style is considered a more advanced technique. It reflects the natural look of old junipers and pines, which have areas of trunk that are totally free of bark. In the wild, this is caused by natural die-back or by lightning. Whatever the cause, the result can be dramatic and exciting. This style can be formed by taking a plant with a thick trunk and stripping part of the bark away to create the driftwood. It can also be formed by using a piece of suitable driftwood and attaching a younger plant to it. This is often called a "wraparound" as the living material is simply wrapped around a piece of dead wood.

Driftwood techniques can be used in several other styles of bonsai, including the literati, informal upright, cascade and windswept styles. If you are going to create a driftwood-style bonsai from a single plant, then you will need one that has a thick trunk so that you can strip away the bark from the main trunk to form the basis of the driftwood.

A much simpler method is to use a piece of collected driftwood or perhaps even the dead trunk of an old bonsai.

If you use the latter, then treat it with a wood preservative which will soak completely into the dead wood. This may need to be repeated several times over a period of months to make sure that the wood is properly protected against the normal decaying process that wood undergoes, particularly when wet. The piece of treated wood will then need to be left to dry thoroughly, so that all traces of any unsafe liquids in the preservative have evaporated away.

Above: A Cedrus deodara *nursery plant and a piece of driftwood, both of which are suitable for creating a driftwood-style bonsai.*

You will need various tools for attaching the plant to the driftwood, including stainless-steel screws, raffia and wire, as well as a power drill. When using power tools, follow the manufacturer's safety guidelines.

Suitable pots for this style vary, but as the form is rugged and primitive, the pot should reflect these qualities.

CREATING YOUR DRIFTWOOD BONSAI

You will need
- Branch cutters
- Knife
- Rake
- Sprayer
- Screwdriver
- Screws
- Raffia
- Wire cutters
- Wire
- Scissors
- Pot
- Mesh
- Soil
- Scoop
- Chopstick

1 Remove the shoots and branches completely on one side of the plant and, using a sharp knife, cut away approximately half of the trunk on the side from which the branches have been removed.

2 Rake out the root-ball (roots) in order to remove excess soil, and trim the roots into a compact system. Spray the roots regularly to prevent them drying out because this style takes a long time to produce. Using a power tool or hand screwdriver, attach the lower trunk to the lower part of the driftwood. Stainless-steel screws are preferable, but brass would be a good second choice.

3 Continue to attach the trunk with screws, making sure that the cut side of the trunk sits adjacent to the driftwood.

4 The trunk can be curved around to the front of the driftwood so that it follows any curving features of the driftwood, and then secured with raffia.

5 When the trunk becomes too narrow to accept a screw, continue to attach it to the driftwood by tying it tightly with raffia.

6 While you are attaching the plant to the driftwood, keep spraying the roots regularly and cover them with a plastic bag to retain moisture. This will assist the tree during the lengthy attachment process.

7 The tree is planted in a suitable pot and secured firmly with wire as described in the repotting section. The most exposed and best-looking part of the driftwood normally forms the front of the bonsai.

8 Some of the branches are removed, with the remaining branches being wired and carefully manipulated into place to create a tree-like shape.

9 With the wiring and shaping now complete, any downward-growing foliage is removed in order to leave the tree with a tidy and compact shape.

11 Close-up of the top of the tree, showing the raffia attachment and branch wiring in detail.

12 The interesting structure of the lower part of the driftwood which will eventually be the main lower trunk of the finished bonsai.

10 This is the back of the driftwood on the upper part of the tree, showing the position of the trunk and branch in relation to it.

Right: *The finished styling shows the basic shape of the tree. This will be enhanced over the following years as the foliage areas bulk out and the real bonsai emerges.*

Twisted Trunk – *NEJKAN*

This style clearly has a very strong Chinese connection because it is followed by many Chinese bonsai artists. Indeed, ancient Chinese artefacts often contain paintings of trees such as this. Many different types of plants can be trained in this style of bonsai, but it is obviously advisable to choose a variety that has a very flexible trunk so that its shape can easily be altered with a suitable application of wire. Once the wire has been added, it is then possible to manipulate the trunk line into virtually any shape you wish, as long as the trunk is flexible enough. The structure of the branches is then styled so that they blend well with the line of the trunk.

The twisted trunk is not a very popular style for bonsai because it does not have a particularly natural appearance. The trunk is actually spiral-shaped, and this can be achieved by using thick wire to manipulate it into place. You will need a tree with a fairly thick trunk that is flexible enough to be curved into the required shape. Use a rake to scrape away the surface soil so that you can check the healthiness of the root system and establish which is the best side to form the front. Select branches that will make a natural-looking tree.

Using branch or knob cutters, remove any unwanted branches so that the full trunk line is exposed. The complete tree is then wired with wires of an appropriate thickness, so that the structure can be formed by gently bending the branches. Always make sure that a single piece of wire is used to travel from the branch around the trunk and along another so that two branches can be anchored by each other. It is important to wire all branches, however large or small, so that every single part of the tree can be

Above: *A mountain pine (*Pinus mugo*) which has been grown in a shallow container for several years to obtain a shallow root system suitable for bonsai training.*

worked into a suitable position. This will ultimately result in a design that is pleasing to the eye.

When the final shape of the bonsai has been achieved, you will need to trim back all the shoot tips lightly in order to encourage the generation of more new buds within the inner parts of the tree.

You will need
- Branch cutters
- Scissors
- Wire
- Wire cutters
- Rake
- Pot
- Mesh
- Soil
- Scoop

CREATING YOUR TWISTED TRUNK BONSAI

1 Tilt the tree by resting the rear of the root-ball on the back edge of the seed tray. This will give a better appearance to the line of the trunk.

2 Use branch cutters to remove the branch that is obscuring the front trunk-line of the tree.

4 Using branch cutters, prune out any long, uninteresting branches.

5 Wire the remaining branches and carefully bend them into place.

3 Cut out all the minor inner branches with a pair of scissors, so that the full extent of the twisted-trunk line is shown at its best.

6 Bend the rest of the branches into place, and trim away excessively long shoots to refine the outline.

Right: *Following the completion of the styling, the bonsai is placed in a pot that reflects the curvaceous nature of the tree.*

Exposed Root – *NEAGARI*

The roots of many trees in the wild are uncovered by years of exposure to natural elements such as rain and wind. Indeed, some elderly trees have a large number of roots exposed, so that the tree looks as if it is standing on stilts. In the world of bonsai, these natural features can be artificially created by growing roots specially for the purpose, but it is easier for novices in the art and culture of bonsai to acquire a plant that already has thickened roots. When visiting plant centres or bonsai nurseries, you will need to examine the root systems of your potential purchase, but be careful not to disturb them too much, unless you are confident that you will buy the tree, because the staff may not be pleased. As with all bonsai, the appearance of this style can be improved by adding some moss to the surface of the soil.

Above: *This trident maple (Acer buergerianum) has been purchased from a bonsai nursery. It is highly suited to the exposed-root style.*

In the exposed-root style, you are trying to copy a natural feature, as you are with all bonsai, whatever the style. Indeed, the first task you must carry out to turn a garden-centre plant into a bonsai is to rake the surface soil away from the roots to expose some of them. This gives the lower part of the tree a mature and established look. You should find a tree that has long, mature roots by probing into the soil before you buy. Virtually any species of tree may be used and a suitable pot would be simple and rugged.

The exposed part of the root system now technically becomes part of the bonsai trunk and must be treated in the same way as normal. The exposed roots will need to be kept clean and free of the moss that will slowly cover the lower part of the trunk if it is not kept in check. A stiff brush, such as an old toothbrush, is ideal for this purpose, but bonsai suppliers will also have a range of suitable brushes that will allow you to access narrow gaps between some of the exposed roots.

Some people are tempted to fill the gap in the exposed-root system with a rock of some kind, but this will only turn your exposed-root bonsai into a root-over-rock style and would defeat the original purpose. It would be acceptable to add a rock alongside the tree, but do not fill in any gaps between the roots.

You will need
- Rake
- Brush
- Root shears
- Scissors
- Pot
- Mesh
- Wire
- Soil
- Scoop
- Chopstick

CREATING YOUR EXPOSED ROOT BONSAI

1 Remove the tree from the pot, taking care not to damage the branches because they can be quite brittle in a trident maple.

2 Rake the soil away to expose the thickened roots that will become the exposed part of the bonsai root system.

3 Brush the main roots clean, using a stiff brush, until the mature part of the root-ball (roots) is completely exposed.

4 Trim the fibrous root-ball with root shears so that the bottom is neat and flat. This will help you to fit the tree into a suitably sized bonsai pot.

5 Settle the tree into a prepared pot with the best roots to the front.

6 Fill the pot with soil using a scoop, and work it around the roots with a chopstick.

Above: *When the roots are securely placed in the pot, the appearance of the soil surface can be improved with the application of some moss to make the finished tree look more natural.*

Clump – *KABUBUKI OR KABUDACHI*

There are several ways that this design can be created, but the most common involves gathering several young trees together and tying them tightly at the base for several years so that they naturally graft together. You must make sure that the trees do not become strangulated. If it looks as though this is likely to happen, then the tie should be released and another applied. This style can be seen quite often in the wild, usually in woodland areas where many seeds have germinated, grown in close proximity, and then grafted together over a number of years. It is a very simple bonsai style to create because it needs little in the way of materials, tools and spare time. Simple young plants will be ideal to use, as they will grow rapidly to produce the desired result.

Above: *Five common beech (*Fagus sylvatica*) hedging plants, which are suitable for creating a clump-style bonsai.*

There are very many plant varieties that are suitable for this fairly simple style. Deciduous trees are recommended in particular because they graft together more easily than coniferous plants. For beginners to bonsai, it would be much better to start with young plants that can be easily obtained from your local plant centre. Small self-seeded plants would also make ideal plant material, but they may be smaller than those plants that are commercially available and your bonsai would take longer to mature.

If you are a little more ambitious, the process described can be carried out on very much larger plants, which will provide a more challenging, and possibly more interesting, final design. You will need a more substantial tying mechanism, such as wire, to hold all the plants together and a larger pot to accommodate the root system.

As with any bonsai styling and arrangement process, you will need to be very patient because the growth rate of plants can vary considerably. Young plants tend to graft together quickly,

while older plants will inevitably be very much slower. Always take your time when constructing any bonsai arrangement and never allow the roots to dry out completely. Simply make sure that you have a water spray to hand, so that regular applications of water can be made to the roots. This will enhance the survival rate of the bonsai following completion.

You will need
- Rake
- Scissors
- Raffia
- Pot
- Mesh
- Wire
- Wire cutters
- Soil
- Scoop
- Chopstick

CREATING YOUR CLUMP BONSAI

1 Remove any roots that appear high up on the trunk, leaving radial roots for development.

2 Remove the thick tap roots completely, so that only fine fibrous roots remain. This will encourage more fibrous roots to develop.

3 Shorten the remaining fibrous roots, leaving a reasonable amount to ensure the survival of the plant.

4 All five plants have been root-pruned and are now ready for assembly into the initial clump design.

5 Using a length of raffia, tie the five tightly together immediately above the root system of each plant.

6 Prepare a shallow, oval pot and then add some soil before carefully placing the clump of trees in the soil.

7 The roots should be worked well into the soil, so that the raffia is approximately level with the rim of the pot.

9 The initial styling of the clump-style bonsai is now complete. The clump will now need to grow and become more refined over several seasons before achieving its full potential as a bonsai.

8 Top up with dry soil using a scoop and work the soil into the root system using a chopstick. Water the arrangement well, allow it to drain and then keep in a shaded place for several weeks.

Right: The finished clump has had the raffia disguised with soil and the completed planting is displayed on a dark wood stand against a suitable background. The five plants will mature so that they all eventually graft together at the base. At this point, the trunk base can be exposed.

Broom – *HOKIDACHI*

This style looks similar to the traditional broom used for sweeping, which is made from a bunch of twigs tied to a wooden handle. As full-size trees, this style can be seen in parks and gardens all over the world. It was initially derived from the natural shape of several varieties of *Zelkova*. It is, therefore, best suited to these trees, but other species can also be successfully grown in this style. Deciduous trees in particular lend themselves to training into broom-style bonsai because they quickly produce a good array of branches that will form a tight, twiggy, upper structure to the tree. Frequent pinching of the leading shoots on all the branches throughout the growing season will lead to excellent branch ramification with very little physical effort.

Above: *An old elm tree* (Ulmus) *that has been prepared with air layering in readiness for developing into a new bonsai.*

The form is based around a straight section of trunk with the branches coming from the top. There may be a continuation of the initial part of the trunk, but it will taper fairly abruptly and have smaller branches emerging along its length.

As each branch is developed, it should take on a finely branched, twiggy form. Frequent pinching out of the shoot tips is one of the most important aspects of the year-by-year improvement of this style, so do not neglect this part of the process.

If the weekly shoot pinching through the growing season from mid-spring to late summer is missed, and the branches become too long, they can be reduced by pruning fairly hard and starting again. If this pinching is carried out regularly, then the emerging leaves will naturally be slightly smaller than the previous batch that have been removed by the pruning process. This means that as time goes by, a spectacular bonsai will develop, as long as the correct pruning regime has been followed.

Never forget that a bonsai will continue growing if it is not controlled. This is especially true of the broom as it depends on concentrated pruning every spring and summer to maintain a compact structure. As the bonsai matures, study it in the winter when it is free of foliage. This is the best time to remove branches that are becoming too dense or are causing confusion.

CREATING YOUR BROOM BONSAI

You will need
- Saw
- Wound sealer
- Branch cutters
- Scissors
- Rake
- Pot
- Mesh
- Wire
- Wire cutters
- Soil
- Scoop

1 Close-up of the root system produced during the air-layering technique. This is one year on from the initial preparation.

2 Using a saw, remove the air-layered section to leave a stump that will eventually produce many new shoots.

3 Cut the top of the stump into a "V" shape to encourage shoots to appear from slightly different positions around the trunk circumference.

4 Close-up of the "V"-cut, which will need to be sealed with a suitable wound sealing paste to assist the plant in the production of shoots. The plant will take some time to produce a suitable number of shoots.

5 On another elm that has already produced a suitable number of shoots, it can be seen how the initial development takes place.

6 The top of the stump needs to be tidied up using branch or knob cutters, and trimmed back to the uppermost shoots.

7 The lower shoots are removed using a pair of scissors until a group of shoots remains at the top of the trunk. The plant is then potted up in a temporary pot so that it can grow on and develop into a proper broom-style bonsai.

Above: *The remaining shoots are all growing at approximately the same level, albeit radiating out around the trunk. These will mature into a dense branch structure that will enhance the tree's appearance.*

INDOOR BONSAI

Most people, when starting out in the bonsai world, often keep their first bonsai indoors because it is a commonly held view that all bonsai are indoor plants. This misunderstanding normally leads to disaster and an instant withdrawal from the bonsai scene. Most bonsai are actually outdoor plants if they are kept in the correct conditions. However, if kept in areas outside their normal habitat, they will need special environmental conditions to ensure their survival. Tropical and subtropical plants will be classified as indoor bonsai when grown in colder areas of the world and temperate climate plants will need special environmental conditions if they are grown in hotter areas. In temperate climates, tropical and subtropical plants will always be called indoor bonsai, but it is not so easy to provide them with the warmer and more humid conditions they require. They will need good light, but not direct sunlight through a window, and a warm, slightly humid atmosphere.

Left: *A weeping fig* (Ficus benjamina *'Wiandii') in the early stages of training, showing the initial wiring process that will help in the formation of the final branch structure.*

Aralia elegantissima

These plants, commonly known as finger aralia, can have one or more trunks and make a very attractive landscape. *Aralia* is a member of the ivy family which consists of trees, shrubs and palm-like plants, some of which have spines. They often have woody stems, even the smaller varieties such as the one described here. This variety is ideally suited to a group situation, as it tends to be upright with a relatively slim trunk. When grouped fairly closely together, a very pleasant indoor forest can be achieved. These plants can be sourced quite easily from plant centres or nurseries and have a compact root structure suited to shallow containers.

When growing bonsai plants in a group, always make sure that the tallest plant is somewhere in the central third of the arrangement and that the rest of the plants get progressively smaller towards the sides and rear.

Trim away all lower side shoots so that the trunks or main stems can be clearly seen. As with all group plantings or forests, the plants should always be placed very close together in order to give a mature feeling to the arrangement. The plants can be split into two groups so that an impression is given of a footpath running through the forest.

Small stones or rocks can be included in the composition to give a more rugged feel to the group and moss or very small plants can be planted under the main trees to enhance the natural look of the forest.

Containers should be shallow and can be rectangular or oval. The pot should not be too bright in colour and should complement the foliage colour of the trees. As with all bonsai

Above: *Suitable* Aralia *plants can be bought from many plant centres and will be sold simply as houseplants; these can be quickly turned into an indoor-bonsai planting.*

containers, it should never clash with the trees in any way, but just be there for growing support and minimal decorative appearance. Pots normally have a subtle glaze or a matt (flat) finish and should, of course, have good-sized drainage holes.

As with all indoor bonsai, it is a good idea to mist regularly to maintain the health and vigour of the trees.

STYLING YOUR *ARALIA ELEGANTISSIMA*

You will need
- Scissors
- Pot
- Mesh
- Wire
- Wire cutters
- Soil
- Scoop
- Chopstick
- Rake
- Rocks

1 Cut off the lower and inner leaves of the plants using a pair of scissors, so that the trunks can be clearly seen. This will immediately open up the stems so that they look like trunks and create a more tree-like effect. It is surprising how different a simple plant can look when the main stem, or trunk, is cleared of foliage. This applies to almost any plant that has a woody stem, and is one of the first features you should look for when choosing a plant for a bonsai.

2 Place in the prepared pot, arranging the seven trunks so that they are slightly spread out at the top.

3 Add extra soil and work well in with a chopstick until the plants are firmly arranged in the pot. Press the soil well into the roots, but do not compact it too tightly because the roots will not be able to breathe.

4 Carefully position several pieces of rock or tufa to give the effect of a miniature landscape. Make sure the pieces of rock are firmly embedded in the soil so they look as if they have always been there. This will greatly enhance the overall appearance of the finished bonsai.

Right: *Once the styling is complete and a stone and some soil decoration have been put in place, the group makes a very attractive indoor bonsai that will give great pleasure as long as the soil is kept just moist at all times. Do not forget to mist spray the foliage regularly as this will help the tree to cope with the drier indoor atmosphere.*

Crassula arborescens

Commonly known as the money tree or jade plant, this is often underestimated as bonsai material. Many species of crassula are available and *C. arborescens* is one of the best. There are many varieties available that have smaller leaves which may be even more suitable as bonsai. Most of them produce flowers at some time in the year and therefore can make very interesting indoor bonsai. Being succulents, they are prone to frosts that will almost certainly kill the plant in a very short time. Some are semi-hardy and may be suitable for cold conservatories (sun rooms) and greenhouses. Most, however, are quite happy outdoors providing they are slowly acclimatized. Crassula can be defoliated and pruned very hard if required and need very little water, so are ideal if they need to be left untended for several weeks.

Crassula arborescens has thick leaves and is strictly a succulent. The leaves and stems hold a large quantity of water, which allows the plant to go for several weeks without showing any signs of wilting. This characteristic makes the plant easy to look after as it needs watering less often than most plants. Even if it dries out, wilts and looks dehydrated, it will almost always recover once watering is resumed.

Propagation is also easy; just break off a leaf, leave until the end is dry (for about four days), and lay it on the surface of some dry soil. In about one month the leaf will have sprouted new roots. Do not water until you can see signs of new growth. Feed as with other houseplants, but only with a weak mixture of fertilizer.

When you are controlling the growth of your bonsai *Crassula*, you should wait until two or three pairs of leaves have been produced and then trim back to just one pair. Each time you do this, the growth pattern will double up. That is to say, each pruned shoot will produce two new shoots.

Above: *This is a typical garden centre or supermarket plant which can be trained into an attractive indoor bonsai.*

Never allow the plant to be exposed to frost, because its high water content will freeze and, on thawing, the tree will just collapse.

Overall, this is a very easy plant for bonsai because it has a compact root system that requires little water. The leaves will become overlarge if too much water is given, so keep watering to a minimum.

STYLING YOUR *CRASSULA ARBORESCENS*

You will need
- Branch cutters
- Scissors
- Rake
- Pot
- Mesh
- Wire cutters
- Soil
- Scoop
- Chopstick

1 Cut off the left-hand trunk using branch cutters, so that the main trunk in the centre is dominant.

2 Clean up the stump, using branch or knob cutters to form a natural-looking trunk base free from excess plant growth.

3 Pull off the lower leaves to expose the line of the tree's main trunk.

4 Having removed the leaves, it is clear that the other low branch should also be removed. This allows you to see the main trunk at its best.

5 Using scissors, reduce the length of the leading shoots.

6 Place in a suitable pot and top up with soil, working it in and around the roots with a chopstick until the soil fills every space.

Above: *Once the styled plant is complete, some moss can be added to the surface of the soil to give a more natural look which will enhance the line of the trunk. New shoots will soon begin to appear from the pruned shoot ends.*

Ficus benjamina 'Wiandii'

This ficus has a compact growth habit and well-proportioned leaves. Plants may have one or more trunks and generally have an interesting root system. Regular misting of the foliage with water is beneficial and the soil should be kept just moist at all times. Feed lightly, but regularly, during the main growing season from spring to autumn. As the shoots grow, prune them back to one or two leaves. This plant will enjoy warm, humid conditions, so it would be ideal for keeping in a conservatory (sun room) or similar surroundings. It is fairly tolerant of slightly dry conditions when allied to higher humidity, as the humidity will help the survival of the relatively thick leaves. A negative aspect of this *Ficus* is that the branches can be brittle and so should be handled with care.

A serious point to note about *Ficus* is that, when pruned, the wounds will produce a sticky white latex solution that is toxic and should be kept away from the eyes and not ingested. This latex solution also appears when the plant is root pruned, so you should be cautious whenever pruning any part of this fig. Always wash your hands thoroughly after you have been working on these plants.

Many varieties and cultivars are now available, so the choice of a plant for bonsai culture is very wide-ranging. There are extremely drooping varieties, as well as more formal upright forms, some with very small rather thin leaves and some with very large, thick leaves. Variegated varieties are also very popular as houseplants, and these, too, will make very interesting and different additions to a bonsai collection.

Ficus can be purchased as single-trunk plants or multiple-trunk specimens in a wide range of sizes, so there should be something available to suit every bonsai grower's taste.

Above: Ficus benjamina *'Wiandii' can be bought from the indoor plant section of most plant centres or superstores. This is good material for training into a indoor bonsai because it is a tropical or semitropical plant.*

Figs can be shaped by pruning or wiring, but take care that you do not break the branches when you are manipulating them after wiring because they can be very brittle. As figs usually have smooth bark, they can be easily damaged if the wire is left on for too long, so check them regularly.

STYLING YOUR *FICUS BENJAMINA* 'WIANDII'

You will need
- Branch cutters
- Wound sealer
- Wire
- Wire cutters
- Scissors
- Rake
- Pot
- Mesh
- Soil
- Scoop
- Chopstick

1 Leaves growing directly from the trunk and branches must be removed to create a clean-looking plant. White latex fluid oozes from cut areas of the *Ficus* family and contact with the mouth or eyes should be avoided at all times.

2 A small amount of wiring has been carried out and excess shoots cut out in order to create a tree-like shape.

3 Use a sharp, clean pair of cutters to remove the excess shoots.

4 This is the final shape of the bonsai, before it is placed in a bonsai pot.

5 The tree has been repotted using the techniques described in the potting section and the dry soil is being worked into the root system using a chopstick. After repotting, water the soil and allow any excess water to drain away.

Right: *The tree blends well with the cream glazed pot and has been displayed on a dark, modern Chinese stand that shows the pot and tree to advantage.*

Myrtus communis

This variety is commonly known as dwarf myrtle, and only young plants are usually available, but it is relatively easy to train as bonsai. If you can buy some small plants, a miniature landscape can be constructed using a combination of plants, soil and rocks. Try to thin out the top growth to achieve a branched structure. It will be tempting to "clip" the foliage, but that would be topiary rather than bonsai. You will also need to be persistent with the thinning-out process because a dense mass of foliage can quickly regrow. Myrtle is relatively small-leaved in most of its forms and is therefore highly suited to this type of miniature landscape. The leaves will become substantially smaller with pruning and over time, and the plants will make attractive small bonsai that are suitable for grouping together.

Above: *These are typical of commercially available* Myrtus communis *plants. They are small, compact and very suitable for constructing a small landscape planting.*

This species requires regular misting to maintain the health of the foliage, particularly in the summer. As with most indoor bonsai, this variety can be placed outside in a shady spot in warmer weather. Water when the soil starts to dry out, but never allow the roots to stand in water as they will quickly rot. Good light is important, but do not place your tree in direct sunlight as this will scorch the leaves.

Because myrtles develop into compact bonsai easily, they can be planted in a variety of arrangements using different rock formations. They grow well in rocks as they have compact root systems and will fit into even the smallest of cavities. They would, however, be more suited to low-lying rockscapes as they generally grow into compact bush-like structures.

Try to be bold and use your imagination when planting any size or arrangement of landscape, as it is individual ideas that produce the great diversity of shapes and forms which make growing bonsai such an inspiring art form.

Pots or containers should be shallow and possibly slab-like in shape. If the pot is too deep, it will dominate the composition, so ensure that the pot is complementary to the bonsai and not overpowering. You will also need to add some ground-cover plants to give a natural and weathered feel to the composition.

STYLING YOUR *MYRTUS COMMUNIS*

You will need
- Rake
- Scissors
- Pot
- Mesh
- Wire
- Wire cutters
- Soil
- Scoop
- Rocks

1 Having removed the plants from their pots, rake away the soil to obtain a suitable root-ball and expose the trunk base. Using scissors, remove some of the lower branches to expose the trunk line.

2 Trim each plant into a tree-like form by shortening the long shoots and branches.

3 Prepare the pot in the normal way and add a layer of soil.

4 Arrange some rocks, in this case tufa, so that there is enough space to plant the trees around them, and add extra soil.

5 Place the medium-size tree on the left and settle it into the pot, using a back-and-forth rotating motion so that the plant is bedded well into the soil.

6 Having placed the smallest tree on the right, plant the largest beside it and to the right of the rock. Ensure that this tree is slightly higher than the others. Never finish with the tops of all trees at the same level.

Right: *The final effect should be that of a miniature landscape which has been in existence for many years, so it will be necessary to add various mosses and tiny plants to the surface of the soil.*

Sageretia theezans

Commonly known as the bird plum cherry, *Sageretia theezans* is a popular species for indoor bonsai. Specimens of this plant are normally sold as fully trained trees. This particular specimen has been allowed to grow on and has lost its original shape. The bird plum cherry originates from the Far East where it is often used as a hedging plant, largely because it grows very quickly into medium-sized, shrubby shapes and even small trees. When fully developed, it produces an excellent, textured trunk that thickens very quickly and eventually forms a good, mature, flaking trunk which is especially suitable for bonsai styling.

These trees have delicate leaves which can lose their moisture quickly and dry out. Regular misting of the foliage should control this situation. The roots develop quickly, so repot every year. As the bark matures and flakes away, it will leave a very attractive patchy yellow and orange colouring that is particularly pleasing when the plant has dropped its leaves.

As with many other shrubby plants, the roots of *Sageretia* develop into very compact structures that are ideal for bonsai culture as they will flourish in shallow bonsai pots. This indoor bonsai can also be kept outdoors during frost-free periods of the year, but, because of its very thin, delicate leaves, it can be very vulnerable to many conditions. Strong wind and strong sun – either separately or, even worse, together – can quickly destroy the foliage, so great care should be taken to avoid adverse conditions such as these.

When it is necessary to prune the thick branches or even the trunk of a *Sageretia*, it will soon become very

Above: *This* Sageretia theezans *has been grown in a pot for several years until suitable for pruning and planting in a bonsai pot.*

clear how hard the wood can be. In fact, it may take several smaller cuts to carry out a pruning operation that would need just one cut if you were working with a plant that has much softer wood. For this reason, you will need to make sure that all your pruning tools are extremely sharp, so that the pruning process is made as easy as possible.

STYLING YOUR *SAGERETIA THEEZANS*

You will need
- Rake
- Branch cutters
- Pot
- Mesh
- Wire
- Wire cutters
- Soil
- Scoop
- Chopstick
- Scissors
- Sprayer

1 Having removed the plant from its pot and raked out the roots very carefully, use branch cutters to cut out the central branch which would otherwise spoil the line of the finished tree.

2 Settle the tree into the pot just off centre and fill up with some soil using a scoop. Work the soil into the roots with a chopstick.

3 Using a pair of scissors, cut back the long shoots, leaving just one or two leaves.

4 Mist the soil and plant to create a high humidity. This species has thin leaves that can dry out quickly after repotting, so do this regularly.

Below: *After placing the finished tree in a crackle-glaze pot and shaping it by pruning, press some moss into the soil surface to add a little more realism to the design.*

DISPLAYING BONSAI

When displaying bonsai indoors, remember that they need an airy position in good light, whereas outdoor bonsai require full light and an open situation. Indoors, bonsai are best displayed on some type of display table, perhaps on a suitable mat. Any background used indoors should also complement the tree, being as plain as possible, so that the tree form is not compromised in any way. Outdoors, bonsai can be displayed on specially built stands or benches. It is important that these are high enough for the trees to be viewed at approximately eye-level.

The choice of pot is also important. Indeed, the size, shape, colour and texture of the pot, whether it is glazed or unglazed, and whether it has bold or insignificant feet, are all features that can make or break the appearance of an individual bonsai. None of these elements must dominate the tree, but they must gently complement and frame it.

Left: *A broom-style Chinese elm (*Ulmus parvifolia*) in an indoor situation. Remember to protect furniture from possible damage from water or pot feet.*

Pots and Containers

To the untrained eye, it may seem that the bonsai pot is just the container in which to grow the tree. Nothing could be further from the truth, however, as the pot is one of the most important parts of the overall effect. The relationship between the pot and the tree is a complex one, and it is most important that the pot blends well with the tree, so that the final composition of tree and pot becomes a complementary and well-balanced single unit. A bonsai in a suitable container can be compared with a classical work of art mounted in a similarly suitable frame. In both cases, your eye should be drawn first by the painting or tree, with the frame or pot later being perceived as the complementary mount. If the reverse is true, then the framing feature will be seen to dominate the intended subject.

Above: *A common beech (*Fagus sylvatica*) in a pot that some might consider too deep, but which works quite well with this tree.*

With bonsai, the pot is the frame, and there should be no conflict over which part of the composition is viewed first. The eye should be drawn first to the lower trunk of the tree, then move up into its apex before considering the pot as framing the whole presentation.

CONSTRUCTION

Bonsai pots will need to be frost-proof if they are going to contain hardy outdoor trees in a temperate climate, and should therefore be made from high-temperature fired stoneware. (Even if trees are to be kept in tropical or subtropical areas, frost-proof pots would be recommended, as they are much tougher.) Pots and containers that are constructed of less sturdy materials, such as mica and plastic, are fine for use by beginners or as temporary training pots, but stoneware pots certainly give the trees a far superior appearance.

Choose pots that have one or more large drainage holes. Larger pots may have a series of small holes around the perimeter of their base; these are for use when you are tying the tree into the pot. The floor of the pot should be flat, so that there are no areas where water can become trapped for any prolonged period.

Make sure that any pots you purchase have good feet. These will raise the base of the pot above the display stand, so allowing free airflow around and under the base of the pot, which will increase the chances of your trees remaining healthy.

Left: *An informal upright Japanese maple,* Acer palmatum *'Nomura', planted in a suitably coloured and shaped pot.*

STYLES OF POT

Bonsai pots are produced in a huge range of different shapes, sizes and colours designed to suit all styles and species. The accompanying pictures show a small range of available pots. When choosing a pot, it is advisable to take your tree to a pot supplier, who will have a wide range of suitable pots, to make sure that you obtain the best container for your individual tree.

GLAZING

As a general rule when choosing a pot, opt for glazed or semi-glazed pots for deciduous trees and matt (flat) or unglazed pots for conifers and evergreens. Bonsai pots should always be unglazed on the inside, as this will help to keep the tree stable within the pot when the roots have grown sufficiently to come into contact with the pot sides. Any external glazing should run over the rim and a short way down the inside edge of the pot.

Above: *A small ceramic Japanese pot that is good enough to display on its own. Only a small, pretty flowering tree would suit this pot.*

Right: *An unusual cascade bonsai in a pot made by the tree's owner, and exhibited at a Bonsai Kai bonsai competition.*

A RANGE OF POTS AND CONTAINERS

There are some general rules to follow when you are deciding which container is most suitable for a particular bonsai tree. Glazed pots of various colours are much better for displaying broadleaf trees, but remember that they must never be very bright in colour. Instead, the colour should blend beautifully with the shade of the foliage or with the colour of the trunk. Unglazed pots, which are available in varying shades of matt (flat) brown or grey, are much more suitable for conifers and evergreen trees. Outdoor trees, which are more likely to be exposed to frosts, will also require a container that is totally frost-proof.

The container that you choose should also accentuate the form and colour of the bonsai specimen, while at the same time not dominating the tree. Think very carefully before choosing your container, and if you are in any doubt, consult an experienced bonsai artist who will help you to select a pot that complements your bonsai perfectly.

Right: *A tall pot such as this is ideal for cascade bonsai because it allows the form of the cascading tree to be seen to advantage.*

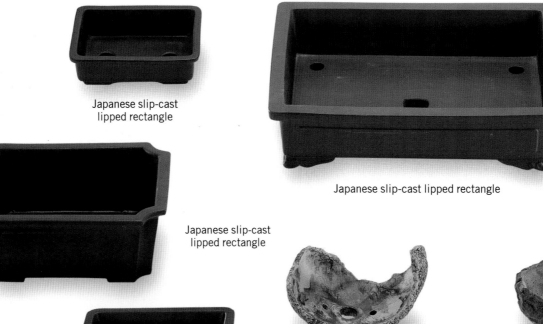

Japanese slip-cast lipped rectangle

Japanese slip-cast lipped rectangle

Japanese slip-cast lipped rectangle

Japanese slip-cast lipped rectangle

English hand-made crescent

English hand-made round

English hand-made
square cascade

English primitive hand-made
shallow round

Chinese decorated
square cascade

English primitive hand-
made shallow crescent

Japanese shallow rectangle

English primitive hand-made
shallow crescent

English primitive
hand-made round

Japanese fluted round slip-cast

English hand-made
rectangle

Japanese slip-cast
lipped rectangle

Japanese slip-cast lipped oval

Japanese shallow
oval

Japanese slip-cast
lipped oval

English hand-made
round

Japanese slip-cast lipped
rectangle

Display Stands

It is very important when displaying any size or style of bonsai to make sure that each element of the display complements the others, as well as the chosen bonsai. This means that the colour and design of any display tables, stands, matting and background should be subtle and blend with the bonsai pot, trunk, foliage and any accent plant involved. Display tables and stands can be purchased from bonsai suppliers or found in stores that sell oriental-style furniture. These accessories will normally be used when displaying any type of bonsai indoors in your own home or at special bonsai exhibitions and shows. All bonsai can be displayed indoors as long as you ensure that outdoor trees are only kept inside for a day or two at the most. As with the pot, the display stand must not dominate the tree.

Above: *This is a typical outdoor display using stands made from pre-treated timber and coloured to taste.*

Display tables should always be carefully selected so that they blend well with each individual tree. They are available in a very wide variety of sizes, shapes, designs and colours and are mostly constructed in various types of wood, from oak and rosewood through to ebony or teak – in fact, virtually any wood can be suitable providing it blends with the tree to be displayed. However, good-quality display tables can be difficult to obtain. If you have the ability and skill, and think you can construct your own display tables, then this may be an easier way forward, as you can then custom-build them to your own requirements.

Instead of formal-style display tables, consider using thin slices of good-quality timber as a form of display. These are probably best suited to displaying groups or forests that are contained in or on a large flat slab or pot. The slice of timber will need to be slightly larger than the slab or pot and be properly finished so that it looks like a quality piece of furniture.

Stand shapes include rectangular, square, round and multi-sided, and range from very low to extremely tall.

Left: *This elegant Chinese elm (*Ulmus parvifolia*) cascade bonsai is being displayed to great effect on a tall Chinese mahogany stand.*

Right: *A modern Chinese tall rosewood stand (left) and an antique Chinese mahogany stand (right), both of which are suitable for cascade-style bonsai.*

Low stands are suitable for most trees, be they formal upright, informal upright, leaning or multi-trunk, while tall stands would normally be used to display cascade or semi-cascade trees, which need the height so that they can cascade down over the side of the stand. The height of the stands depends largely on the overall height of the tree. Again, if you have the facilities, knowledge, skill and ability to produce your own display stands, then you can tailor-make them to suit a specific bonsai.

Above and right: *The photographs here show clearly how important the choice of stand is for your bonsai. Low and tall stands have been used to display the same bonsai, but, because the tree is a cascade, it is much better suited to the tall stand.*

Below: *Clockwise from top right: English oak rectangle; Chinese mahogany round; English oak rectangle; Chinese rectangle (stained softwood).*

Below right: *Rectangular rosewood stand from Taiwan (top) and a Japanese oak rectangular stand from Nihonmatsu City (below).*

Slabs and Rocks

Bonsai are traditionally grown in pots and containers of a certain depth in order to enclose the root structure of each individual tree. However, this is not always the case, because some styles of bonsai can actually benefit from being planted on a thin, flat slab made from stone or slate. If this technique is required, then the bonsai will need to be securely attached to the slab because there are no sides for support as there are with a pot. Suitable slabs can be made of slate, sandstone or, in fact, any type of real rock, because artificial slabs which are made of concrete will almost certainly never look as attractive. Slabs that are made from clay in the same way as pots can be very good and, if made by a good potter, they will look as good as any natural rock.

Ideally, these flat slabs should be formed of a material that is strong enough to take the weight of the individual planting involved. Although the pieces of rock need to be thin for aesthetic reasons, they must not be so thin and weak that they break when they are transported.

Above: *Although this bonsai is in the process of being repotted, it can still be displayed on the slab on which it is resting after repotting.*

There are many types of rock for this purpose, but the best is slate, which is structurally very strong. Sandstone can be very weak when in thin section, so this may not be very suitable, although if a thicker slab were needed, it might be satisfactory.

If you find natural stone slabs hard to find, then a good bonsai potter will make you a slab, provided he or she has a good-sized kiln. You can make an artificial slab using a metal frame covered in glass fibre with a sand-and-cement surface that has been coloured to create the appearance of natural rock.

You might find stone slabs locally, but good bonsai suppliers will be able to advise you. Look out for natural products, such as real sandstone or slate. A visit to a local quarry or stonemason could reveal suitable pieces of stone. As a last resort, you can buy reinforced concrete slabs (the type normally sold as paving), but these are heavy and do not look natural enough.

Left: *A "mame" box (Buxus sempervirens) displayed on a thin piece of slate. This image was taken at an RHS bonsai show in London.*

SLAB PLANTING A *COTONEASTER* 'CORAL BEAUTY'

1 Select a good-quality specimen of *Cotoneaster* 'Coral Beauty' from a plant nursery.

2 Remove approximately three-quarters of the upper growth and half of the root-ball (roots). Carry out a trial placement of the pruned and styled plant on a sandstone slab.

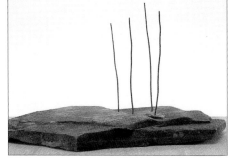

3 Drill four "tying-in" holes through the slab using a power drill and a masonry drill bit. Always wear safety glasses or goggles when you are using power tools.

4 Pass two pieces of wire through the holes from under the slab.

5 After carrying out initial pruning, place the plant on the slab between the wires.

6 Twist the ends of the two pieces of wire tightly together to secure the tree to the slab. Cut off the spare wire ends.

7 Contour the root-ball by adding a small amount of soil and cover the soil completely with moss in order to create a natural effect.

8 The final arrangement of the bonsai with its slab is pictured here on a suitable surface and against a striking purple background. The tree, soil mound and slab all complement each other beautifully.

Accessories

There are many accessories that can be used with bonsai. These range from stands to labels, and must always complement the bonsai that is on display. Other types of display material, such as bamboo matting, gravel, stone or slate, as well as many other substances, may also be used in the display of bonsai, and you can use a selection of these items to design suitable settings for your bonsai. In all instances, when using accessories such as those already mentioned, consideration must be given to the style, shape, size, colour of both the bonsai and the pot in which it is planted. None of these accessories should clash with or detract the viewer from looking at the bonsai, as it is the bonsai that is always the most important part of each display. That said, all items must be complementary to each other.

Some people like to include all sorts of accessories around their bonsai, but, if too many items are introduced, there could be confusion as to what is the most important item on view, which should always be the bonsai. Therefore, there should never be any item that is not connected with that bonsai, as it will inevitably detract from the appearance of the tree. For example, small figures or figurines incorporated alongside or on the soil of a bonsai are totally inappropriate, as they would catch the eye first and distract the viewer from the beauty of the bonsai.

Above: *This indoor bird plum cherry (*Sageretia theezans) *bonsai has been grown in a glazed pot and displayed on a cut-rush mat.*

MATS

You can use various styles and textures of matting as a base for bonsai as long as they complement, not distract from, the tree itself. You might like to try rush or bamboo matting. Again, it is important to choose matting with a colour and texture that complements the choice of container.

LANTERNS

Stone lanterns can be used in a garden situation where one or, at the most, two (depending upon the size of your garden display area) can be placed strategically alongside some bonsai display stands to give an oriental look to your garden. Any more than two would overdo the situation.

LABELS

Bonsai will benefit from having name labels next to them so that anyone viewing them can instantly identify the species and variety. Any labels should

Left: *Broom-style Japanese grey bark elm (*Zelkova serrata) *on a dark bamboo mat that was chosen to complement the style of pot.*

be subtle and the information they display should be kept to a minimum so that the appearance of the bonsai is not compromised.

OTHER DISPLAY ELEMENTS

The time and application that goes into the creation of bonsai trees means that you will want to display them to the best effect. Top-dressings, such as moss and gravel, various fabrics as well as many other substances may well be suitable for use in the display of bonsai. A potted bonsai can be displayed on a thin layer of grit, which can be acquired in many different colours and sizes to suit your tree.

Above: Frankenia thymifolia *accent plant on a hexagonal stand that matches the pot shape. The label is typical of that used at exhibitions.*

Above: *Moss is used as an accessory for decorating the soil surface and is essential for giving a natural look to the completed arrangement.*

Accent Planting

Accent or complementary plants are used to enhance the natural appearance of a bonsai. Full-size trees growing in the wild have various other plants and natural objects around them, including wild flowers, grasses, mosses, lichens and even stones or rocks, some of which may have very interesting shapes. We can draw on these natural features for inspiration when searching for items to display with a bonsai specimen, so creating a more exciting arrangement for the viewer that does not detract attention from the tree itself. Small plants are the most suitable as accents for the majority of displays because their size does not overpower the bonsai. Much larger plants can be used as accents in an outdoor display where they can be used on the ground at the base of a single bonsai display stand.

Suitable material that can be used as accent plants include the dwarf forms of *Equisetum*, *Miscanthus* and *Pennisetum*, as well as *Ophiopogon planiscarpus* 'Nigrescens', *Hakonechloa macra*, *Acorus gramineus*, *Imperata cylindrica*, *Aruncus aethusifolius* and some dwarf forms of *Astilbe*. Many other plants are also suitable for use as accent plants, including daisies, gentians and dandelions, as well as very small bamboos.

In all cases, the accent plants should be potted in complementary containers in just the same way as the bonsai pots complement the trees. When choosing plants as accents for bonsai, it is possible to collect plants from the garden or from woodland areas, as well as buying from plant centres. It is easy to develop a blinkered view when deciding on a plant variety as an accent so try to be open-minded and look at any type of small herbaceous or alpine plant. You may be surprised to find that there are many more plants available than you first imagined which would be suitable.

Below: *Korean hornbeam* (Carpinus laxiflora*) with a cyclamen accent plant. Both are displayed on a slice of polished yew wood.*

Above: *Sisyrinchiums make good accent plants. The botanist Theophrastus used the word sisyrinchium for a plant related to the iris.*

Right: *This Japanese black pine (*Pinus thunbergii*) is being displayed with a wild violet accent plant. The rustic accent pot blends well with the rugged trunk of the bonsai.*

SUITABLE ACCENT PLANTS

Above: Frankenia thymifolia *with its russet-coloured foliage is planted here in a deep, hexagonal, matt (flat) brown pot and displayed on a complementary hexagonal rosewood stand.*

Above: Aruncus aethusifolius *growing in a shallow, primitive-style pot. This is a large accent plant and for this reason is more suited to an outdoor display.*

Above: Hakonechloa macra *'Alboaurea' is quite a large plant with red stems and stripes within the leaves, so the chosen red pot shows off the plant superbly.*

Above: Astilbe × crispa *'Lilliput' has fern-like leaves and eventually upright stems with pale pink flowers. Again, this is a fairly large plant, planted in this case in a primitive-style pot.*

Above: Ophiopogon planiscarpus *'Nigrescens' is a very attractive, almost black-leaved plant. The pot is more decorative than normal because it matches well with the curly leaves.*

Above: Any small or alpine variety of cyclamen will make a very good accent plant for use with bonsai. Here, a cyclamen is planted in a pot and displayed on a rosewood stand.

Suiseki

These are decorative stones. In traditional Japanese settings, bonsai and *suiseki* are often positioned very close to each other when these two art forms are displayed together. They may, in fact, be regarded as an art form in their own right. Suitable stones can be collected from almost anywhere, such as beaches, river beds, mountain areas, quarries, garden centres and even from your own garden. The main criterion is that each stone must have an interesting shape that can tell a story of its own. Its appearance should also give the impression of a mountain or cliff or other natural features such as these. If the stone has a vein running through it, this might even represent a mountainside with a waterfall or other similar watery outlet.

Above: *English Lake District quartz formed into an interesting shape that closely resembles a craggy mountain peak.*

It is thought that the first *penjing* (the original Chinese form of tree and rock landscapes) and *gongshi* (viewing stones) were given to the Empress Regent Suiko of Japan by the Chinese imperial court around AD592–628. These stones were considered to be of great interest to the Japanese aristocracy by virtue of their amazing shapes, which included various features that resembled mountains, caves, waterfalls and many other natural-looking features. They tended to be in the form of stones that emulated the massive, almost vertical, mountains of China. This type of decorative stone became very popular with the Japanese for many hundreds of years.

The Samurai warrior class came to power in Japan in the late Kamakura Period (1183–1333). The teachings of Zen Buddhism became widely accepted by the Samurai as a result of the highly active trading that took place between China and Japan. The disciplines of Zen Buddhism – including austerity, meditation and intuitive insight – meant that apparently simple items in keeping with this philosophy, such as stones with interesting but subtle shapes and colours, were much sought after.

This preference was further emphasized by Zen monks during the Muramachi Period (1338–1573), when the stones were cleaned of all other elements, such as soil, dirt and possibly plant material, thus accentuating their simple but interesting detail.

Over a considerable period of time, stones came to be selected that suggested, by their form, representations of natural landscapes, such as mountains, valleys, caves and waterfalls etc. The Zen monks had a powerful influence over the Japanese ruling class, and these stones were considered to lead to spiritual refinement, enlightenment and inner awareness.

During the Edo Period (1603–1867), the wealthy merchants who came to the fore began to challenge the

Left: *A piece of* ibigawa *rock, displayed here as an accent to an* Acer palmatum *'Kiyohime', which is showing the beautiful branch ramification of its winter form.*

aristocracy with their interest in *suiseki* and began collecting and competing with them for these stones. During this period, Japan became extremely isolated as a result of closing its borders to all outsiders, but this closure meant that the Japanese arts expanded and flourished without influence from other countries, religions and regimes.

The Meiji period (1868–1912) saw a lull in the interest in *suiseki* largely because of the decrease in wealth of the Samurai and upper classes, but in some ways it began to develop. It was during this period that *suiseki* first came to be classified and given names for certain shapes and styles.

From the middle of the twentieth century, interest in *suiseki* began to regenerate, and it spread into the international arena, as did bonsai. It continues to rise in interest today, so much so that there are now *suiseki* societies, clubs and associations throughout the world.

DIFFERENT *SUISEKI* STONES

Above: *Beautiful slate* suiseki *resembling a mountain with vertical rock faces and sheer drops.*

Above: *Japanese* ibigawa *stone which has many different colours, interesting textures and caves.*

Above: *Coastal rocky island with interesting, water-shaped erosion and textures in a sea of fine white gravel.*

Above: *This Californian jade mountain stone has intriguing caves, waterfalls and sheer rock faces.*

Above: *Another slate* suiseki *with a graduating slope that leads to a dramatic vertical rock face.*

Above: *Very interesting mountain range that culminates in a typically high, imposing alpine peak.*

Indoor Displays

Whatever the climate of your area, and whatever types of tree you have, at some time you will want to display one, some or all of your bonsai indoors. You will need to make sure that the trees you select are in pots suitable for the surroundings in which they are to be displayed. You will also need to take into account the amount of light there is, as well as any direct source of heating, since these aspects may well affect the health of the bonsai in question. With contemporary styling in our homes comes the need to try different ideas when planting and displaying bonsai indoors. Trying different, minimalist containers and placing trees in various rooms can bring a whole new meaning to a bonsai display, but never forget the importance of good light and humidity.

Above: *Broom-style Chinese elm (*Ulmus parvifolia) *on a table by a north-facing window, a good source of natural light.*

Bonsai should be kept in the correct environmental conditions for the species of plant being grown. Their position also depends very much upon where you live in relation to the natural growing environment of any particular bonsai that you are growing. They will always need to be in receipt of very good natural light, but not placed on a windowsill where the sun can shine directly on to the tree because this could lead to irreparable damage to the bonsai.

It is advisable to place your trees on a table or bench that is covered with a suitable piece of fabric or any sort of natural material that will enhance rather than detract from the appearance of the tree. The tree can then be placed on a smaller table or mat of some description on top of the chosen fabric or natural material. None of these props should detract from the tree in any way: they are simply meant to contribute to the satisfactory display of the tree.

TYPE OF ROOM

A bonsai can be displayed in virtually any room in the home, as long it is checked carefully and regularly to see if it needs watering or feeding and whether the atmospheric conditions are right. You will also need to ensure that it is pruned correctly. Central heating can severely affect any plant when kept indoors, as the conditions will be far too warm and dry for successful plant growth. This can be overcome, to some extent, by mist-spraying with water.

The best room for displaying a bonsai is obviously one in which the bonsai can be seen by you and any friends or visitors, such as the sitting room. However, this is not the best room as far as the atmospheric conditions are concerned and, for this reason, a kitchen, bathroom or anywhere that may experience a certain amount of humidity is

Left: *Twisted-trunk Chinese elm (*Ulmus parvifolia) *planted in a clean, contemporary container and displayed in a bathroom which will provide good humidity.*

Above: *This bird plum cherry (Sageretia theezans) has been displayed to good effect in a curved dish and placed on a sideboard.*

preferable. Indeed, the best rooms in which to display bonsai are the kitchen and bathroom because they have an inbuilt humidity as a result of the water systems in place there.

Tropical and sub-tropical plants may be kept in slightly warm and humid indoor conditions for quite long periods of time, but hardy temperate trees can remain indoors for only a maximum of one or two days before they begin to show signs of stress. If you have to spray the foliage of any tree while it is being displayed indoors, you will need to take care that water droplets do not fall on to polished wood surfaces, especially if the piece of furniture is of any value.

Right: *This Chinese elm (Ulmus parvifolia) has been planted in a traditional pot and placed in a kitchen near to a window in order to obtain good natural light.*

DISPLAY TABLES AND STANDS

The tables upon which bonsai are displayed will need to vary in style depending on the tree that has been chosen for display. For example, if the tree is powerful and masculine in form, then it will need a stand or table that is strong and powerful, though not so dominant that it detracts from the main appearance of the tree. Similarly, if the tree is soft and feminine in appearance, then the stand should have similar features so that it complements and does not overpower the tree. The stand should always be complementary to the tree that is being displayed and should never appear to be the main item in the display; nor should it be of a completely opposing colour or design. If the tree has a simple shape, then the stand should be simple. If the tree is more complex, then a more complicated design may be suitable.

TRADITIONAL BONSAI DISPLAYS

Traditionally, in Japan, bonsai are displayed in a specially designed area called a *tokonoma* or alcove, which can be quite a large construction. It is basically a bench with sides and background within which any object of interest can be displayed. The description given here is very basic, but the finished *tokonoma* must have simple, crisp, clean and elegant features. Most people do not have the space at home to construct this type of alcove display area, and therefore the most likely place to find this type of display will be at a horticultural show, such as the Chelsea Flower Show, or a major exhibition that deals only with bonsai and related subjects.

In Japan, there are many different shapes and sizes of *tokonoma*, depending on their intended use. Some are used in a teahouse and others for displaying such items as

bonsai. The most common version used for bonsai display is called "Kekomi-doko"; it has a wooden floor usually covered with tatami matting and basically looks like a step up from the surrounding normal floor.

Above: *Tree of a thousand stars (*Serissa foetida*) standing on a cabinet. Ensure that protection for the polished surface is supplied.*

Right: *The variegation of this weeping fig (Ficus benjamina 'Variegata') is picked up by the white of the table on which it is displayed.*

Right: *You can display an outdoor bonsai indoors for a maximum of a day or two as it cannot tolerate indoor conditions for longer.*

Left: *A* Podocarpus *bonsai has been displayed on a mantelpiece. This is possible as long as there is not a burning fire beneath it. This would certainly be very dangerous to a bonsai. This type of display situation should only be temporary.*

Right: *Several trees have been placed indoors on a long, heavy, timber shelf. This looks rather attractive, but the thickness of the shelf tends to dominate the trees.*

When you are displaying a bonsai in such an alcove or *tokonoma*, it is important that the bonsai is placed on a suitably sympathetic stand or table along with an accent plant, which must also be placed on a suitable stand. In traditional *tokonomas*, there is often a scroll of some description hanging on the back wall. All the items in the display must complement each other. If, however, you are simply displaying a tree for your own enjoyment in your home, then you can place a bonsai on a normal piece of furniture, as long as this does not overpower the appearance of the bonsai specimen.

MODERN BONSAI DISPLAYS

With the advent of more minimalist decor in our interiors, there has been a natural progression into a similarly minimalist style for bonsai planting and displays. So, why not try out some different types of pots, such as glass containers and vases, variously shaped bowls and wooden dishes for

Right: *Sacred bamboo (*Nandina domestica*) growing in a piece of rock. Good light and humidity must be maintained.*

displaying your bonsai? These containers can all be displayed on modern pieces of furniture made of any type of material such as glass or various plastics, but always remember that good light is required for healthy plant growth. Try standing your bonsai on a shelf in a bathroom,

kitchen or sitting room, by all means, but always make sure that any polished wood surfaces are meticulously maintained. An office desk is often used to display a bonsai, but, unless it is near to a window, it will not be very good for the tree because of the low light levels.

SINGLE SPECIMENS AND GROUPS

Whether you have only one tree or many, it is worth making the effort to display your bonsai to best advantage. When showing more than one bonsai in a particular place, try to arrange them so that they complement each other, with pots of varying heights and sizes that are suitably positioned. When displaying several trees in a line, it can be difficult to find a suitable tray for them all, so you may have to find individual trays or dishes on which to stand each tree, as this will be a good way to protect your furniture from damage by water.

BACKDROPS

It is important to use relatively plain backgrounds or backdrops behind bonsai or *penjing* so that you do not detract from the impact of the tree. The tree is always the most important feature at all times and a very busy background may distract the viewer.

Left: Serissa foetida, *tree of a thousand stars, with a bowl of potpourri as an accessory, standing on a polished wood table, which should be protected.*

Above: *Japanese black pine* (Pinus thunbergii) *placed on a windowsill. As it is an outdoor variety, it can only be kept indoors for one day.*

Outdoor Displays

Display stands for bonsai kept outside can be very varied and much more rustic in appearance than stands for indoor bonsai. Whatever style of stand you choose, give the trees the dignity they deserve by placing them on good-quality display units. Do not forget the background that will be behind your collection of trees. If they are displayed in your garden in front of a hedge or other trees, you may not even be able to distinguish them. Try to set them against a fence or even a plain painted wall, so that they can be seen in all their glory. When displaying bonsai against a wall or fence, it is also important not to place the trees too close to the background because the tree will "search" for the best light and grow in one direction away from the background. You should also turn your trees regularly to avoid this problem.

Above: *A purple Japanese maple (*Acer palmatum*) displayed in front of garden plants will be lost in the background, unless it is backlit, as here.*

OUTDOOR BENCHING AND STANDS

Benches made from timber that has been treated with a plant-safe preservative are ideal. They can be supported on timber stands, legs or even concrete, brick or stone blocks. Reinforced concrete slabs are also suitable if they are available and can be laid across the top of concrete block stands to create a long-lasting display. Remember that most timber has a limited lifespan because it is subjected to all types of weather, so any timber benches will need to be replaced every 5–10 years, depending on how well they have been maintained.

Strong display benching is very important, and it is well worth making sure that the size and weight of any benching used is suitable for the trees to be displayed. The most suitable height at which to display your bonsai trees is approximately eye-level, so that you can look into the trees from just above the level of the pot rim. Remember that if you were viewing a full-size tree, you would be looking at it from just above ground-level, so when viewing a bonsai you must use the same criteria by imagining that you are looking at your trees with the eye of a suitably scaled-down person.

DISPLAYING A LARGE OUTDOOR COLLECTION

If you have a large collection outdoors, then it may not always be possible to provide benching that can be used to display a variety of trees at the correct

Left: *Bonsai should be displayed so that their features can be clearly seen. A split-level stand such as this can be used to display trees of different sizes perfectly.*

Above: *Part of the author's collection of bonsai at Leonardslee Gardens, West Sussex, England, where the trees are on permanent display on a variety of stands.*

height. It may, therefore, be a good idea to vary the height of the stands to suit each tree. Your main aim should be to provide a pleasing overall effect, while allowing easy access for all general maintenance purposes. If you have several large trees, using a table-top that can be rotated will prove to be a considerable advantage because you will need to turn the trees from time to time in order to maintain even growth all round.

Right: *A typical bonsai display belonging to a Japanese bonsai grower, showing heavy timber benches of varying heights. Heavy-duty benches are required if each bench has to support a large number of bonsai.*

Above: *A large, old Japanese white pine (Pinus parviflora) in a garden situation and displayed on timber decking next to a small pool. This situation will help any bonsai by providing it with additional humidity. The deck should always be raised substantially above ground-level to prevent possible damage by animals.*

Left: *Many bonsai nurseries use this type of concrete block-and-timber display bench as a good way of showing off their trees to customers. Each tree should never be too close to its neighbour.*

SUITABLE BACKDROPS

Any bonsai will look its best if it is displayed against a suitable backdrop. On earlier pages, the points that need to be considered when displaying bonsai indoors have been discussed. Most of these are the same for outdoor bonsai, although there are other points that you will also need to consider.

Backgrounds for bonsai are normally made from natural materials such as timber, stone, or other varieties of plant. In the case of timber, the most common is some sort of fence and, if you regard bamboo as a type of timber, then this too can be used to form a flat, fence-style background. If you would like to use a wall as a backdrop for bonsai, then remember that it should

always be very plain so that it is not confused with the tree displayed in front. Indeed, a brick or stone wall may be very distracting behind a bonsai, so it is best to paint it with some pale-coloured paint. Should the wall be of an uneven texture, it may also be necessary to render it to achieve a smooth, uninterrupted surface. When the rendered wall is painted, it will provide an excellent solid backdrop, allowing the bonsai trees to stand out so that their true forms can be truly appreciated.

If there needs to be any form of joint in a fence or wall, then it is preferable for these to run vertically, rather than horizontally. Horizontal lines will detract from the appearance of any

Above: *A beautiful Japanese maple (*Acer palmatum*) placed on a small table in a private garden. In this instance, the tree is standing in an open position, so that it does not become confused with the background.*

bonsai because they will "cut through" the form of the tree, whereas vertical lines or joints will accentuate the line of the tree.

If you have hedges in your garden, then you will need to position your bonsai specimens so that they are far enough away from the hedges to stand out and be clearly seen. If you place the trees too close to any form of hedge, however, the whole picture will become very confusing and rather uninteresting.

Any background must always be high enough to allow the whole tree to be viewed in front of it and not so short that the top of the fence, wall or hedge simply cuts across the top of the tree.

Backgrounds to a bonsai display can be a very controversial talking-point because what seems acceptable to one person does not always please another. For this reason, it is actually very difficult to define what is good and what is bad as a backdrop. Be prepared to try something new, by all means, but remember that the bonsai tree must remain the most important feature at all times and you should do all you can to ensure that its appearance is never compromised.

OTHER POINTS TO CONSIDER

If you are designing a purpose-built bonsai display area in your garden, then you will need to give careful consideration to the backgrounds so that the correct environmental conditions are achieved for your bonsai specimens. For example, both sides of a wall or fence can be used to provide a background for two different displays

Right: *European olive (*Olea europaea*) that has been grown as a garden bonsai, although it does not follow the proportional relationship between the plant and the pot, as is customary with traditional bonsai specimens.*

of bonsai, as long as you can ensure that the trees can flourish in the conditions in each area.

Many other accessories, such as lanterns and wind chimes, can be included in an outdoor display, but these should be kept to a minimum. Also ensure that they do not distract the viewer from the bonsai, which should be the main feature.

It is sometimes difficult for people to understand the concept of bonsai as an art, but the most important point to note when you are displaying bonsai of any description is that all backgrounds and accessories must complement the bonsai so that the viewer can appreciate the beauty of this living art form.

Left: *An 80-year-old Japanese white pine (*Pinus parviflora*) on an outdoor bench.*

Above: *Japanese maple (*Acer palmatum*) growing in a temporary training pot until its final bonsai form is achieved.*

Above: *Japanese white pine (*Pinus parviflora*) on a timber stand in front of a painted brick wall that distracts the eye slightly from the bonsai.*

Above: *Japanese white pine* (Pinus parviflora) *trained as a garden bonsai in a pot that is not normally suitable for a traditional-style bonsai.*

Above: *Chinese juniper* (Juniperus chinensis) *in an English handmade pot that shows off the cascade styling to perfection.*

Bonsai Shows

Many of the best bonsai are in private collections and are rarely seen by members of the public except when they appear at horticultural shows or special bonsai exhibitions and conventions. It is at these special events that the owners of such collections have the opportunity to display their bonsai when they are looking their very best. Such shows and conventions occur in most parts of the world and it is worth attending one of these events to see top-quality bonsai correctly displayed by very experienced bonsai growers and collectors. Most people who exhibit at bonsai shows and competitions are amateur growers who are members of their local bonsai club or society and who may have been growing bonsai for anything from a few months to many decades.

Above: *This Virginia creeper (*Parthenocissus*), with its ivy-like leaves, belongs to a member of Bonsai Kai and is an unusual subject for bonsai.*

One of the most well-known shows at which you can view bonsai is the Royal Horticultural Society's Chelsea Flower Show. This takes place in late May every year in the grounds of the Royal Hospital in London. At this show there are normally about six bonsai exhibits staged by both professional and amateur bonsai growers, as well as bonsai societies.

Below: *General view of a Bonsai Kai members' competition at one of the Royal Horticultural Society's London shows.*

The Chelsea Flower Show is the world's most prestigious horticultural show and normally draws people from most countries around the world. It is considered to be the pinnacle of any grower's life to be invited to exhibit at this show and, to date, the author and his wife have exhibited eighteen times consecutively and been awarded six Gold Medals.

Similar gardening shows, as well as shows devoted purely to the exhibition of bonsai, take place all over the world and are very well patronized by people from all nations. This is because bonsai is such a very absorbing and popular pastime.

When displaying bonsai at a show or exhibition, it is absolutely critical that every piece of equipment involved in the display, including the bonsai tree, is complementary to every other item, such as stands, backdrops, *suiseki*, accent plants and table coverings.

POINTS TO CONSIDER WHEN SHOWING BONSAI

- Your bonsai trees should be correctly trimmed so that they are presented at their very best and do justice to your efforts. Bonsai judges are very meticulous in their observations.

- The pot must be suitable for the tree in terms of design and colour and the pot and tree should be in balance.

- The pot must be thoroughly clean; its appearance can be enhanced by a light application of oil or leaf-shine to the pot's outer surface.

- Foliage on the tree must be clean and free from any type of pest or disease. Check well in advance to be certain of a healthy-looking tree for the show.

- If there is any wire or other shaping aid on a bonsai, it must be unnoticeable when viewed from any angle.

- The soil surface should always look as natural as possible, with moss or other very small ground-cover plants strategically placed. Grit is not recommended as a soil decoration.

Above: *A variety of bonsai on show at a Royal Horticultural Society spring show in London. This club competition is open to all members who are amateur bonsai growers.*

Left: *The author judging the Bonsai Kai bonsai competition at the 2005 spring show organized by the Royal Horticultural Society.*

THE BONSAI YEAR

Throughout the year, bonsai trees can change dramatically in appearance. Some trees, such as junipers and pines, may not look that different from one season to the next, but those that produce prominent flowers and fruit, as well as those that change their foliage colours every season, can be breathtaking to look at. Most trees look different as the seasons pass, but many deciduous trees, such as maples, often develop brilliantly coloured leaves in both spring and autumn. It is this spectacular transformation throughout the seasons that captures the imagination of so many bonsai enthusiasts. Even if you have just one or two flowering or fruiting bonsai, this will certainly make an interesting contribution to your collection.

Left: *This Oriental hornbeam (Carpinus laxiflora) group is just beginning to attain its autumn colour. From green summer foliage, it progresses through a mixture of yellow, orange and red.*

Spring

Early spring brings about the first signs of active growth in your trees following their dormant period throughout the winter months. This certainly makes it one of the busiest times in the bonsai year. In the northern hemisphere, spring encompasses the months of March, April and May whereas, in the southern hemisphere, spring covers September, October and November. In real terms, this means that the work which needs to be carried out in spring varies by six months over the two areas of the world. It is important to make sure that all necessary procedures for this period of the year are carried out so that the health of your bonsai is not compromised. General housekeeping tasks, such as watering and feeding trees, as well as maintaining the cleanliness of trees and pots, are all necessary in spring.

Above: *A relatively young Japanese crab apple (*Malus floribunda*) with delicate spring flowers. These become small fruits in autumn.*

SPRING CARE

Most deciduous trees should have been repotted in late winter, but, if there are a few still to be done at this time of year, then they must be dealt with as soon as possible. Any sign of hard frosts means that freshly repotted trees may need to be provided with some form of protection. You can easily do this by placing your bonsai in a garden shed or perhaps a cold greenhouse or cool conservatory (sun room) until the threat of frosts is over. Just before the buds break, any repotting required should be done, so make sure that you have everything prepared in order to repot your bonsai when the time is right.

Some pruning can be carried out now because this is by far the best time of the year for tidying up both deciduous and coniferous trees. In the case of deciduous trees, it is easy to see any twigs or branches that have died back or need removing just before the buds burst. So, trees should be trimmed now so that they start the year in good shape. When the shoots begin to extend, cut them back to one pair of leaves in order to maintain a compact growth pattern.

Wire for shaping can be applied now to conifers, such as pines (*Pinus*) and junipers (*Juniperus*), but preferably not to deciduous trees. These should not be wired until a little later in the year when the sap is flowing freely because they will be more flexible if branch bending is required. Monitor any wire on trees at all times of the year; it can be surprising how quickly the branches swell. Remove any wire that appears to be cutting into the bark.

Left: Acer palmatum *'Deshojo' with its late-spring leaf colouring, which fades from pink at bud-break to bronze in the summer.*

Fertilizer must never be applied to recently repotted and/or root-pruned trees because this can easily result in severe damage to the roots that were pruned during the repotting process or to very young, freshly growing roots.

Watering should be of a moderate nature and only when it is required, but it will be necessary to increase the amount of water as the weather begins to warm up with the approach of summer. Freshly potted trees must also never be over-watered because they can easily become waterlogged. This is because freshly pruned roots do not take up moisture until the new young roots begin to develop.

BONSAI FEATURES IN SPRING

Spring is a very colourful and vibrant time of the year for bonsai, and for plants in general for that matter, so you should make the most of the huge variety of fresh and beautiful colours both of foliage and of any blossom that may appear.

Foliage colours in spring can vary from brilliant pink to bright yellow or green and almost any other colour variation that you can imagine. The really brilliant colours are normally courtesy of deciduous trees because conifers and evergreen plants are generally not so colourful at this time of year. Japanese maples (*Acer palmatum*) will produce some of the most spectacular spring leaf colours with such a wide range of colours available that it would be impossible to classify them all here.

The leaf forms of the spring growth of this type of plant are also very varied. As the leaves unfurl, they present a multitude of shapes that cannot be easily matched by any other variety of tree used for bonsai culture.

Flowers are another very important and colourful aspect of spring within the bonsai world. There are many different species of plant suited to bonsai growing that will produce flowers of many different shapes and

Above: *This* Acer palmatum *'Deshojo', with its brilliant pink colouring, will draw admiring comments throughout early spring.*

Left: Prunus incisa *'Kojo-no-mai' in mid-spring showing its delicate flowers that are closely followed by the fresh new leaves.* ▷

colours. The size of blossom on bonsai is crucial to the overall look of the tree, so it is necessary to research the eventual size of the flowers before you embark on a bonsai that will produce flowers.

Most flowers are too large in proportion to the plant when grown in a miniature form such as that encountered with bonsai. Look out for small-flowered plants, such as crab apple (*Malus*) and flowering cherry

Below: *Informal upright Japanese crab apple (Malus floribunda) in mid-spring with an abundance of white flowers.*

(*Prunus*), which will give a balanced feel when the plant actually produces its flowers. It is also important that you do not forget that many flowering plants will also go on to develop fruit later in the year. The size of any eventual fruit on the bonsai specimen must also be taken into account when you are choosing a plant from which to create and style a bonsai.

Whatever aspect of your bonsai is important in spring, it must always be considered for its balance relating to the size of the tree, as well as the size, shape and colour of any flowers that may develop.

SEASONAL FEATURE PLANT: WISTERIA

Wisteria, when it is grown naturally to its full size as a climber, is perhaps one of the most spectacular hardy plants in the world. When it is used in an open garden or decorative situation, wisteria is normally seen growing against a garden wall or fence, or even cladding the side of a house.

Wisteria is native to China and Japan and can provide some of the most spectacular spring floral displays in its native habitat or in a garden. The flowers consist of long, pendulous racemes of fragrant, pea-like flowers that hang in dense clusters, giving the plants a weeping appearance. The flowers, which appear in late spring and early summer, vary in colour from white and mauve through to blue and are often at their best when the new leaves are just beginning to break behind them. This provides a breathtaking and stunning start to the garden year and should you be lucky enough to own a bonsai version it will give your collection a much-needed boost of spectacular colour. Wisteria flowers also have the added bonus of a deliciously intoxicating scent.

Because of its pendulous appearance when it is in flower, the wisteria is usually grown as a weeping-style tree. The racemes of flowers, depending on the variety, can be from as little as 10cm (4in) to as much as 1m (40in) in length, with the longer ones being preferred for a weeping-style bonsai.

Because of their long flower formation, wisteria are best grown as informal upright, slanting, weeping, semi-cascade and cascade-style bonsai. They are also normally grown as fairly large specimens because of the size and scale of the flowers.

Bonsai wisteria need protection from frost in the winter as they have rather thick, succulent-like roots that can be very easily damaged if the temperature drops below about

-5°C (23°F). During the summer months, a wisteria bonsai will need copious amounts of water and, during the really warm parts of the summer, it is advisable to stand the pot in a shallow tray of water so that the plant has a continuous supply of water throughout this hot period. It is most important that wisteria bonsai are never allowed to dry out completely. This is, of course, a rule that applies to all bonsai, although some species can tolerate a certain amount of dryness. However, in general, allowing a bonsai to dry out can quickly result in its death.

You will need to feed your wisteria bonsai about once a week following flowering until midsummer, commencing again in early autumn through to late autumn. Repot wisteria bonsai every two to three years and prune back to two buds following flowering in the summer, as well as in the autumn.

To obtain good flowering plants, propagation should be carried out using hardwood cuttings or grafting in early spring or by air layering from late spring to early summer using the techniques described in the appropriate section of this book. Propagation from seed produces plants very quickly, but they do require anything from seven to ten years to produce flowers whereas the other propagation methods should produce flowers the following year.

KEY TASKS FOR SPRING

ROOT PRUNING AND REPOTTING

- Root-prune and repot any deciduous trees as soon as possible, although most should have been done in late winter. Make sure that all repotting is done before the buds break.

- Never apply fertilizer to recently root-pruned and repotted trees, as this could damage roots pruned during the repotting process.

- Protect freshly repotted trees by placing them in a shed or unheated greenhouse until all threat of frost has passed.

PRUNING

- Tidy up deciduous and coniferous trees. With deciduous trees, it is easy to see twigs or branches that have died back or need removing before the buds burst. Trimming them now means they start the year in good shape. When shoots begin to extend, cut back to one pair of leaves to maintain compact growth. With some conifers, such as juniper (*Juniperus*) or larch (*Larix*), pinch out any new soft shoot tips. This encourages more shoots to grow and the process can be repeated. With pines (*Pinus*), pinch back new candles by about two-thirds when they reach about 2.5cm (1in).

WIRING

- Apply the wire for shaping to conifers such as pine (*Pinus*) and juniper (*Juniperus*), but preferably not to deciduous trees. These should not be wired until a little later in the year when the sap is flowing freely. This means that the trees will be more flexible if the branches need to be bent during the shaping process.

WATERING

- Water moderately when required, increasing the amount as the weather warms up, but never over-water freshly repotted trees.

Summer

June, July and August constitute the summer months in the northern hemisphere, whereas in the southern hemisphere, summer is the period that includes December, January and February. All repotting should have been finished by the beginning of the summer. If you have trees in your collection that require a different pot for display purposes only, then it is possible to remove them carefully and plant them in a more suitably sized pot. Do not seriously disturb the roots; simply loosen them slightly and place the bonsai in its new pot, filling in the gaps with fresh soil. It is not advisable to repot any trees during the summer months, but, if this is necessary, then careful consideration of the placement and care of the trees is very important immediately following repotting.

Above: Acer palmatum *showing the colour variation that appears on the leaves as a result of stronger sunlight. The balance would improve if the lower right branch were removed.*

SUMMER CARE

Most trees should be growing at their maximum rate at this time of the year and any rapidly extending shoots will need to be pruned, trimmed or thinned on a regular basis. Deciduous trees will need their shoots cut back to one or two pairs of leaves and the buds on conifers should be carefully plucked out as they begin to swell and extend. The use of wire for training purposes can be brought into the equation now and applied to most species of tree at this time of year. However, it is vital that you always remember to keep a close watch on wire that was applied earlier in the season and remove any that appears to be cutting into the tree or if you think the branch or trunk has already become set in its required position. If, after removing any wire, you find that the branch or trunk springs back towards its original position, then you will need to rewire for a few more weeks or months.

Watering daily is required as the weather gets warmer. If it becomes very hot, then watering may be needed more than once each day and extra care should be taken of very small trees. At all times, the condition of the soil needs to be monitored and the bonsai watered if required.

When there is a sudden burst of torrential rain, your trees will not necessarily have gained sufficient water. Trees with a heavy foliage canopy can shed rain rather like an umbrella, so water beneath the canopy directly on to the soil.

Feeding is also very important at this time of the year and most trees will need to be fed throughout the summer months, making sure that you lower the amount of nitrogen applied as you progress from late summer into the autumn.

Left: *Japanese hornbeam* (Carpinus laxiflora) *in full foliage which will remain rich green in colour throughout the summer. Note the close proximity of the trunks in this group.*

Above: *This Japanese maple* (Acer palmatum) *is displaying its beautiful summer colouring. Maples undergo many colour changes through the year.*

BONSAI FEATURES IN SUMMER

This is an interesting time in the bonsai calendar, with many unusual trees making an appearance. You can, for example, create stunning bonsai from fruiting plants such as kumquats and olive trees (*Olea europaea*). Flowering bonsai include fuchsias, while the summer foliage of more traditional bonsai can also provide a burst of colour, including the fresh green Japanese hornbeam (*Carpinus laxiflora*) and the beautiful colour variations of certain varieties of Japanese maple (*Acer palmatum*).

SEASONAL FEATURE PLANT: RHODODENDRON

This genus includes some of the most spectacular varieties of flowering plant. Azaleas fall within this genus and, contrary to popular opinion, there is no botanical difference between azaleas and rhododendrons. A large number of species originate in Japan and many named varieties are now available. Their hybridization and propagation has been taking place in Japan over the last four centuries with the evergreen Satsuki azaleas being the most popular. These have a wide range of flower sizes and colours. The Kirishima or Kurume azaleas also make beautiful bonsai and have smaller blooms than the Satsuki, which makes their proportions appear much more in keeping with bonsai sizes.

Rhododendrons can be trained into most bonsai styles, except broom, and of course the larger-flowered varieties are more suitable for larger bonsai. Those with smaller flowers are generally grown as small bonsai, but when grown as large bonsai they will appear to be much more in proportion.

These plants are acid-loving, needing an ericaceous compost (acid soil mix) for the best results and watering with rainwater in areas with a hard water supply. Protect them from heavy rain

Above: *A small* Rhododendron *bonsai with pale pink, double flowers. This bonsai has a very chunky trunk and has been placed in a* similarly rugged-looking pot. This tree has been developed from the stump of a very much larger plant.

when in flower as the blooms damage easily. Remove the new shoots after flowering. Give a lighter shoot prune in midsummer to encourage new flower buds for the following spring.

Rhododendrons need repotting and root pruning once the flowers have dropped. There will be few repotting problems as they have a compact, fine, fibrous root system. Keep them in partial shade, giving little water in winter, and feeding fortnightly in spring, leading up to the flowering period.

Rhododendrons can be propagated either by air layering or softwood cuttings in early summer and quickly produce vigorous new roots. A good way to obtain a *Rhododendron* bonsai is to find an old plant in the garden, prune it hard back to the main trunk, lift it from the ground and pot it into a temporary container. Once re-established, it quickly puts on new growth that can be selectively pruned to produce a good bonsai in two or three years and a very good bonsai in ten years.

SEASONAL FEATURE PLANT: FUCHSIA

As the interest in using hardy, woody, shrubby perennials for bonsai increases, plants such as fuchsias have been found to exhibit good woody growth that eventually develops into a mature, tree-like form given the correct pruning and shaping.

A very common method of growing fuchsias is with a tall straight stem, supported by a cane. Side shoots are continually pinched off until a tall,

GROWING A BONSAI FUCHSIA

1 Remove the plant from its pot and tease the potting compost (soil mix) from around the roots of the plant using a fork or rake.

2 Using a sharp pair of scissors or secateurs (pruners), carefully cut away approximately two-thirds of the roots.

3 Cut down a plastic flowerpot to leave a small, low pot that will provide a temporary training pot for the fuchsia.

4 Repot the fuchsia, holding the plant upright and trickling charcoal-rich, gritty potting compost around the roots.

5 Gently firm down the potting compost, using a stick to ensure that all the spaces are filled. Water the fuchsia.

Above: *This young bonsai fuchsia is clearly in the early stages of shaping and styling, and there is further work to be done. If you want to* encourage a "windswept" growth form, then *you can lay the plant on its side or at an angle for a couple of weeks.*

thick stem is produced, before finally pinching out the lead shoot to encourage a twiggy, branched canopy of blooms.

The training of fuchsia bonsai is very similar to this procedure in that some side shoots are removed leaving a few selected shoots in suitable positions so as to form a tree-like trunk and branch structure.

Fuchsias are indigenous to South and Central America and are therefore not totally hardy in a temperate climate, although a few varieties are able to withstand some degree of frost.

To avoid die-back of the trunk and branch structure, growth must be maintained throughout the winter months and this can be achieved by making sure that the plant retains its foliage throughout the colder part of the year. It is therefore recommended that fuchsia bonsai be given winter protection where the temperature remains below 6–7°C (43–45°F).

As with other flowering bonsai, varieties with small leaves and flowers are preferred because they create a

lifelike and balanced specimen. In the same way as the chrysanthemum, fuchsia bonsai can be trained in all the usual bonsai styles with informal upright and cascade being two of the most frequently grown forms. Most shaping and styling can be achieved by pruning to shape rather than using wire because fuchsias are capable of developing compact, twiggy structures by constant pruning of the shoot tips. At all times, remember that the flowers normally appear from the tip of the shoots and, therefore, as the flowering

Left: Fuchsias are becoming increasingly popular as subjects for pruning and shaping into highly decorative bonsai.

season approaches, care should be taken not to remove any forming flower buds.

When in bloom, fuchsia bonsai can be spectacular, being covered in brightly coloured, pendulous flowers that last many weeks before sometimes developing richly coloured seed pods. As with any bonsai that produces fruit or seed pods, it is not advisable to allow too many to remain on the plant as it can overpower the appearance and overtax the strength of the tree.

The normal method of propagation is by softwood or semi-ripe cuttings taken from the parent plant in mid-summer. These should be inserted into good-quality cuttings compost (soil mix) and kept in a slightly shaded place until the first signs of growth are observed. The cuttings can then be moved to larger pots to establish a good root structure and initial top growth.

KEY TASKS FOR SUMMER

ROOT PRUNING AND REPOTTING

• All root pruning and repotting should have been finished by the beginning of the summer, but if there is a tree that seems to be too large for its pot, just repot it without pruning the roots at all. Avoid seriously disturbing the roots by just loosening them slightly, then place the tree in its new pot and fill the gaps with fresh soil.

PRUNING

• Prune, trim or thin rapidly extending shoots of your bonsai regularly, as most trees should be growing at their maximum rate at this time of year.

• Cut the shoots of deciduous trees back to one or two pairs of leaves, and carefully pluck out buds on conifers as they begin to swell and extend.

WIRING

• Most species of tree can be trained by wiring at this time of year, but keep a close watch on any wire you have already applied and remove any that appears to be cutting into a tree.

• Remove any training wires if you think a branch or trunk has already become set in its required position. If, after removing any wire, you find that the branch or trunk springs back toward its original position, you will need to rewire for a few more weeks or months.

WATERING

• Water regularly as the weather gets warmer, and every day should it become hot. You may need to water more than once each day if the temperature becomes very hot.

• Take special care if your trees are small and in very small pots.

• In all cases, keep a very close watch and monitor the soil regularly, watering if it begins to dry out. Do not be fooled into thinking that a sudden burst of torrential rain will provide your trees with sufficient water.

• Some trees have a heavy foliage canopy that can shed rain just like an umbrella, so be vigilant and water beneath the canopy and on to the soil.

FEEDING

• This is an important time of year for feeding and most trees will need to be fed throughout the summer. Ensure you lower the amount of nitrogen applied as late summer passes into autumn.

Autumn

A northern hemisphere autumn covers the months of September, October and November and a southern hemisphere autumn takes place in March, April and May. The rate of growth in most plants begins to slow down in early autumn, dropping off to almost nothing by late autumn. Deciduous leaves will change colour and eventually fall, leaving the trees bare during winter. The inner leaves will be the first to fall, as these were the earliest to develop, leaving those on the ends of the branches to fall last. Some conifers change foliage colour for the winter, so do not think that some of your trees may be dying – they are just acquiring their autumn colours. Root growth will slow right down, and any buds that have already formed for the following year will harden up with the colder weather to prepare for winter.

Above: *An informal-upright Japanese holly* (Ilex crenata) *with the bright red berries that remain on the tree from autumn to winter.*

AUTUMN CARE

You can continue pruning pines (*Pinus*) and junipers (*Juniperus*), but avoid pruning deciduous trees in early autumn, as this can induce a spurt of new growth that can be damaged by early frost. When growth has stopped, the pruning or trimming of shoots is not necessary, with the exception of some conifers like junipers and cryptomerias. The shoot tips of some species can be pinched out one last time before winter sets in.

Wiring is not generally necessary in autumn, but if some conifers like pines still need to retain their wire, you must keep a close watch on them as they often produce a late burst of growth and may well suffer serious damage from wire that has been inadvertently left in place. Should this appear to be happening, the wire must be removed as soon as possible.

Do not apply wire in late autumn; in fact, it is more beneficial to remove it, allowing your trees to have a rest during the colder winter months.

With the cooling of the weather, the need to water will drop almost completely away as the trees are going into a temporary dormancy. Look at and check the condition of the soil daily and apply water sparingly if required. When deciduous trees have shed their leaves, they will need very little water as transpiration through the leaves will have ceased, but remember that very strong, cold winds can dry the soil just as quickly, if not quicker, than strong sun, so you may need to protect conifers that retain

their foliage by placing them under cover. Two applications of nitrogen-free fertilizer should be given to most trees in the autumn to harden off the current year's growth. One should be applied in mid-autumn. This is an excellent way of helping to protect your trees in winter.

Left: *A spectacular* Acer palmatum *specimen, displaying the brilliant red leaves that are such an important feature of any display during the autumn.*

Above: *Autumn colour varies tremendously with species and variety, and this Japanese grey bark elm* (Zelkova serrata) *has beautiful golden-yellow foliage at this time of year.*

BONSAI FEATURES IN AUTUMN

This is one of the most colourful periods in the bonsai year, with many trees going through stunning colour changes. The Japanese grey bark elm (*Zelkova serrata*), for example, has golden foliage in the autumn, while Japanese maples (*Acer palmatum*) can be relied upon to provide a stunning display of colour. Early berries are also a feature of autumn, with the bright red berries of the Japanese holly (*Ilex serrata*) making a welcome appearance.

SEASONAL PLANT FEATURE: CHRYSANTHEMUM

Growing chrysanthemum as bonsai is relatively recent. It has become popular in Japan over the past three centuries and is beginning to gain a foothold worldwide. This form of bonsai-growing is a little quicker than normal in that the finished product can be achieved in a reasonably short time. It can, however, take much longer than this to create a mature-looking tree.

The art of producing any bonsai relies on the plant producing a woody trunk and branch structure that looks very old. In the case of a chrysanthemum, the plant should develop the mature characteristics, such as roots, trunks and branches, within the first year of training.

Being a perennial flowering plant, it produces blooms each year and, as with any other flowering bonsai, you need to choose varieties that produce small, compact flowers. Over several hundred years of chrysanthemum cultivation, many miniature flowering forms with characteristics suitable for bonsai have been developed. These include short internodal growth, compact habit, multi-branching habit, strong root and trunk growth, and the all-important profusion of long-lasting blooms on very short stems.

Chrysanthemum varieties for this type of culture should also have very pliable young growth that allows for easy manipulation and styling into tree forms.

Above: *Japanese hornbeam* (Carpinus laxiflora) *planted in a group and displaying its initial autumn colour of yellow progressing through to brilliant red. This group holds its changing coloured foliage for many weeks.*

Left: *This is a root-over-rock* Chrysanthemum, *showing how the roots cling to the rock. The rocks are normally soft building blocks that are easily carved into any shape with grooves to accommodate the roots.*

Developing a chrysanthemum for bonsai is no more difficult than using any other type of material as the techniques involved are the same as those already described. Using techniques such as wiring, pruning and pinching could well produce an acceptable result in between ten and fifteen months, depending on the skill and vision of the grower.

As the chrysanthemum tends to grow quicker than any other tree or shrub, it is possible to make changes or correct mistakes that will improve the overall appearance of your chrysanthemum bonsai. As it takes relatively little time to produce an attractively shaped bonsai, it need not be a massive disaster if the odd failure occurs as a new plant can be formed fairly easily.

Flowers can vary in colour from pure white through yellow and orange to pink and red. Continual pinching out of the shoots will produce densely flowering pads of colour, which will last for anything up to two months.

Chrysanthemum can be trained in all the usual bonsai styles and make spectacular displays throughout mid-

Left: Chrysanthemum *plants trained over artificial rock make for a very natural root-over-rock display.*

and late autumn each year. The chosen plants should be of the hardy varieties and kept outside for as long as possible, placed under cover for protection in the most severe winter conditions.

Propagation is normally carried out using cuttings or stolon growth. The use of cuttings is very popular for propagating chrysanthemum as many plants can be produced from a single stock plant. Cuttings should be approximately 7.5–10cm (3–4in) in

length with five or six leaves. The lower two leaves should be removed before the cutting is inserted into the cuttings compost (soil mix).

Stolons are shoots that emerge from the crown of the root system of a mature plant and can develop either just above or just below the soil surface. Propagation from stolon growth generally provides a more vigorous plant and is more suited to much larger styles of *Chrysanthemum* culture. Like normal cuttings, these are carefully removed from the parent plant using a sharp knife or scalpel and inserted into a good-quality rooting compost as with cuttings.

SEASONAL FEATURE PLANT: CRAB APPLE (*MALUS*)

The crab apple is a popular plant that can be styled into a most attractive flowering and fruiting bonsai. Remember that the smaller flowering and fruiting varieties are most suitable for bonsai, so that the correct balance

Right: *Large* Chrysanthemum *bonsai created from a piece of dead tree stump with flexible-stemmed* Chrysanthemum *plants being trained up the rear and into the branch structure to create an impressive exhibit.*

Above: *The apex of a crab apple bonsai with fairly well-proportioned fruits.*

Left: *Very attractive Nagasaki crab (*Malus cerasifera*) with individual fruits showing various colours as they mature.*

between tree size, foliage, flower and fruit is maintained through the year. One of the most common varieties used for bonsai work is *Malus cerasifera,* or the Nagasaki crab, as it produces both dense foliage and masses of compact clusters of flowers, followed by reasonably small fruits.

The crab apple is normally grown as an informal upright bonsai that often resembles a full-size apple tree, only in miniature, but other styles can be successfully created if desired.

Some varieties have relatively smooth bark, while others may develop a knobbly, gnarled bark structure. As with any tree with a smooth bark, extreme care must be taken to avoid damage as a result of any wiring used in the training process.

Most varieties of *Malus* are totally hardy, but when grown as bonsai in shallow pots, they may require some light winter protection for their slightly tender, succulent roots. With full-size trees growing naturally in the

ground, these roots would normally be below the frost level in the soil and the plants would therefore be considered hardy.

As *Malus* produce a prolific number of fibrous roots, plants should be repotted every year in spring before the flower buds begin to break. The soil, as with most bonsai, should be an open, gritty, free-draining compost (soil mix) that allows good fibrous root development, which in turn will result in a strong, healthy flowering plant.

KEY TASKS FOR AUTUMN

PRUNING

- Prune pines (*Pinus*) and junipers (*Juniperus*).

- Avoid pruning the deciduous trees in your collection in the early autumn because this could induce a sudden spurt of new growth, which could be severely damaged by an early frost.

- Once all plant growth has stopped in the autumn, no more pruning or trimming will be necessary, except perhaps of some conifers, such as junipers and cryptomeria.

- Pinch out the shoot tips of some species one last time before the winter.

WIRING

- Look out for wiring on some of your conifers such as pines which often produce a late burst of growth and may be damaged by wire left in place. Remove the wire as soon as possible. Generally speaking, it is beneficial to remove any wiring to give your trees a rest during the colder winter months.

WATERING

- Assess the condition of the soil daily and apply water sparingly if this is required. Deciduous trees will need almost no water, but conifers that retain their foliage are vulnerable to strong, cold winds, so place them under cover for protection.

FEEDING

- Give two applications of nitrogen-free fertilizer to most trees in late autumn to harden off the current year's growth. and to protect your trees through the winter months.

REMOVING DEAD LEAVES

- Pick up any leaves that fall on the soil surface, the surrounding display benches and the ground below.

- Regularly remove all dead leaves that become trapped in the branches.

- Keep the trunks and branches of all your trees clean and free of all algae and moss.

Winter

The winter months cover December, January and February in the northern hemisphere and June, July and August in the southern hemisphere. It is a quiet time for your bonsai, but there will still be some general maintenance required and, unless you live in a reasonably mild area, you will need to protect your trees from severe weather. Do not, however, over-protect hardy varieties that would normally survive well in your area. Winter is a time to study trees that have lost their leaves and assess their structure with a view to deciding what can be done to improve them. It is not advisable to carry out severe pruning, however: leave this until early spring when the wounds will heal quicker. Conifers and any other evergreens will need to have old, dead internal foliage removed to allow light and air to penetrate.

Above: *Looking at this* Acer palmatum *'Deshojo' in winter allows the true form to be seen and it is now that any structural changes which may be required can be identified.*

WINTER CARE

Wiring and pruning should not be carried out in early winter. However, at a time when deciduous trees have dropped all their leaves, it is a good idea to look closely at the form of all your bonsai trees with a view to making an assessment of which branches may need to be pruned or adjusted in the early part of the following spring. Assess whether branches or trunks need to be reshaped or if any major or minor branches need to be removed altogether in order to improve the overall appearance of the tree.

Bonsai trees left out in the open will not need watering from mid-autumn through to late winter because they should receive enough water from dew, mist, rain, and even snow. However, bonsai need to be monitored at all times to check on the moisture levels around their roots. Should any appear dry, then it is advisable to give them a splash of water in order to maintain a "just-moist" situation in the soil. If they become too wet, they can be placed under cover, but you should still ensure that they are open to all atmospheric conditions except rain until they dry out a little. A good tip is to prop up one end of the pots of your bonsai with a brick or something similar so that they are tilted to one side. Any excess water will then quickly drain away, returning the root system again to that "just-moist" situation that will ensure a healthy tree throughout the winter.

Left: *The pale bark of this Japanese beech* (Fagus crenata) *looks striking in winter. It has been recently pruned and rewired.*

Right: *Korean hornbeam* (Carpinus laxiflora*)*
following the shedding of its foliage gives a
very good view of the excellent structural form
of the tree.

Some bonsai growers always tilt all their trees throughout the winter months and place as many deciduous trees under rain protection as possible.

Hardy bonsai will come to no harm if they become covered with a blanket of snow; it will actually keep the root-ball (roots) at a more even temperature. However, if there is a heavy snowfall where large amounts of snow collect on bonsai branches, then it is always advisable to knock the snow away so that its weight cannot damage the branches in any way.

Preparations for the onset of spring will need to be made during the winter. Start by sourcing any new pots that may be required, along with new soil and all accessories such as grit, wire, tools and anything that you think may be useful for the coming new bonsai season. All of these items may

be needed when you begin repotting in early spring, so make sure you have all the materials you may require. Sift and mix the necessary soils, grit and humus so that repotting can be started in late winter, but always be careful to protect freshly potted trees from frost.

Outdoor bonsai can be very attractive in their winter form and make an excellent short-term indoor display, as long as you remember that they can be indoors for only a very short time and then only where the temperature is fairly low in a room with an airy atmosphere.

Tropical or subtropical trees are better suited for indoor use during the winter and they will need warmer and more humid conditions than their outdoor counterparts.

Left: *During the winter Japanese beech*
(Fagus crenata*) can retain their leaves in a*
bronze form and these will need removing in
the spring if they do not fall naturally.

Right: *This is the attractive winter form of a Japanese maple* (Acer palmatum). *Its broom style clearly shows in its winter silhouette. Bonsai can be attractive all-year-round.*

YOUR BONSAI IN WINTER

Winter is the ideal time to sit and study your trees because there will be little or no apparent activity. Trees, of course, do not stand still and there will always be something happening over the winter period in readiness for the new season. It is important to understand exactly what happens during a tree's so-called dormant period. For example, buds will be setting and the roots settling down and getting ready to leap into action when temperatures begin to rise in early spring.

The autumn application of a low- or zero-nitrogen fertilizer will have begun to do its work in the preparation of both roots and buds. It will have helped to harden up the previous year's growth and will therefore take the trees through the winter months without too much stress caused by any very cold weather.

During this time, you will be able to take stock of the individual style and structure of each tree, especially the deciduous trees that have shed their

leaves. Now is the time to decide which, if any, branches will need to be adjusted or removed. However, you will probably carry out the most severe pruning in early spring as the healing rate of wounds is much greater in

spring than winter. The growth rate of all your trees will have slowed down, so callousing of wounds will not take place and the risk of infections leading to decay within the tree's structure will be higher than in spring.

KEY TASKS FOR WINTER

PLANNING WIRING AND PRUNING
- Do not carry out wiring and pruning in early winter, but this is a good time to look closely at the form of all bonsai trees, now that deciduous trees have dropped all their leaves. You can then make an assessment of which branches may need to be pruned or adjusted in the early part of the following spring.

WATERING
- Bonsai trees that are kept out in the open should not need watering, as they should receive enough water from dew, mist and rain. You should, however,

give them a splash of water if they become dry. If they become too wet, place them under cover, in the open, until they dry out a little.

- Prop up one end of your bonsai pots so that they are tilted; any excess water will then quickly drain away.

OUTDOOR CARE
- Hardy bonsai will come to no harm if they are covered with a blanket of snow; in fact, it will keep the root-ball (roots) at a more even temperature. Remove heavy snow from any branches, however, as the weight could damage them.

ROOT PRUNING AND REPOTTING
- Prepare for the onset of the spring now by sourcing any suitable new pots and containers that may be required, along with sufficient new soil for the root pruning and repotting processes that need to take place during the following year.

- Sift and mix the necessary soil ingredients, and make sure you have everything you need before starting work on any deciduous trees that need this treatment. Be careful to protect any freshly root-pruned and repotted trees from frost.

SEASONAL PLANT: FLOWERING HAZEL (*HAMAMELIS*)

Flowering bonsai specimens, such as hazel (*Hamamelis* × *intermedia*) are very popular, but the choice of plant needs to be considered very carefully because not every flowering or fruiting tree or shrub is suitable for bonsai.

It is important to know that when you are applying the normal techniques used for bonsai training, the foliage usually tends to decrease in size with age. It is equally important to remember that, unlike the foliage, neither the flowers nor the fruit of any plant will reduce in size due to any type of pruning or any other bonsai technique. It is therefore absolutely essential that you select trees that have naturally small flowers and fruit and which will be in proportion to the size of bonsai that you are growing. Care should also be taken to ensure that the growth which will bear the flowers is not pruned off before it blooms.

Hamamelis is now available in many varieties which produce autumn leaf colours ranging from yellow, orange and red, and flowers in brillant yellow, orange and rusty red.

Left: *Hardy* Hamamelis *x* intermedia *showing the highly attractive flower formations covered with ice. It would be preferable to remove any snow from the branches before it freezes into an ice block.*

STYLING A FLOWERING HAZEL (*HAMAMELIS* × *INTERMEDIA*)

1 The unpruned plant has a nice even shape, making it a suitable subject. Remove any inward-growing branches with scissors.

2 Using a pair of side cutters, prune out the very long top growth from the plant.

3 Scrape away the soil with a rake to see where the roots begin to flare out. This will ensure the best blend of trunk to soil surface.

4 Place the tree in a prepared pot and secure in place with wire.

Above: *The finished tree is potted up in a cream glazed pot, which blends with, but does not detract from, the impact of the flowers. Given several years of pruning and shaping, the structure of this tree will improve dramatically.*

BONSAI DIRECTORY

This section provides a comprehensive list of plants that can be trained and styled into bonsai. This is a guide only as there are many other plants that are suitable; in fact, almost any plant that produces a woody main stem will have characteristics that are suitable for bonsai growing. For many of the plants described, there is a photograph of the typical foliage shape and colour, as well as descriptions of the texture of the bark and the colour of the flowers and fruit where applicable. The styles of bonsai to which the plant is most suited are given where relevant, as is a recommendation of the preferred size for the bonsai, which will depend upon the characteristics of each plant. The details provided on each plant also include its country of origin and the environmental conditions in which the plant should be grown.

Left: *The beautiful late spring appearance of an* Acer palmatum *'Deshojo'. This shows every detail of a most attractively foliated plant highly suited to bonsai culture.*

A to Z of Bonsai Plants

Acer buergerianum
Trident or Three-lobed maple

Smooth-barked deciduous tree, eventually producing flaking bark that exposes attractive red-orange patches. Leaves are dark green, paler underneath and three-lobed, turning red, orange or yellow in autumn. An excellent plant for bonsai as it responds well to hard pruning, resulting in a dense, twiggy growth pattern. Slightly tender in winter as it produces rather fleshy roots, but it should not require much winter protection if it is grown in good, open, granular soil.
Country of origin Japan and Eastern China
Suitable bonsai styles Informal upright, slanting, twin trunk, group, root-over-rock
Environmental conditions Hardy in temperate climates; slight protection required below -5°C (23°F). Z5–9

Acer palmatum
Japanese maple

Deciduous tree growing to about 8m (25ft) in the wild. This is one of the most popular and easy-to-grow plants for bonsai culture. The leaves are bright green with paler undersides, have five to seven deeply divided lobes and turn red in autumn. There are hundreds of cultivars of Japanese, European and American origin, some of which are listed separately in this plant directory. Other good cultivars

Acer buergerianum

include 'Osakazuki' (with brilliant red leaves in autumn) and 'Senkaki' (which has bright coral-pink young shoots in the winter). They are all hardy and need protection only in the most severe conditions.
Country of origin Japan and Central China
Suitable bonsai styles Informal upright, slanting, cascade, twin trunk, group, root-over-rock
Environmental conditions Hardy outdoors in temperate climates. Z5–8

Acer palmatum 'Deshojo'
Japanese maple

This is one of the most popular cultivars of *Acer palmatum* and is a deciduous tree that has bright carmine-red leaves in the very early stages of spring. The five-lobed leaves develop into rich red at the start of summer, changing to red/green in late summer and brilliant red in autumn. The red leaf colour will be retained for a longer period if the bonsai is kept in very good light conditions for as long as possible.
Country of origin Japan
Suitable bonsai styles Informal upright, slanting, cascade, twin trunk, group, root-over-rock
Environmental conditions Hardy outdoors in temperate climates. Z5–8

Acer palmatum 'Kamagata'

Acer palmatum 'Kamagata'
Dwarf Japanese maple

A dwarf deciduous cultivar with mainly five-lobed, sometimes only three-lobed, green leaves edged in rich or rusty red in spring, changing to brilliant light green in summer. Autumn colours range from yellow to orange and sometimes red, and remain on the tree into late autumn.
Country of origin Japan
Suitable bonsai styles Informal upright, group
Environmental conditions Hardy outdoors in temperate climates. Z5–8

Right: *Acer palmatum*

Acer palmatum 'Deshojo'

Acer palmatum

Acer palmatum 'Kiyohime'
Dwarf Japanese maple
A dwarf cultivar of *Acer palmatum* of low, compact, spreading habit with small, five-lobed, green leaves edged with orange-red in spring, changing to rich green in summer, and then yellow, orange and red in autumn. This is one of the earliest deciduous trees to break bud in spring and one of the last to drop its leaves in the autumn.
Country of origin Japan
Suitable bonsai styles Twin trunk, broom, clump
Environmental conditions Hardy outdoors in temperate climates. Z5–8

Acer palmatum 'Shindeshojo'
Japanese maple
The name means "new Deshojo" because this plant is a later selection of cultivar than 'Deshojo'. It has many more brilliant flaming or crimson leaves in the early stages of spring as the leaves unfold. The five-lobed leaves retain their red colour well into summer, changing to reddish-green in late summer and a mixture of orange and red in autumn. As with 'Deshojo', the leaf colour will be retained for a longer period when the tree is placed in very good light conditions for as long as possible.
Country of origin Japan
Suitable bonsai styles Informal upright, slanting, cascade, twin trunk, group, root-over-rock
Environmental conditions Hardy outdoors in temperate climates. Z5–8

Aralia elegantissima
Finger aralia
This plant has attractive straight stems when young, with deeply cut, purple-brown, more or less deeply serrate, somewhat pendulous leaves, not dissimilar to those of *Acer palmatum dissectum*. The juvenile stage can be up to 1.8m (6ft) or so in height, unbranched with many leaves. The stems and petioles are smooth, with leaves up to 23cm (9in) long and 2.5cm (1in) wide, narrowing from the middle to the tip. The juvenile stage is best for bonsai use.

Country of origin New Hebrides
Suitable bonsai styles Groups
Environmental conditions Half hardy; protection required below -5°C (23°F). Z10

Berberis thunbergii
Barberry
A round and compact shrub that can reach a height of approximately 1.2m (4ft), barberry has a strikingly different appearance in the various seasons. It has pale to mid-green leaves that turn a brilliant red in the autumn. Long clusters of pale yellow flowers, which appear in mid-spring, are followed by small, scarlet-red berries. Two other good varieties of barberry which are suitable for bonsai are 'Atropurpurea', with rich purple-red leaves throughout spring and summer, and 'Atropurpurea Nana', which has similar leaves, but a more compact habit.
Country of origin Japan
Suitable bonsai styles Informal upright, clump, semi-cascade, cascade, twin trunk
Environmental conditions Totally hardy in most areas. Z5–9

Bougainvillea spectabilis
Bougainvillea
Tender, shrubby, climbing, deciduous plant, with spiny growths and dark green elliptic leaves. Long flower panicles with magenta bracts are produced from

Bougainvillea glabra

mid-summer to early autumn and there are many varieties with various shades of colour from cerise and scarlet through to deep pink. Its very rigid twigs and branches mean that bonsai shaping is normally achieved by simple pruning techniques. *B. glabra* (often known as the paper flower) is an evergreen or semi-evergreen, rambling climber that has clusters of floral bracts in shades of cyclamen purple in the summer.
Country of origin Brazil
Suitable bonsai styles Informal upright, semi-cascade, cascade
Environmental conditions Tender in temperate areas with minimum temperature of 10°C (50°F). Z10

Berberis thunbergii 'Atropurpurea'

Buxus sempervirens

Buxus sempervirens
Common box

A hardy, evergreen, slow-growing shrub with a bushy habit. It has dark green, glossy leaves as well as inconspicuous, honey-scented, pale green flowers in mid-spring. Box is commonly used for closely clipped hedges and topiary and is therefore highly suited for bonsai use, as the clipping procedure promotes the dense twiggy structure required for bonsai.

Country of origin Europe, North Africa and Western Asia

Suitable bonsai styles Informal upright, clump, twin trunk, broom

Environmental conditions Totally hardy. Z6–9

Carpinus betulus
European hornbeam

Deciduous tree with oblong, pointed, deep green leaves, turning to various shades of yellow in autumn. Catkin-like fruits sometimes appear when it is grown as a bonsai. Commonly grown as hedging around fields, it responds well to hard pruning, producing compact growth suitable for most bonsai styles.

Country of origin Europe and Asia Minor

Suitable bonsai styles Informal upright, slanting, twin trunk, group

Environmental conditions Hardy outdoors in temperate climates. Z5–9

Carpinus laxiflora
Japanese hornbeam

Deciduous tree growing to 15m (50ft), with pointed green leaves which turn to yellow, orange and red in autumn. Excellent for bonsai training as this plant responds extremely well to shoot pruning and quickly develops a good twiggy form. Catkin-like fruits sometimes appear when it is grown as a bonsai.

Country of origin Japan and Korea

Suitable bonsai styles Most styles, but normally informal upright, slanting, group or forest

Environmental conditions Totally hardy outdoors in temperate climates, but may need some protection from extreme heat in tropical areas. Z5–9

Cedrus deodara
Himalayan cedar

Evergreen tree of pendulous habit, with rich green to grey-green, very sharp, needle-like leaves. Not as good for bonsai training as *Cedrus libani* but can produce acceptable results with persistent effort. Can be very sparse in foliage if consistent and regular shoot pruning is not carried out properly.

Country of origin Western Himalayas, Afghanistan and Eastern Nepal

Suitable bonsai styles Informal upright, cascade

Environmental conditions Hardy outdoors in temperate climates. Z7–9

Cedrus libani
Cedar of Lebanon

Large evergreen tree growing to 45m (150ft) in natural conditions, with roughly horizontal branches and mid-green, sometimes bluish, needle-like leaves. Provides very good material for bonsai, especially the dwarf variety 'Brevifolia'. Produces cones, but often when grown as bonsai they are too large and so out of proportion with any miniaturized tree.

Country of origin Syria and south-east Turkey

Suitable bonsai styles Formal upright, informal upright, literati

Environmental conditions Hardy outdoors in temperate climates. Z7–9

Carpinus laxiflora leaves

Carpinus laxiflora stems

Cedrus libani subsp. *atlantica*

Cedrus libani 'Brevifolia'

Cedrus libani subsp. *atlantica*
Atlas cedar

Evergreen subspecies of *Cedrus libani*, but with slightly ascending branches. Needle-like leaves can be dark green, blue-green or blue-grey. Another good plant for bonsai, as it develops dense, twiggy foliage when pruned using bonsai techniques.

Country of origin North Africa (Atlas Mountains)

Suitable bonsai styles Formal upright, informal upright, literati

Environmental conditions Totally hardy outdoors in temperate climates and will not need any protection from extreme heat as originates from very hot areas. Z7–9

Cedrus libani subsp. *atlantica* 'Glauca'
Blue Atlas cedar

Another very good plant that can be developed into high-quality bonsai. This is the blue form of the *Cedrus libani* subsp. *atlantica*, which has silver-blue, needle-like foliage and is generally known as the blue Atlas cedar. There are many slightly different forms of this plant, which include weeping and fastigiate versions.

Country of origin North Africa (Atlas Mountains)

Suitable bonsai styles Formal upright, informal upright, literati

Environmental conditions Hardy outdoors in temperate climates. Z7–9

Celtis bungeana
Nettle tree or Hackberry

This is a deciduous tree which reaches a height of 15m (50ft) in the wild. It has oval leaves that are glossy and dark green. The smooth, light grey bark is damaged easily if the tree is wired during bonsai training, so wiring is not recommended for this particular plant. *Celtis australis* is a very similar plant, but it has oval to lanceolate, rough, dark-green leaves that are downy on the underside.

Country of origin Central and northern Asia

Suitable bonsai styles Formal upright, informal upright, twin trunk, group

Environmental conditions Hardy in most temperate areas of the world. Z2–9

Cercis siliquastrum
Judas tree or Love tree

This is a deciduous tree or shrub that grows naturally to approximately 10m (30ft). It has maroon young shoots with rounded, matt, grey-green leaves which turn bright yellow in the autumn. Pale rose to rich magenta, pea-shaped flowers on very short racemes break from naked old wood in late spring and are then followed by flat seed pods which are similar in shape to mangetout (snow peas). These seed pods turn brown and are retained well into the following year.

Country of origin Eastern Mediterranean

Suitable bonsai styles Informal upright

Environmental conditions Hardy in temperate climates. Z8–9

Cercis siliquastrum developing seed pods

Cercis siliquastrum foliage

Chaenomeles japonica

Chrysanthemum

Chaenomeles japonica
Japanese or Maule's quince

This delightful spreading, deciduous, thorny shrub grows to approximately 1m (3ft) in height. It has mid-green, ovate to round leaves. The flowers, which resemble the flowers of apple trees, can be orange-red, scarlet or crimson and are borne on the old wood from early to late spring. The flowers are followed by apple-shaped yellow fruits, which are sometimes tinged with red.

Country of origin Japan

Suitable bonsai styles Informal upright, clump

Environmental conditions Hardy in temperate climates. Z5–9

Chamaecyparis obtusa
Hinoki cypress

This is a slow-growing evergreen tree which reaches approximately 40m (130ft) in height when growing in the wild. The hinoki cypress bears blunt, deep green, scale-like leaves, with silver-white undersides, which are sweetly aromatic when they are crushed. The bark has a brown, flaky, very attractive appearance and can be peeled to reveal deep reddish-brown colouring. There are several dwarf forms available, all of which are highly recommended for bonsai.

Country of origin Japan

Suitable bonsai styles Formal upright, informal upright, twin trunk

Environmental conditions Hardy in temperate climates. Z4–8

Chamaecyparis pisifera
Sawara cypress

Evergreen tree that has bright, mossy-green foliage in fern-like sprays, with fine silver-white undersides. The foliage is acridly aromatic when it is crushed. The bark is rusty-brown and peels into thin strips that can be removed, as with *Chamaecyparis obtusa*. Makes excellent material for bonsai training as it develops a very compact form with correct shoot pinching.

Country of origin Japan

Suitable bonsai styles Informal upright

Environmental conditions Hardy in temperate climates. Z5–8

Chrysanthemum

About 20 species of scented herbs, often woody at the base. Flowers range in size, but the best varieties for bonsai will have the smallest flowers. Flowers usually borne in autumn and remain on the plant for several weeks. Results will be achieved in less time than most hardy, woody varieties of plant. Suitable varieties include 'Hokuto' (red), 'Ohko' (yellow) and 'Sumi' (yellow).

Country of origin Europe and North Africa

Suitable bonsai styles Groups, informal upright, formal upright, root-over-rock, root-in-rock

Environmental conditions Half hardy; protection required below -5°C (23°F). Z8–9

Chamaecyparis obtusa

Chamaecyparis pisifera

Cotoneaster × suecicus 'Coral Beauty'

Crassula arborescens

Cotoneaster horizontalis
Cotoneaster

This is a deciduous shrub with a flat-growing habit and a striking, herringbone-like branch structure. The broad, glossy, dark green leaves turn brilliant red in the autumn. Depending on the atmospheric conditions, some or all of the leaves may remain throughout the winter period. The very small pink flowers, which appear during the spring, are followed by cheerful red berries in the autumn.
Country of origin Western China
Suitable bonsai styles Informal upright, semi-cascade, cascade, root-over-rock
Environmental conditions Hardy in temperate climates. Z5–9

Cotoneaster × suecicus 'Coral Beauty'

Evergreen, low-growing, spreading shrub with oval, bright green leaves and outstanding brilliant red berries in autumn. This is a very good plant for bonsai culture as it can be easily pruned into shape with very little need for wiring, and can tolerate virtually any weather conditions imaginable.
Country of origin China
Suitable bonsai styles Semi-cascade, cascade, any form of rock planting
Environmental conditions Very hardy. Z5–9

Crassula arborescens
Jade or Money tree

Named from the Latin *crassus*, which means thick or swollen, and refers to the succulent nature of the plant. There are many species and varieties, but *C. arborescens* is one of the most widely available. Leaves are oval, thick and succulent and are borne in opposite pairs. Clusters of very small white flowers appear on vertical stems in the leading ends of shoots from late autumn to early spring.
Country of origin South Africa
Suitable bonsai styles Informal upright, twin trunk
Environmental conditions Minimum temperature of 10°C (50°F). Ideal low-maintenance indoor bonsai. Z10

Crataegus monogyna
Common hawthorn or May

This is a thorny, deciduous, very hardy small tree with glossy, lobed and toothed, very dark green leaves. Bears dense clusters of white flowers in late spring followed by dense clusters of small crimson haws in autumn. Numerous very hard thorns, which can grow to 2–2.5cm (¾–1in) in length, appear on most of the shoots; these can prick your hands when

Crataegus monogyna

Cryptomeria japonica

Cryptomeria japonica 'Tens Sans'

you are training this plant as a bonsai specimen, so take great care. *C. laevigata* is similar to *C. monogyna*, but it can have white, pink or red flowers and bright crimson, double flowers as in the cultivar 'Paul's Scarlet'.

Country of origin United Kingdom and Europe

Suitable bonsai styles Informal upright, semi-cascade

Environmental conditions Hardy in temperate climates. Z5–7

Cryptomeria japonica
Japanese red cedar

This is an evergreen tree with mid- to dark green, needle-like leaves which turn bronze in the winter, but remain green on some cultivars. The thick, peeling bark is red-brown. Dwarf varieties, such as 'Jindai-sugi', are highly recommended for bonsai culture. The different varieties of the Japanese red cedar can vary considerably in their habit, but when the shoots are pinched out regularly, very dense growth patterns will result.

Country of origin Japan and China

Suitable bonsai styles Formal upright, group

Environmental conditions Extremely hardy in temperate climates, but when grown as a bonsai, it will benefit from a slightly shady position. Z6–9

Fagus crenata
Japanese beech

Large deciduous tree with long, pointed buds leading to pointed, soft green leaves in spring, changing to glossy, mid- to dark green leaves in summer, and then russet in autumn. When trained as bonsai, the leaves are retained throughout the winter, eventually falling in spring. It has a very smooth, pale grey bark. There are many species of beech, all of which would make good bonsai.

Country of origin Japan

Suitable bonsai styles Formal upright, informal upright, twin trunk, clump, group

Environmental conditions Hardy in temperate climates. Z4–7

Fagus sylvatica
Common or European beech

This is a very large, long-lived, deciduous tree with ovate, pointed, wavy-margined foliage, which is bright green in spring, turning mid-green in the summer and yellow to russet in the autumn. When grown as bonsai, the russet leaves remain in place until bud-break in spring. As with the Japanese beech, this tree has smooth grey bark, but in a slightly darker shade of grey.

Country of origin Europe

Suitable bonsai styles Informal upright, twin trunk, clump, group

Environmental conditions Hardy in temperate climate and very tolerant of most conditions. Z4–7

Fagus sylvatica

Ficus benjamina

Ficus benjamina 'Variegata'

Ficus benjamina
Weeping fig

An evergreen tree with pendulous branches and slender, pointed leaves that are soft green when young, maturing to dark glossy green. The bark is grey. Aerial roots often appear, particularly when kept in humid conditions. During pruning, the wounds will produce a sticky, white latex solution that is toxic and should not be ingested.
Country of origin India
Suitable bonsai styles Informal upright, cascade, twin trunk, clump
Environmental conditions Maintain temperature above 10°C (50°F) in winter. Z10

Ficus benjamina 'Variegata'
Variegated weeping fig

Evergreen tree similar to *Ficus benjamina* but with leaves that are green with creamy-white variable edges.
Country of origin India
Suitable bonsai styles Informal upright, cascade, twin trunk, clump
Environmental conditions Maintain temperature above 10°C (50°F) in winter. Z10

Ficus microcarpa
Indian laurel, Curtain fig, Malay banyan, Chinese banyan or Glossy-leaved fig

This plant was previously misnamed *Ficus retusa* and is often still known by this name. It is an evergreen tree with a spreading crown and ascending branches, from which many aerial roots descend to form curtains around the trunk. The glossy leaves are similar to *Ficus benjamina*, but darker green, and the bark is grey and rougher. As with *F. benjamina*, pruning produces a white, toxic latex solution.
Country of origin India
Suitable bonsai styles Informal upright, cascade, twin trunk, clump
Environmental conditions Maintain temperature above 10°C (50°F) in winter. Z10

Fuchsia
Lady's ear drops

There are over 100 species of procumbent, erect or climbing shrubs or small to medium trees in this genus. The leaves are alternate, opposite or in whorls. Flowers are solitary and axillary, or gathered into terminal paniculate groups and are often drooping, tubular, and with nectar at the base. Flowers vary in size from about 5mm to 10cm (¼ to 4in) in length and come in a large variety of colours from white to deep purple. The flowers form the most spectacular part of these plants in bonsai. Suitable varieties include 'Tom Thumb' or 'Lady Thumb'.
Country of origin Central and South America, Mexico, New Zealand, Tahiti
Suitable bonsai styles Groups, informal upright, formal upright, root-over-rock, root-in-rock, cascade
Environmental conditions Half hardy; varieties require protection below -5°C (23°F). Z8–9

Gingko biloba
Maidenhair tree

This ancient deciduous tree is thought to have been around for about 200 million years and is now often grown as a curiosity because of its historical value. It has leathery, fan-shaped leaves, partially divided in the middle and similar to the maidenhair fern. Leaves are pale green in spring, dark to mid-green in summer and brilliant gold in autumn. Once the leaves have turned gold, they drop very quickly.
Country of origin China
Suitable bonsai styles Informal upright, twin trunk, broom
Environmental conditions Hardy in temperate climates. Z5–9

Fuchsia

Hamamelis × intermedia
Witch hazel

A cross between *H. japonica* (Japanese witch hazel) and *H. mollis* (Chinese witch hazel). Medium-sized shrub with broad leaves which are 10–15cm (4–6in) long. Autumn leaf colours are yellow with tints of red and orange. Flowers are butter yellow, 2.5cm (1in) or so in diameter, with crumpled petals, borne in midwinter. Various forms have different flower colours, ranging from pale yellow through orange to deep rust red.

Country of origin China, Japan, North America and Europe
Suitable bonsai styles Formal upright, informal upright
Environmental conditions All varieties totally hardy. Z5–9

Hamamelis mollis 'Pallida'

Ilex crenata
Japanese or Box-leaved holly

Evergreen shrub or small tree with dark green leaves and numerous lustrous, small white flowers followed by small, glossy black fruits. Ideal for bonsai culture because of its small leaves, flowers and fruit and its easy persuasion, by pruning, to form tight twiggy growth.

Country of origin Japan and Korea
Suitable bonsai styles Informal upright
Environmental conditions Hardy in temperate climates. Z6–8

Ilex serrata
Japanese winterberry

This deciduous shrub has mid-green leaves and small pink flowers. The flowers are followed by small red berries in autumn. It is widely used for bonsai in Japan, but seldom seen in other countries. It responds well to pruning and produces good, branched growth patterns, making it an ideal subject for bonsai culture.

Country of origin Japan and China
Suitable bonsai styles Informal upright
Environmental conditions Hardy in temperate climates. Z6–9

Jasminum nudiflorum
Winter jasmine

A deciduous shrub with a rambling growth pattern and dark green leaves. Fragrant yellow flowers are borne on previous years' growth from winter to early spring. It develops a rough bark at a young age.

Country of origin Northern China
Suitable bonsai styles Informal upright, slanting, semi-cascade, cascade, root-over-rock, exposed root
Environmental conditions Extremely hardy and tolerates sub-tropical and tropical conditions. Z6–9

Ilex serrata

Jasminum nudiflorum

Juniperus chinensis
Chinese juniper

This is an evergreen bushy tree that has dark green, scale-like adult foliage with needle-like juvenile leaves internally or when the plant is severely pruned. The insignificant flowers develop into small, blue-black fruits. The bark is red-brown in colour, peels very easily and can be lightly brushed in order to give a beautiful reddish appearance. There are many cultivars of Chinese juniper to choose from, some of which carry the scale-like adult foliage and others that bear only the needle-like juvenile foliage.

Country of origin China

Suitable bonsai styles Informal upright, cascade, group

Environmental conditions Hardy in temperate climates. Z5–9

Juniperus communis
Common juniper

This is a densely branching evergreen tree or shrub which has needle-like foliage, deep green on the outer surface with a blue-white band on the inner surface. The fruits of the common juniper are berry-like and green in appearance, ripening to blue-black in approximately two years. It is not one of the easiest trees to form into a bonsai, but it will make a superb specimen with persistence.

Country of origin Europe, Asia and North America

Suitable bonsai styles Informal upright, semi-cascade, cascade

Environmental conditions Hardy in temperate climates. Z3–7

Juniperus chinensis

Juniperus horizontalis
Creeping or prostrate juniper

Evergreen, low-spreading, mat-forming species developing into thick cushions with grey-green leaves; it may produce dark blue cones. There are many cultivars in various shades of green that will provide very good material for bonsai production.

Country of origin North-east America

Suitable bonsai styles Semi-cascade and cascade

Environmental conditions Hardy in temperate climates. Z3–9

Juniperus procumbens
Procumbent juniper

Evergreen species with maroon-brown bark and light green foliage. This is an excellent plant for bonsai, especially the very compact variety 'Nana' or any of the less common varieties that are now available in plant centres and nurseries.

Country of origin Japan

Suitable bonsai styles Semi-cascade and cascade

Environmental conditions Hardy in temperate climates. Z5–9

Juniperus rigida
Needle or Temple juniper

This small evergreen tree reaches a height of 15m (50ft) in the wild and is highly sought-after by bonsai enthusiasts. It has yellow-brown peeling bark and very sharply pointed, needle-like, bright green leaves, which have a blue-grey line in a dorsal groove. The cones mature in about two years into spherical, dark purple, eventually black, berry-like fruit.

Country of origin Japan, Korea and northern China

Suitable bonsai styles Formal upright, informal upright, driftwood

Environmental conditions Hardy in temperate climates. Z6–9

Larix decidua
European larch

This is a deciduous conifer with bright green needle-like leaves on the young shoots and in whorls on spurs on the older growth. The young shoots are yellow-brown in colour, with grey-brown bark which matures to flaking plates. The female flowers are red-purple, developing into small, woody cones which can remain on the trees for many years. The cones are small enough to be in proportion when they are allowed to remain on larger bonsai specimens.

Country of origin Central Europe

Suitable bonsai styles Formal upright, informal upright, cascade, group or forest

Environmental conditions Hardy in temperate climates. Z3–6

Right: *Juniperus chinensis*

Juniperus horizontalis

Larix decidua

Larix kaempferi
(syn. *L. leptolepis*)
Japanese larch

Deciduous conifer with rusty-brown, fissured and scaly bark and red-brown shoots. These are grey at first, but eventually bear needle-like green leaves that are slightly broader than *Larix decidua*. The small squat cones that are produced in profusion are retained on the branches for several years. A very good plant for bonsai as it responds extremely well to any bonsai styling technique.

Country of origin Japan

Suitable bonsai styles Formal upright, informal upright, cascade, twin trunk, group

Environmental conditions Hardy in temperate climates. Z5–7

Lespedeza bicolor
Bush clover

Bushy, woody shrub with vivid green leaves that are paler beneath. Small flowers can be in short racemes or terminal clusters and are purple-rose or rose-violet. A very attractive plant that is relatively easy to care for and will produce a good-looking bonsai in a fairly short time.

Country of origin Japan, China, Manchuria, Korea and Taiwan

Suitable bonsai styles Informal upright, twin trunk, broom, root over rock

Environmental conditions Normally hardy but susceptible to die-back in very cold conditions.

Lonicera nitida
Hedging honeysuckle

Dense, branched, evergreen shrub growing to about 3.5m (11ft), with young purple shoots carrying ovate to rounded glossy dark green leaves. Insignificant cream to white flowers from early to mid-spring followed by shiny, semi-translucent, blue-purple, globular berries in late spring and early summer. Has the potential to make superb bonsai.

Country of origin China

Suitable bonsai styles Informal upright, semi-cascade, twin trunk, windswept

Environmental conditions Hardy in temperate climates. Z7–9

Malus floribunda

Lonicera pileata
Shrubby honeysuckle

Low-growing, often prostrate, evergreen or semi-deciduous shrub with young purple shoots. Leaves are shiny, mid- to dark green. Inconspicuous yellow-white flowers on underside of shoots in the spring are followed by semi-translucent, amethyst-coloured, globular berries in late spring. A first-class plant for bonsai training, this species develops a flaking woody trunk while still quite young.

Country of origin China

Suitable bonsai styles Informal upright, semi-cascade, twin trunk

Environmental conditions Hardy in temperate climates. Z5–9

Malus floribunda
Japanese crab

Deciduous tree or shrub growing up to 10m (30ft) with mid-green, toothed leaves. Flowers are abundant along the length of branches in spring, beginning deep pink in bud, fading to pale pink with white inside, and followed by yellow fruits in autumn. Makes a good flowering bonsai, but is not easy material from which to achieve a pleasing tree-like shape.

Country of origin Japan

Suitable bonsai styles Informal upright

Environmental conditions Hardy in temperate climates with some frost protection being required when the flowers are about to break. Z5–8

Lonicera nitida

Morus alba
White mulberry
A small, rounded tree with downy young shoots eventually bearing glossy, bright green leaves with serrated edges. Flowers are white-green, leading to green-white fruit, ripening to pink or dark red with a sweet but poor flavour. Capable of producing, with persistence, a good, rough-barked, twiggy bonsai.

Country of origin China

Suitable bonsai styles Informal upright, twin trunk, broom, root-over-rock

Environmental conditions Relatively hardy but needs protection in very serious winter conditions. Z5–9

Myrtus communis
Myrtle
A much branched, erect shrub, to 3m (10ft), with dense, dark lustrous green foliage that is strongly scented when crushed. The fragrant, slender flowers are white or pink-white, 2.5cm (1in) in diameter and up to 2.5cm (1in) long. Fruit is blue-black when ripe. Widely cultivated from ancient times with its native range therefore uncertain. Many different varieties are now available, most with fragrant flowers and small leaves, which are suitable for bonsai culture.

Country of origin North Africa, Mediterranean and south-west European countries

Myrtus communis

Olea europaea

Suitable bonsai styles Informal upright, formal upright and groups

Environmental conditions Half hardy; protection required below -5°C (23°F). Z9–10

Nandina domestica
Sacred or Heavenly bamboo
An upright evergreen or semi-deciduous, multi-stemmed shrub, with green leaves tinged with red when young and turning to red-purple in autumn. Profuse flowers are followed by red, pea-sized fruits that remain in place for long periods. Will not produce classical bonsai styles, but makes for an interesting variation in a collection.

Country of origin Japan

Suitable bonsai styles Informal upright, clump, twin trunk, group, landscape

Environmental conditions Hardy, but young shoots can be damaged by frost. Z7–10

Olea europaea
European, Common or Edible olive
Multi-branched evergreen tree that grows to 7m (23ft), with grey-green leaves that are silvery beneath. Off-white, fragrant flowers turn to red, followed by purple-black fruit. Makes a good indoor bonsai because the normal habitat is dry and arid.

Country of origin Mediterranean

Suitable bonsai styles Informal upright, broom

Environmental conditions Hardy down to freezing, but could be damaged below this temperature. Z9–10

Picea mariana
Black spruce
Medium-sized evergreen tree with red-brown bark and densely arranged blue-green needles. The dwarf variety 'Nana' is highly suited for bonsai, as it is very compact with short, blue-green needles. Excellent for small group plantings and rock landscapes, where the trees can be pruned into very mature-looking designs.

Country of origin Canada

Suitable bonsai styles Root-on-rock, landscape

Environmental conditions Very hardy in temperate climates and will need no protection at all in any area. Z3–6

Picea mariana 'Nana'

Pinus parviflora

Podocarpus macrophyllus

Pinus parviflora (syn. *Pinus pentaphylla*)
Japanese white pine

Evergreen tree with blue-green, short needles in fives on the upper side of shoots. The bark is smooth and grey-black, developing small plates when it is mature. This is one of the classical varieties from which bonsai are grown and it can be very long-lived in the bonsai form.
Country of origin Japan
Suitable bonsai styles Informal upright, slanting
Environmental conditions Hardy in temperate climates. Z6–9

Pinus sylvestris
Scots pine

Extremely hardy evergreen tree with grey-green needles borne in pairs. The bark is thin, red-brown and flaky when young, exposing rusty-brown colouring beneath, and becomes thick and plate-like with extreme age. Superb tree for bonsai

Pinus sylvestris

culture because of its hardiness and willingness to be manipulated and pruned. Particularly good for literati-style bonsai.
Country of origin Europe, Siberia and Eastern Asia
Suitable bonsai styles Formal upright, informal upright, semi-cascade, cascade, literati, driftwood
Environmental conditions Hardy in temperate climates. Z3–7

Pinus sylvestris including 'Beuvronensis', 'Jeremy' and 'Watereri' syn. 'Nana'
Dwarf Scots pine

These are compact, slow-growing varieties of the Scots pine, all having shorter needles than the species *Pinus sylvestris*. 'Beuvronensis' has blue-tinted needles, 'Jeremy' has green needles, and 'Watereri' has rich blue-grey needles. They are all grafted on to rootstocks of *P. sylvestris* and exhibit features that make them ideal for bonsai training.
Country of origin Europe
Suitable bonsai styles Formal upright, informal upright, semi-cascade, cascade, literati, driftwood
Environmental conditions Hardy in temperate climates. Z3–7

Pinus thunbergii
Japanese black pine

This is an evergreen tree with black-grey, furrowed bark and orange-yellow young shoots. The dark green needles are borne in pairs of two and are densely arranged on the shoots. This pine makes good material

for bonsai and is much prized in Japan. It is grown less abundantly as a bonsai specimen outside Japan, but it is still very popular with bonsai enthusiasts worldwide.
Country of origin Japan and Korea
Suitable bonsai styles Informal upright
Environmental conditions Hardy in temperate climates. Z5–8

Podocarpus macrophyllus
Big-leafed podocarp

Evergreen tree or shrub with densely arranged, mid- to dark green leaves that are tinged yellow beneath. Normally sold as an indoor tree in temperate areas, but is totally hardy and makes a good evergreen bonsai. The leaves are slightly long, but they do reduce in size with time.
Country of origin Japan
Suitable bonsai styles Informal upright, semi-cascade, cascade
Environmental conditions Suitable for both indoors and outdoors in most areas. Z7–10

Pinus thunbergii

Prunus cerasifera
Cherry plum

Deciduous, tree-like, sometimes spiny shrub with bright green leaves. The small, pure white, solitary flowers on twigs in late winter and early spring are followed by red to yellow, cherry-shaped fruit. This makes a good flowering bonsai, but it is not easy to maintain this particular plant in a good tree-like shape.

Country of origin Asia Minor and Caucasus
Suitable bonsai styles Informal upright
Environmental conditions Hardy in temperate climates. Z5–9

Prunus spinosa
Blackthorn or sloe

Very spiny, dense, bushy shrub or tree, which has dark green leaves. Masses of small, snow-white flowers in early and mid-spring are followed by small green fruit in late spring, turning to black damson-like fruit (sloes) in late summer and early autumn. The fruit is used to make sloe gin. In the right hands, the plant will make a handsome bonsai.

Country of origin Great Britain, North Africa and north Asia
Suitable bonsai styles Informal upright
Environmental conditions Hardy in temperate climates. Z5–9

Prunus yedoensis
Tokyo cherry

A cross between *P. × subhirtella* (winter flowering cherry) and *P. speciosa* (Oshima cherry). This small tree, growing to 15m (50ft), is mainly upright with smooth bark and young ascending branches. The leaves, up to 12cm (4½in) in length, are vivid green above and paler beneath. The pure white flowers can be 4cm (1½in) across. The fruits are round, pea-sized and black when ripe. 'Shidare Yoshino' ('Pendula') has a weeping habit with snow-white flowers.

Country of origin Japan
Suitable bonsai styles Informal upright, formal upright.
Environmental conditions Mostly hardy, but protection required to prevent frost damage to opening flower buds. Z6–8

Prunus yedoensis

Pyracantha

Punica granatum
Pomegranate

Deciduous shrub or small tree with glossy, pale green leaves and often spiny branches. The funnel-shaped flowers are orange-red and the fruits are spherical, up to 12cm (4½in) in diameter, with many seeds in a fleshy, sweet, edible coating. There are several cultivars, the best of which is the dwarf variety 'Nana', which makes a good small bonsai.

Country of origin Eastern Mediterranean to Himalayas
Suitable bonsai styles Informal upright, semi-cascade, twin trunk, group, raft, root-over-rock
Environmental conditions Able to endure only light short frosts; otherwise hardy. Z8–10

Pyracantha
Firethorn

Extremely hardy evergreen shrub closely related to *Cotoneaster* and *Crataegus*. Depending on variety, the leaves range from entire to crenate. Flowers are white on most varieties, but the fruits vary from yellow through to brick red and are borne in dense clusters throughout. Excellent, hardy material from which beginners can learn the art and culture of bonsai.

Country of origin South-eastern Europe to China
Suitable bonsai styles Informal upright, semi-cascade, cascade, twin trunk, broom, root-over-rock
Environmental conditions Very hardy in all climatic conditions and will endure wide-ranging temperatures. Z6–9

Rhododendron 'Double Pink'

Azalea

Quercus robur
English oak, Common oak or Pendunculate oak

Large, long-lived tree with grey-brown, deeply fissured bark and dark green leaves that have rounded lobes. This is not one of the easiest trees to turn into a bonsai, but is worth the effort because of its popularity as a well-known tree. There are many oaks that are not suitable because they have quite large leaves which are difficult to miniaturize for the purposes of bonsai.

Country of origin Great Britain through Europe to Russia

Suitable bonsai styles Informal upright, twin trunk, group

Environmental conditions Hardy, but roots can be slightly tender when potted as bonsai. Z5–8

Rhododendron indicum
Satsuki azalea

This is an evergreen shrub with dark, glossy green leaves. There is a profuse display of wide, funnel-shaped flowers in mid-summer, ranging from white through to deep pink, sometimes variously striped, depending on the variety. There are hundreds of cultivars and varieties, available from most good garden centres, but the smaller-flowered varieties are best suited to bonsai.

Country of origin Japan

Suitable bonsai styles Informal upright

Environmental conditions Hardy in temperate climates. Z5–8

Rhododendron obtusum 'Amoenum'
Kirishima azalea

This is a semi-deciduous, small-leaved rhododendron which has dark green leaves and small, magenta flowers. The Kirishima azalea is particularly good for bonsai culture because of its small flowers and its good response to bonsai shoot-pruning techniques. It is widely planted in large ornamental gardens and is, therefore, a possible source of very old plants from which to make excellent bonsai specimens.

Country of origin Japan

Suitable bonsai styles Informal upright, slanting, group

Environmental conditions Hardy in temperate climates. Z5–8

Sageretia theezans
Bird plum cherry

Evergreen shrub with shiny, mid-green leaves and insignificant, green-white flowers followed by small blue berries. Stiff, straight branches produce compact twiggy growth when regularly shoot-pruned. Indoor bonsai of this species, which are imported from China, need to have their foliage sprayed regularly to encourage healthy growth.

Country of origin Central and southern Asia; some regions in North America

Suitable bonsai styles Formal upright, informal upright, multi-trunk, slanting, semi-cascade, cascade

Environmental conditions Need winter protection below 12°C (54°F). Z5–8

Right: *Rhododendron*

Quercus robur

Sageretia theezans

Styrax japonicus

Serissa foetida

Serissa foetida
Tree of a thousand stars

This is an attractive evergreen shrub with dark green leaves. It also bears small, double, white, rose-like flowers.

Country of origin South-east Asia

Suitable bonsai styles Most normal bonsai styles, but best for informal upright and broom

Environmental conditions Needs winter protection below 15°C (59°F). Z9–10

Styrax japonicus
Snowbell or Silverballs

This is a deciduous shrub or small tree, which grows up to approximately 10m (30ft) in height, with elliptic to oblong, slightly toothed, glossy, dark green leaves. The bark is attractive because of its smooth, sometimes flaky, appearance and the flowers are generally white in colour. Snowbells are very popular in Japan as bonsai specimens and are rapidly gaining popularity among bonsai enthusiasts in other parts of the world.

Country of origin China and Japan

Suitable bonsai styles Formal upright, informal upright

Environmental conditions Extremely hardy in temperate climates, but, when grown as a bonsai, will benefit from a slightly shady situation. Z5–9

Taxus baccata
Yew

This is a very long-lived evergreen tree which is native to many areas of the northern hemisphere. The bark is brown-tinged purple, smooth, but also slightly flaky. The attractive leaves are glossy and dark green. This plant makes extremely good material for creating bonsai specimens and will respond reliably to all bonsai styling and training techniques.

Country of origin Europe, North Africa (Atlas Mountains) and Asia Minor

Suitable bonsai styles Formal upright, informal upright, twin trunk, clump, group, windswept

Environmental conditions Very hardy. Z6–7

Ulmus glabra
Wych elm

Large tree to 40m (130ft) with a wide spreading, open crown and smooth bark, becoming fissured when very old. Leaves 5–16cm (2–6¼in), oval and occasionally three-lobed at the apex. Leaves uneven at base, partially covering the petiole, rough, dull green above and lighter green beneath. Flowers formed in dense clusters with red stigmas and the fruit up to 2.5cm (1in), broadly elliptic with a notched apex.

Country of origin North and Central Europe to Asia Minor

Suitable bonsai styles Informal upright, formal upright

Environmental conditions Totally hardy in most areas of the world. Z5–7

Taxus baccata

Ulmus parvifolia

Wisteria floribunda

Ulmus parvifolia
Chinese elm
This is a deciduous tree when it is kept outdoors, but it is an evergreen when it is treated as an indoor bonsai. Chinese elms have rich green leaves with toothed margins and often develop interesting corky bark.
Country of origin Many temperate areas of the world
Suitable bonsai styles Informal upright, semi-cascade, cascade, twin trunk, broom
Environmental conditions Mostly hardy, but those elms that originate from southern China and Taiwan should be considered as indoor bonsai in temperate areas. Z5–9

Ulmus procera
English elm
Deciduous tree with mid- to deep green leaves that turn bright yellow in the autumn. It is popular with bonsai enthusiasts because it responds well to all bonsai techniques.
Country of origin Great Britain, western and southern Europe
Suitable bonsai styles Informal upright and group
Environmental conditions Hardy in temperate climates. Z5–8

Wisteria floribunda
Japanese wisteria
Hardy, deciduous, climbing shrub with light to mid-green, pinnate leaves, each with 12 to 19 leaflets. Fragrant, violet-blue flowers in 24–30cm (10–12in) drooping racemes. White and pink forms available.
Country of origin Japan
Suitable bonsai styles Informal upright
Environmental conditions Hardy in temperate climates. Z4–10

Wisteria sinensis
Chinese wisteria
Hardy, deciduous, climbing shrub with dark to mid-green, pinnate leaves, with up to 11 leaflets. Dense, 20–30cm (8–12in), pendulous racemes of fragrant, mauve flowers. White and double mauve-flowered forms available.

Country of origin China
Suitable bonsai styles Informal upright
Environmental conditions Hardy in temperate climates. Z5–9

Zelkova serrata
Japanese grey bark elm
A large deciduous tree that can grow to over 30m (100ft). It has mid-green leaves that turn yellow-orange and red in autumn. The bark is smooth and grey, and prone to damage if wired during bonsai training.
Country of origin Japan
Suitable bonsai styles Informal upright, broom, group
Environmental conditions Hardy in all temperate climates and will endure wide ranging temperatures. Z6–8

Ulmus glabra

Wisteria sinensis

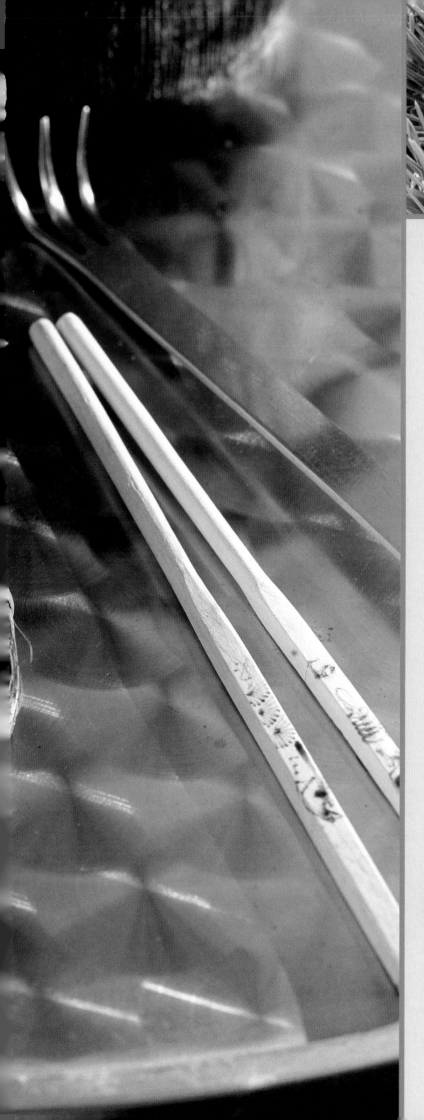

CARE AND MAINTENANCE

Wherever you decide to display your bonsai collection, you must make sure that all of your trees and pots are clean and tidy, so that anyone viewing them sees them at their best. To achieve this top-quality appearance, there are a few basic procedures that you will need to follow closely. For example, the pots containing the trees that you wish to display should be washed thoroughly and dried. You should also make sure that the trees themselves are clean and free of any pests and diseases, as well as free of damaged foliage. If you are planning to exhibit any of your bonsai specimens, you should always ensure that they look their very best; if this is not possible with any of your trees, then it is advisable not to include them in a display or exhibition.

Left: *Pliers, scissors, a brush, chopsticks and a rake form a typical range of tools that may be required when root pruning and repotting a collection of bonsai.*

Environmental Conditions

Once you have decided that you want to own a bonsai, you will have to choose between buying a ready-made tree and styling your own. In either case, you will also need to decide whether you wish to keep the bonsai indoors or outdoors because you need to select the type of tree that best suits the chosen environment. Growing, training, styling and general maintenance techniques for both indoor and outdoor bonsai are virtually identical; it is only the environmental climate that is different. All outdoor trees are happy to be grown in their natural climatic conditions, but when they are moved to a position with different conditions, such as those that occur in other parts of the world, they may need special treatment to maintain an environment more akin to that of their natural habitat.

The local climatic conditions in the area of the world in which you live will inevitably determine the type of trees you can keep indoors or outdoors. Wherever you live, it is generally trees that naturally grow outdoors in your area that will be most suitable as outdoor bonsai, while those from different climatic conditions to the area in which you live, such as tropical or sub-tropical in a temperate climate, will need to be kept indoors or in controlled environmental conditions.

INDOOR BONSAI

Trees to be kept indoors normally need warm conditions with fairly high humidity, which can often be difficult to achieve in centrally heated homes. They will also need to be kept in very bright conditions, but not in front of a sunny window, as this could result in serious drying-out of the foliage.

Their situation means that indoor trees often require extra humidity in and around the foliage. You can supply this by placing the tree, in its pot, on a

Above: *Deciduous bonsai stored in a rain-free environment from late autumn to winter, so that moisture levels of the roots can be monitored.*

layer of absorbent granules within a shallow tray or dish. Keep the granules constantly moist so that as the water evaporates from the granules it drifts up and around the foliage, slowing down the transpiration rate of water from the leaves and therefore decreasing the risk of the leaves drying out and shrivelling up.

Left: Ficus benjamina *bonsai used as a table decoration. Remember that this variety needs good light and humidity.*

Above: *Japanese black pine* (Pinus thunbergii) *kept temporarily indoors. This can done only for a maximum of one or two days.*

OUTDOOR BONSAI

Trees to be kept outdoors in a temperate climate will always be those species and varieties that are hardy in those climatic conditions. They will normally be able to accept very cold conditions (from about -10°C/14°F) up to quite hot summer conditions (30–40°C/86–104°F).

If hardy trees are placed under cover during normal cold winters, they may become slightly tender and could be susceptible to damage from late spring frosts when they are removed from that winter protection. It is therefore advisable not to protect such trees too much, as it could lead to greater problems than might be caused if they were left outdoors throughout the winter.

Deciduous trees will need much less water in the winter, as they will not have any foliage to keep supplied with fluid. It may therefore be necessary to give only a light splash of water every month over the winter period. You must, however, always keep a close watch on the moisture levels, as total drying out could be a disaster and result in the death of the tree.

Above: *A very useful outdoor display area, incorporating several different heights of stand that show off a variety of different bonsai.*

Left: *A bonsai on a timber deck next to a pond will be provided with extra humidity.*

Left: *This is winter housing for bonsai, with the slightly more vulnerable trees placed beneath the bench for added protection from the elements.*

Watering

As with all plants, water is vital to the survival and healthy growth of bonsai. If bonsai are kept outside, then rainfall will supply some of their needs, but if they are kept inside, they will be totally reliant on their owner for their water supply. This may seem obvious at first, but it is a fact that cannot be overstated because so many people find it difficult to assess the watering needs of bonsai, whether they are indoor or outdoor varieties. It is therefore crucial that the correct watering regime is carried out in order to maintain the health and vigour of any type of bonsai. Bonsai must never be allowed to dry out or become waterlogged because it can prove fatal in both instances. The death of a bonsai is demoralizing when you consider the time and effort that goes into creating it.

Above: *Use a watering can with a very fine rose attachment when applying a light watering to the soil of a bonsai.*

OUTDOOR BONSAI

Although outdoor trees will benefit from rainfall, you should not think that if it rains, even heavily, watering will be unnecessary. A tree may have a very heavy foliage canopy, similar to an umbrella, which even heavy rain cannot penetrate, and so the soil may not get wet at all. You will therefore still need to supply your bonsai with water, making sure that it is applied under the foliage canopy and on to the soil itself. Even a tree with a small canopy, and therefore one more suited to being watered naturally, may still need hand-watering, since the fact that most bonsai are grown in fairly shallow containers means that they will be able to retain little of the rain-water they receive.

Keep the soil moist at all times, but never water it to such a degree that the soil and roots become waterlogged because this could quickly result in the roots getting too wet, which will encourage root rot and possibly the death of the tree.

A watering can with a fine rose is ideal, but if your collection of bonsai is very large you can use a hose with a fine rose attached.

The frequency of watering will depend on many things. Strong wind or sun, or a combination of both factors, can be lethal to bonsai, as the soil can quickly dry out. For this reason, you should monitor moisture levels in the growing medium every day in the summer, spring and early autumn.

Right: *Here, a rooted cutting is being watered in using a pressure sprayer, so that the plant receives only a very light watering. This will prevent any disturbance of the fresh soil.*

Left: *A good-quality galvanized watering can with a fine rose is ideal for watering bonsai.*

1 Fill a bowl with water and immerse the pot in the water until the bubbles cease to rise; remove from the water and leave to drain.

2 Use a watering can with a fine rose in order to water the soil and roots. If the soil is very dry, use several applications of water.

3 The same watering can may be used to water the foliage weekly, particularly if there has not been any rain for a while.

4 You can also water with a pressure sprayer or with a hose fitted with a fine rose. Never water with a high-pressure hose.

INDOOR BONSAI

So-called indoor trees require a somewhat different approach to watering. It is very easy to water any indoor bonsai: simply place the whole container in a bowl of water, completely submerging both the container and the soil. Leave the plant submerged until the air bubbles stop rising to the surface, then remove the container from the water, place it on a suitable surface, and allow any excess water to drain away.

You can also water indoor bonsai with a small watering can, preferably one fitted with a very fine rose, but be careful that the pots are not standing on a piece of valuable furniture that will be damaged by having water splashed on its surface.

Take the tree outdoors or to a kitchen draining board or even to the bathroom where moisture in the area will not create a problem. Feeding can also cause problems with furniture, so at all times take care with these tasks. For this reason, it is advisable to apply a dry granular fertilizer to the soil surface of your indoor trees.

Feeding

Regular feeding with the correct type and dose of fertilizer, and at the correct intervals throughout the year, is just as important to bonsai as watering. In fact, feeding is absolutely essential if good, healthy growth is to be maintained. Like all plants, bonsai will take up a certain amount of the fertilizer's nutrients in the soil, but watering will leach away any fertilizer that is left in the soil. This means that a regular input of nutrients is required. Although fertilizers are absolutely necessary to the health of your bonsai, they should always be used sparingly, so that the trees do not put on a massive amount of "forced" growth that will make it difficult to maintain their compact nature. Conversely, too little feeding leads to unhealthy specimens that will struggle to survive.

Above: *A good, balanced general-purpose fertilizer will provide most bonsai with healthy foliage and roots throughout the year.*

Fertilizers can be purchased in a variety of forms, including liquids, slow-release granules and soluble powders. Some of these can be applied as foliar feeds by spraying them on to the foliage with an atomizing spray or by watering them into the soil using a watering can. Pellets can be placed on the soil surface or pushed into the soil and covered over.

Fertilizer pellets that are specially formulated for bonsai can be obtained from specialist bonsai suppliers; they normally take the form of a rapeseed cake. They are a slow-release organic fertilizer that will supply nutrients, and therefore all the necessary feeding requirements, to bonsai for several weeks or months.

When using liquid feed, apply only the recommended dose, or less. Frequent applications of half-strength fertilizer, say once a week or once every two weeks through the spring and summer, will ensure that your trees receive a gentle feeding regime. Once autumn approaches, a feed of very low- or zero-nitrogen content will be required to harden off the current year's growth, which will help your trees to survive better over the winter.

FERTILIZER CONTENT

Most widely available fertilizers contain nitrogen (N), phosphorus (P) and potassium (K), and this combination is usually quoted on the packet as an NPK ratio, such as an NPK of 6:12:10 (which means 6 parts of nitrogen to 12 parts of phosphorus to 10 parts of potassium).

Nitrogen is absolutely essential for vegetative stem and leaf growth, and it is the constituent part of a fertilizer that is responsible for the rich green colours of the leaves. Too much nitrogen will not be good for bonsai, as their growing method means that they do not need to have masses of long, lush, green shoots. Although bonsai need healthy green shoots, they should

Left: *An application of low- or zero-nitrogen fertilizer can be given in late summer and early autumn. This is necessary to harden off the current season's growth in readiness for the winter.*

1 You can apply liquid fertilizers to the roots using a watering-can. Dilute recommended fertilizers as specified.

2 Make sure the fertilizer has been absorbed into the water, then apply the mixture to the soil with care.

3 Pellets made of rapeseed cake can be applied by laying them on the soil surface with tweezers or fingers, about 5cm (2in) apart.

4 After placing the pellets on the soil surface, water over them to start the feeding process which will last two to three months.

be encouraged to grow with short internodal lengths by feeding them with a fertilizer with a relatively low-nitrogen content.

The phosphorus content of a fertilizer is mostly responsible for healthy root growth, but it also helps with bud formation, protection against diseases and poor winter conditions.

Potassium, which is often known as potash, will help to encourage the formation of flowers and fruit. This is also the most essential component in fertilizers in the fight against various diseases. It will also assist with hardening off any new growth produced throughout the season before the winter.

Most commercially available fertilizers contain all three main nutrients, plus some trace elements that will maintain good, healthy growth. There is just one type of fertilizer that is normally available only through specialist bonsai nurseries, and this is a late-autumn feed with an NPK of 0:10:10.

FEEDING GUIDE FOR BONSAI

(Number of applications per month in brackets)

SEASON	COMMONLY GROWN SPECIES		FLOWERING BONSAI
	Liquid and foliar fertilizer	Slow-release fertilizer	Type of Fertilizer
Midwinter			
Late Winter			
Early Spring	High Nitrogen (1)	3 months release (1)	
Mid-spring	High Nitrogen (2) Balanced (1)		Balanced (2)
Late Spring	Balanced (3)		Balanced (1) Tomato/rose fertilizer (2)
Early Summer	Balanced (4)	3 months release (1)	Tomato/rose fertilizer (4)
Midsummer	Balanced (4)		Tomato/rose fertilizer (4)
Late Summer	Balanced (2)	Low Nitrogen (2) Low Nitrogen (1)	Low Nitrogen (2) Tomato/rose fertilizer (2)
Early Autumn	Low Nitrogen (1)	Low Nitrogen (4)	Low Nitrogen (4)
Mid-autumn	Low Nitrogen (1)	Low Nitrogen (2)	Low Nitrogen (2)
Late Autumn	Low Nitrogen (1)	Pines only (1)	Low Nitrogen (1)
Early Winter			

General Maintenance

Whether you grow your trees purely for pleasure or display them at bonsai shows and exhibitions, you will want to make sure that your bonsai look their best at all times. Poor maintenance can result in plants that look untidy, unkempt and generally of reduced quality, so make sure you keep your trees clean and tidy following the instructions below, so that the very best impression of your trees is given to anyone viewing them. If any of your trees cannot be seen at their best, then it is advisable not to include them in a display or exhibition. You will find that the cleaner your trees are, the less likely they are to be infested with insects of any kind, or to be susceptible to attacks from fungal or viral diseases that could prove to be highly problematic to your trees.

POT MAINTENANCE

The pots containing all the prized bonsai specimens that you intend to display or exhibit should be washed thoroughly and also dried. If you encounter a problem when cleaning your bonsai pots, then a kitchen scouring pad is an ideal aid for scrubbing dirty pots and will remove algae, calcium deposits and any stubborn dirt.

To enhance the appearance and colour of a pot, spray it with a leaf-shine product. This dries quickly and gives the pot a very natural appearance; it also tends to protect the pot against the return of any algae, deposits and dirt. Alternatively, you can wipe over the pot with some vegetable oil, using a lint-free cloth so that no small particles of lint are left behind to spoil the effect.

Above: *Despite having large drainage holes, the flat base of a bonsai pot tends to retain a lot of water. This Chinese juniper* (Juniperus chinensis) *is tilted for winter drainage.*

TREE MAINTENANCE

It is also important to make sure that the trees themselves are clean, free from any pests and diseases, and have no damaged foliage. These factors are unsightly and will compromise the appearance of your bonsai display.

Remove any damaged leaves or foliage by pinching them off with your fingers or with a pair of tweezers. You can also simply snip them with a pair of scissors. If they are difficult to reach, then you may need to use a pair of scissors with extra-long blades. If there is any die-back within the branch structure, remove it using scissors for small items and branch or knob cutters for larger pieces.

You may find that over a period of time, there is a build-up of dirt, moss, algae, lichen or even insects on some of the trunk and branch structures of your trees. Brushing with a stiff brush and water will easily remove all of these problems. Spraying with water

Left: *Various bonsai on temporary benches for winter storage under cover.*

CARING FOR YOUR POTS

1 Brush the surface of the soil in order to remove any debris, such as dead leaves, and top up with more soil if required.

2 Add some moss and press it into the surface of the soil while spraying. This helps the moss to establish quickly and results in a very natural look.

3 Brush the sides and rim of the pot to remove any loose dust, and then wash off any dirt that still remains.

4 Using a lint-free cloth that has been soaked with vegetable oil, wipe the pot to bring out its texture and colour.

MAINTAINING YOUR TREES

1 Remove any odd bits of dead bark from the trunk with a pair of tweezers in order to create a clean appearance.

2 Brush the trunk clean with a dry, stiff brush. You can use an old toothbrush if necessary.

3 Using the brush and some water, clean off any algae from the tree.

4 Spraying with water while you are brushing will help to wash away any loose debris.

while brushing will also help to wash away any unwanted debris that is spoiling the effect.

If any loose pieces of bark are unsightly, carefully remove them from the trunk with your fingers or with tweezers, making sure that you do not damage any features of the tree's trunk that could ultimately enhance the overall appearance of the tree. If there are any signs of disease or insect attack, you should take all the necessary steps to stop any recurrence of such a problem and it would be best not to exhibit the tree until the problem has been completely cleared up.

REFINING TECHNIQUES

As bonsai mature, they will always need some form of refining and pruning to keep them looking their best. When refining broad-leaf trees, minor adjustments can be made to the shape using wiring techniques. Young shoots sprout from various places on trunks and branches, and some of these will need to be removed to maintain the mature look of the tree. Tidying up old pruning cuts, removing dead branches and thinning out the branch structure are all essential to ensure continued improvement of your bonsai.

As with deciduous trees, refining techniques for conifers include pruning shoots, cutting out unwanted branches and thinning foliage, as well as the introduction of jin, shari and other artificial aging processes. The relationship of one branch to another and the space between them is important, because this enables the tree to be seen at its best. Creating spaces between branches also allows the sunlight to reach all the foliage and this will lead to healthier, more compact growth. Pinch out young growth with your fingers but use scissors for hardened growth.

SOIL MAINTENANCE

The condition of the soil surface is also very important, not only for the general health of your bonsai trees, but also for their overall appearance when you are preparing for an exhibition. Removing fallen leaves or needles from the soil surface is a high-priority task, along with removing any moss and troublesome weeds such as liverwort and pearlwort. These should be removed as soon as possible so that they do not over-run the roots of your trees. Liverwort is generally a sign that the soil is too wet, while pearlwort can quickly choke the tree's roots, since its own roots can go deep into and under the root-ball, quite often blocking the

drainage holes in the pot. This makes the soil too wet, which can in turn lead to the development of large areas of liverwort.

You can deal with most of these problems by picking out any small, individual plants that are not wanted with a pair of tweezers and then brushing the surface of the soil clean with a suitable brush.

WINTER STORAGE

Whether or not your bonsai need protection for the winter depends on the climate in which you live. If your trees are going to be exposed to conditions below freezing, then you may have to take extra precautions.

These may include placing the trees in a greenhouse, shade tunnel or just under the display benching.

When placing bonsai trees under benches, it is advisable to put them on some form of timber staging to keep them off the ground. You will also need to provide extra protection at the front, sides and back of the benching. Small trees can be placed in containers filled to the brim with peat so that the root-ball and pot are covered. These methods for extra-winter protection should only be carried out if it becomes necessary because over-protecting normally hardy species can lead to problems with new growth in the spring.

REFINING BROAD-LEAF TREES

1 Using a pair of concave branch cutters, remove any stubs left from previous pruning.

2 Cut out any small adventitious shoots with a pair of scissors.

3 Apply wire to those branches that cover the front of the tree.

4 Reposition the branches to give a balanced appearance, and seal all the cuts with wound sealer.

REFINING CONIFERS

1 Use a pair of scissors to remove all downward-facing growth.

2 Similarly, remove all upward-facing growth in order to produce a clean outline.

3 Using branch cutters, prune out any large or heavy growth from the inner part to show the main branch at its best.

4 Gather up the foliage in bunches and pinch the tips off using your fingers or a pair of tweezers to thin out the leaves.

CREATING A HYGIENIC ENVIRONMENT

1 Leaves and rubbish on and around your bonsai trees can harbour all sorts of unwanted insects and diseases.

2 The removal of rubbish not only makes the trees look better, but it keeps them healthier too.

3 Here, you can see that the pot is dirty and there is fallen foliage on the surface of the soil.

4 The removal of debris, and the cleaning and oiling of the pot, will keep the tree healthier, as well as improving its overall appearance.

STORING YOUR BONSAI OVER WINTER

1 Trees can be placed on timber slats beneath the normal bonsai benches for added protection through the winter months.

2 Cover the front and sides (and rear if it is open) with greenhouse shade netting. Here, it is partially covered to show the placement of the trees, but it will be completely covered when the temperature falls below freezing.

3 You can provide added protection for the roots of your bonsai by placing them in a box or basket filled with organic matter.

4 Here, the two trees have their pots and roots protected from severe winter frosts. Water sparingly during the winter months.

Pests and Diseases

Most bonsai are created from hardy shrubs and trees and are therefore not very susceptible to many pests or diseases. Instances of both of these will occur, however, and so it is important to know what to do. The actual process of identifying a pest or disease is very important and, if this is done correctly, then a suitable remedy can be applied. Cleanliness is the best form of attack that you have. In fact, good hygiene practices will normally keep most pests and diseases under control. This should avoid the unnecessary use of insecticides and pesticides. Pesticides can be dangerous and most bonsai growers would recommend the use of such chemicals only as a very last resort. If you do decide to apply pesticide, ensure that you have properly read the instructions and are wearing suitably protective clothing.

Above: *Aphids can be a real problem because they can quickly take over a plant, sucking the sap from its stems, leaves and fruit.*

PESTS

There are a few pests that can be a problem to bonsai trees, as follows:

Vine weevil

This insect is difficult to eradicate. The vine weevil larvae act by devouring the root system of a plant and can quickly kill a tree. They feed on the roots and destroy the tree's lifeline. The larvae will strip the roots bare right up to soil level. It will not be obvious that there is a problem until the tree shows signs of stress, begins to wilt and then dies. The soil should be treated at regular intervals with a suitable product to prevent infestation by these fat, creamy white, maggot-like larvae. Repot your bonsai regularly each year, if appropriate, with fresh soil in early spring just before the buds begin to break. If you discover vine weevil larvae when repotting, wash the roots clean of all soil, destroy any larvae, and repot the bonsai in the usual way.

The adult vine weevil is difficult to spot, as it hides away during the day, emerging only at night when it climbs to the top of plants to eat notches from the edges of the leaves. Treatment with a soil insecticide will deal with the larvae, or you can go out at night with a torch, collect the adults and destroy them.

Scale insect

This is another creature that can be very difficult to find until the limpet-like shell lifts to reveal a fluffy, sticky, white mass on its underside. Scale insects are one of the most difficult pests to get rid of if they get a hold in any indoor bonsai collection.

The application of a systemic insecticide should prevent this insect from becoming a problem for your bonsai, or you can physically remove the adults one at a time, although that process can be very time-consuming and laborious. A cotton bud (swab) soaked in methylated spirits (methyl alcohol) and used as a removal tool is also a very effective way to remove scale insects from the trunks of your bonsai. Alternatively, brushing with a stiff brush such as an old toothbrush

will also remove them. This technique may, however, simply transfer the insects to the soil, from where they could reappear later on, so treatment with a systemic insecticide is probably the only true solution to this rather difficult problem.

Aphids

These can be a serious problem, as they colonize plants and systematically suck the sap from stems, leaves and fruit. They are especially attracted to early spring growth on trees such as Japanese maples (*Acer palmatum*). The first indication that there is an infestation of aphids is usually when the leaves begin to curl up and become distorted. They come in a variety of colours, but the most common are greenfly, blackfly and whitefly. The latter is one of the most troublesome pests that attack indoor bonsai, but regular applications of a systemic insecticide will usually eradicate them from most plants.

The woolly aphid can be a serious problem on pine, larch and beech trees, and manifests itself as a white,

Vine weevil larvae   *Vine weevil adult*

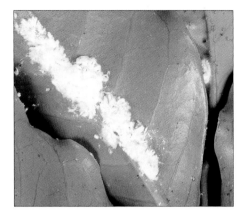

Soft scales

Brown scale insects

White soft scale insects

Young scale insects

Leaf-cutter bee damage

Caterpillar

fluffy, sticky mass. On pines and larch it appears among the needles and is very difficult to remove without applying a systemic insecticide; on beech trees it appears on the underside of the leaves. Once again, the application of a systemic insecticide should be sufficient to deal with this problem.

Leaf-cutter bee
These can be a problem to the bonsai grower, but not one that will cause any serious damage. It will definitely not result in long-term damage to any tree. The symptoms of leaf-cutter bee infestation are large, circular notches cut into the edges of leaves. This is carried out by the leaf-cutter bee and only disfigures the foliage. There is no control method other than removing the damaged leaves. This will, of course, act in the same way as leaf pruning, and will simply encourage more leaves to grow.

Caterpillars
Many varieties of caterpillar can attack the foliage of your bonsai plants. The easiest method of controlling these unwanted visitors is simply to pick them off by hand and destroy them. Alternatively, you can place them on another plant in your garden, so that they eat the foliage of something other than your prized bonsai specimens.

Snail

Snails and slugs
These cause a lot of damage in a short time, so it is important to discourage them from areas around your bonsai by making sure that there are no hiding places for them. They do most damage at night or when it is wet, so keep everything clean by removing dead and unwanted leaves from areas near your trees, especially if you do not wish to use dangerous chemicals.

Slug

▷

DISEASES

These are less frequently encountered than bonsai pests, mostly taking the form of leaf disorders. These can normally be controlled by removing and destroying affected leaves and stems. However, regular applications of a good systemic fungicide will control the most common diseases.

Powdery mildew

This is a white dusty growth that appears on leaf surfaces and young stems, and can be treated by regular spraying with fungicide.

Damping off

This condition is where seedlings begin to rot at the base of the stem, resulting in the seedling falling over and then dying. Spray with a copper-based fungicide.

Rust

This unsightly disease appears on leaves as slightly raised orange/yellow spots. If you see this tell-tale coloration, then quickly remove any affected leaves and destroy them. You should also spray the bonsai specimen with a zinc-based fungicide.

Verticillium wilt

This is a disease that causes die-back in maples. It attacks the sapwood and is difficult to detect, and most trees should be treated with a systemic fungicide as a preventative measure.

Peach leaf curl

This can be a problem on trees belonging to the *Prunus* family and appears as reddish-brown blistery shapes on the leaves. These quickly multiply, causing the leaves to curl up into distorted shapes. Treat with a copper-based fungicide.

Powdery mildew

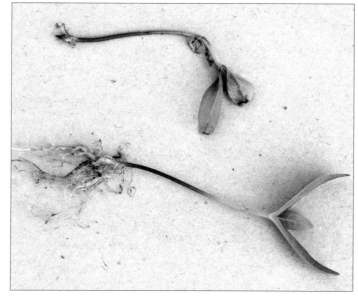

Damping off

Rust

Verticillium wilt

Peach leaf curl

Grey mould

Grey mould

This is a fungus that occurs on the leaves of plants that are kept in conditions of high humidity. It is possible to control it by increasing ventilation and spraying with a systemic fungicide. Always make sure that you adhere closely to the directions on the packaging, and if there are any safety precautions, follow them to the letter.

A NOTE ON SPRAYING

Although you may not use insecticides or fungicides, it is worth noting that regular spraying with them will keep most pests and diseases under control. If an infestation builds up in your bonsai, then some sort of remedy will be required. Systemic remedies are normally sprayed on to the plant using an atomizing sprayer, and precautions should be taken to prevent inhalation of any of these types of spray, as they can be very dangerous to humans, animals and fish.

Systemic insecticides and fungicides act by being absorbed into the tissues and sap of the plant, which then transport them around the entire plant, giving protection for up to about six weeks at a time. Systemic solutions will need to be applied about three to four times during the growing season, but care should be taken not to apply them when the leaves are very fresh, as the chemicals can damage them. Another reliable form of deterrent is to spray your trees with a winter wash, which will destroy any overwintering eggs, larvae, insects and fungi. This means that you will not be plagued with problems in the following spring.

Below: *Garden centres and supermarkets sell a wide range of garden chemicals. Always follow the manufacturer's instructions, wear protective clothing and store products safely.*

Calendar of Care

Throughout the year, you will need to carry out various tasks in order to maintain the health, appearance, growth and general well-being of your bonsai, whether they are indoor or outdoor varieties. Keeping the trunks, branches, soil surfaces and pots clean is just one element of a general maintenance programme that needs to be followed at all times, regardless of season and weather. If any of the following tasks are ignored, you may run into serious problems later in the year or even later in the life of your bonsai specimens. So, make sure that you clean your tools and equipment thoroughly and keep a constant look-out at all times for any signs of distress in your plants, and you will eventually reap great rewards from your bonsai collection.

Above: *Japanese maple (*Acer palmatum*) in a pot ideal for future bonsai training. Check water content of the soil daily to prevent drying out.*

EARLY SPRING

• As the days lengthen, many trees will begin to come out of their dormant period. This will be evident in the swelling of buds, although some bonsai will not start any new growth yet. Keep a close watch on all trees from now on, and repot when each tree is ready. Most trees will not need larger pots because, once their roots have been pruned, they will fit into the same pot, as long as it is still suitable for that tree. Before repotting, allow the tree's root-ball (roots) to dry out a little, as this will help when removing old soil and adding new.

• Watering may need to increase as the weather warms up, but be careful not to overwater.
• Begin to take hardwood cuttings towards the end of early spring, as well as sow seeds in trays of good open soil to encourage root growth on both seedlings and cuttings.

MID-SPRING

• Hardy trees can be taken out from their winter quarters if they have been under any sort of cover. Remember that hardy trees require winter cover in only the most exceptional circumstances.

• Most repotting should have been completed by now, but some conifers can be left until late spring before being repotted.
• If your trees have been left out throughout the winter, their buds will be hardy and should not suffer from late frosts. However, some species, such as Japanese maples (*Acer palmatum*) or anything that has delicate new leaves, may need a little protection from any late frosts.

CARING FOR YOUR BONSAI IN SPRING

Early Spring: *Clean, spread out and prune roots of cuttings prior to potting into larger pots.*

Mid-spring: *Tidy up the shape of all bonsai as they start growing to achieve a neat outline.*

Late Spring: *Repotting a three-year-old cutting into a training pot to obtain good root growth.*

- Watering will now need to be stepped up, as trees are beginning to get into their full growing mode.
- Applications of fertilizer should be started now, as trees will be requiring their first nutrients of the year. The first application of slow-release feed can be given now, but avoid applying fertilizer to freshly root-pruned trees. Leave them for three to four weeks before feeding so as to avoid any root scorch by the fertilizer.
- Tidy up the shape of your bonsai as they begin to grow so that their appearance remains satisfactory.

LATE SPRING

- All bonsai should be in full active growth by now, and daily watering may be required from now on to avoid allowing any trees to dry out. Be careful not to overwater pines (*Pinus*), as this can make them grow too rapidly and produce needles that are too long and look out of proportion to the trees. For this reason pines must definitely be kept on the dry side.
- Feed weekly with liquid fertilizer if you have not given a slow-release application in mid-spring.
- Trees will vary enormously in the strength of their growth, and pruning will have to be carried out to suit each individual tree so that a good shape is always maintained.

Above: *Fresh growth on a* Cryptomeria japonica *a few weeks after the shoots have been pinched out in midsummer.*

Both light and heavy pruning can be carried out in late spring, as most trees are in full growth mode and any pruning cuts will heal very quickly.
- Shaping using wire is acceptable at this time of year on most trees, but take care when applying wire so that you do not damage growth that is important to the shape of your trees.
- If there are any conifers still to be repotted, get this done quickly so that they have a good period of time to re-establish themselves before winter sets in once again.

EARLY SUMMER

- This is quite often one of the hottest times of the year, and with the correct watering and feeding regime, most bonsai will be at their peak growth rate.

- Maples will require almost daily pinching out of shoot tips so that their form, compactness and tight growth are maintained throughout.
- Early summer is a good time to defoliate any deciduous trees that need this treatment, as there is enough time before autumn to ensure that the second set of leaves can reach maturity.
- All root pruning and repotting should have been carried out by now except in very rare emergency situations.
- Take softwood cuttings now. Insert them into a good-quality cuttings compost (soil mix) and provide them with some shade to avoid drying out the soil and any leaves left on the cutting.
- While your bonsai may be growing fast, so too are the weeds, so it is a good idea to remove any unwanted plants from the soil surface as soon as possible. Never allow them to mature and seed, as this just allows them to proliferate.
- Watch out for insects and diseases from now on as most flourish in the warmer weather. Apply systemic insecticides or fungicides when this is necessary, but avoid their use if at all possible because they can be dangerous to adults, children, pets and fish if correct precautions are not taken.

CARING FOR YOUR BONSAI IN SUMMER

Early Summer: *Deciduous trees can be defoliated now.*

Midsummer: *Apply wire to any bonsai that require it.*

Late Summer: *Continue to prune as needed by pinching out shoots with fingers or tweezers.*

MIDSUMMER

- Weather conditions are similar to the early summer, and most bonsai activities are the same. Pruning, pinching, wiring, watering, feeding, etc may all need to be carried out.
- Indoor trees can be placed outdoors now, as they will benefit from the fresh air and good light at this time of year. Give them slight shading when they are first placed outside, then move them into full sun once they have hardened off.
- Continue to take softwood cuttings as well as semi-ripe cuttings and place them in trays.
- Do not root prune or repot other than in extreme emergencies.

LATE SUMMER

- The growth rate of bonsai will be starting to slow down, and overnight dew and some slightly misty evenings mean that some may require less watering now.
- Continue to prune where needed.
- Slow down on feeding, and use low-nitrogen fertilizer at about two-weekly intervals. The low-nitrogen fertilizer will help to harden off the current year's growth, so aiding the trees' survival through the winter.
- Conifers can still be repotted towards the end of late summer, but make sure that enough time is left before the winter for the roots to make

Above: *Autumn is a time of year when you can enjoy the spectacular colour of deciduous bonsai foliage.*

some new growth before winter sets in. If this root growth does not happen, then the tree could sit in wet soil, with cut root ends, which will make the tree vulnerable to root rot during the winter months.

EARLY AUTUMN

- Bonsai will have mostly stopped growing by now, so you will need to water less. Monitor the situation, however, and water where necessary. Give an application of low- or zero-nitrogen fertilizer, as this will help with winter survival.
- Wiring can still be carried out, but is not advisable. Think about removing wire to give the trees a rest and to avoid any damage in winter. Watch pines closely if they still have wire on them, as they often put on a spurt of

growth from early autumn onwards; the wire will become embedded in the bark, with disastrous results. Avoid this by removing wire in good time.

MID-AUTUMN

- Very little watering needs to be done in mid-autumn, as overnight dew and autumn mists will supply a reasonable amount of water.
- Deciduous trees will begin to show some beautiful autumn colour and also to drop a few of their leaves. Some of these trees will look spectacular and should be placed where their beauty can be admired.
- Take all indoor trees back under cover and supply them with some mild heating and humidity.
- Apply the last low-nitrogen feed of the year.
- Carry out any pruning needed to tidy up the shape of your trees.
- Keep all trees clean and remove any fallen leaves from the soil surface, as well as around and under bonsai benches and stands. This will help to deter unwanted pests and diseases.

LATE AUTUMN

- There is very little to do now except for tidying up fallen leaves and giving a splash of water where needed. Make sure that any winter shelter areas are ready so that trees can be moved to them quickly.

CARING FOR YOUR BONSAI IN AUTUMN

Early Autumn: *Prop up one end of the pots to assist drainage and prevent waterlogging.*

Mid-autumn: *Autumn colour is now at its best. Place your trees where they can be seen.*

Late Autumn: *Begin to provide some winter protection, but only in the most severe conditions.*

EARLY WINTER

- This is probably an even quieter month in the bonsai world than late autumn, but bonsai should always be checked regularly, whatever the time of year, to make sure that there are no problems developing. This is a good time to study the structure of your trees, especially that of deciduous trees, as all the foliage has dropped, leaving the branch formation easy to see. An assessment can be made now of any serious pruning required that can take place in spring just before growth restarts. So, once you have recovered from the seasonal festivities you can begin to think ahead to the New Year and all that is needed to once again bring your trees to their best for the spring.

MIDWINTER

- This is normally the coldest time of the year, and there is very little need for watering outdoor trees, though they should be checked regularly and given a splash of water if required. Indoor bonsai continue to grow over the winter period despite taking a little bit of a rest, and they will need regular light watering to keep them just moist at all times.
- Feeding is not required on outdoor trees, but light, regular doses of fertilizer can be given to indoor or less hardy varieties.

Above: *Even in winter, you still need to water your bonsai plants. You cannot simply rely on rainfall at this time of year.*

- Tidy up twigs of both indoor and outdoor trees if you did not do this during late autumn.
- Conifers can be very vulnerable to the effects of strong, cold winds at this time of the year, especially if their root-ball becomes frozen. They will still need to be watered in order to keep the foliage going, and, if the soil is frozen, it will have the same effect as drying out in the summer. (If any of the root-balls of your conifers freeze for more than five days, it is advisable to thaw them out gently by placing the affected plants in a cold greenhouse or shed until they have thawed, then leave them for a few days so that the trees can take up water before returning them to their normal outdoor position.)

- Apply wire to trees such as larch (*Larix*), as it is easier to do this when there is no foliage on the tree, but do not wire deciduous trees such as maples, as they can be very brittle at this time of year.
- There will be no need to begin root pruning or repotting during midwinter, although the pots, soil and any other materials and tools relating to repotting and root pruning should be prepared at around this time.

LATE WINTER

- Conditions in late winter are very similar to those in midwinter, and it is wise to keep deciduous trees a little on the dry side while never allowing them to dry out completely. This can be achieved by placing your outdoor trees under a roof cover.
- Continue to prepare potting supplies and make sure bags of soil are open to allow the soil to dry out, as it is better to use totally dry soil for repotting. If trees show signs of buds swelling, then repot before they begin to break bud. Following repotting they may need some frost protection, as cut root ends are very vulnerable.
- Some heavier pruning can be dealt with now, as the new growth is beginning and wounds will heal fairly quickly.

CARING FOR YOUR BONSAI IN WINTER

Early Winter: *Check on the shape of your bonsai trees regularly in winter.*

Midwinter: *This is a good time of year to admire the structural framework of bonsai.*

Late Winter: *Provide some winter protection for your bonsai trees outside.*

Glossary

Accent plant Separate planting of small plants such as bulbs, grasses or herbaceous plants. Normally arranged alongside a bonsai in a formal display.

Acid soil Soil with pH less than 7.0

Adult foliage Mature leaves of a plant that has distinctly different juvenile and mature foliage

Adventitious Shoots originating from parts of a plant other than the growing points. Usually found on older wood

Air layering Technique used to produce new roots from a wound on a branch or trunk by covering the wound with sphagnum moss

Akadama Japanese red clay, granular, nutrient-free, general-purpose soil

Alkaline soil Soil with a pH over 7.0 or rich in lime

Apex The crown of a tree

Apical Shoot at the tip of a branch or bud at the tip of a shoot

Axil The angle between leaf and shoot

*Chinese elm (*Ulmus parviflora*)*

Back budding New buds within the branch structure that have been encouraged by pruning the tip growth

Bark Protective outer layer of trunk and branches formed by the cambium and dead cells on the outside of the tree

Bole The trunk of a tree between ground level and the lowest branch

Branch cutters Japanese pruning tool with single, concave cutting edges used for pruning branches. Sometimes known as side cutters

Broad-leaved Trees that have relatively broad and flat leaves as distinct from needles

Bud Embryonic shoot protected by scales formed by modified leaves

Bunjingi Literati-style bonsai, usually a tall, slender, freestyle and flowing tree with a few branches normally in the upper trunk

Buttress Base of the trunk from where the surface roots emerge

Callus New growth developed over a wound

Cambium A thin, growing layer between the bark and the heartwood that is responsible for producing new bark on the outside and new wood on the inside throughout the growing season

Candle New tip growth on pines

Canopy The foliage of the outer and upper parts of the tree

Chokkan Formal-upright style, normally with a straight vertical trunk and horizontal main branches

Clamp Tool used to bend heavy trunks or branches

*Variegated fig (*Ficus benjamina *'Variegata')*

Collected tree Tree taken from the wild or a garden, which is suitable for training into a bonsai

Compost (potting mix) Normally a mixture of humus, sand and grit used as the growing medium and sometimes described as soil

Conifer Usually evergreen trees bearing needle like leaves and cones

Cross Hybrid plant resulting from deliberate cross-fertilization between species or varieties

Crown Uppermost part of tree, sometimes referred to as the apex

Cultivar Garden variety of a plant identified by certain characteristics when propagated vegetatively or from seed

Cut-leaved Description of a plant which has leaves with finely divided segments

Cuttings Plant shoots used for propagation

Deciduous Trees or shrubs that lose their leaves in the autumn

Defoliation Complete leaf removal to encourage the growth of smaller leaves

Dendrology The study of trees

Die-back Deterioration of shoots or branches normally caused by drought, disease or incorrect pruning

Dormancy Period of rest for plants during the winter months, and the condition of seeds before germination

Drainage mesh Normally plastic, mesh that is used to cover drainage holes in bonsai pots

Drawn Plants that have characteristic extended, spindly growth caused by overcrowding or poor light

Dwarf Genetic mutation producing plants of small compact habit

Ericaceous Plants normally requiring acidic growing conditions

Evergreen Plants bearing foliage throughout the year

Eye level The ideal viewing position for bonsai. This should be between one third and two thirds of the way up the trunk

Fertilizer Substance that provides essential nutrients for plant growth

Fruit Part of a plant that carries its seeds. Usually includes pod-like seed cases, berries, nuts and fleshy fruit

Fungicide Substance for controlling fungal diseases

Fukinagashi Windswept-style bonsai emulating a tree in nature that has been exposed to the elements

Genus Group of plants with common structural characteristics

Germination Earliest stage in the growth of plants from seed

Girth Circumference of a tree trunk measured at chest height on full-size trees and just above soil-level in bonsai

Habit Characteristic growth pattern of a plant

Half-hardy Plants requiring some winter protection

Han-Kengai Semi-cascade bonsai style, normally with horizontal trunk or just dipping below the horizontal

Hardening off The process of introducing plants grown under protection to normal outside conditions

Hardwood Mature shoots used for cuttings and the term used for timber from broad-leaved trees

Hardy Plants that can survive severe conditions outside during winter

Heel cutting The base of a side shoot after it is pulled away from main stem

Hoki-Zukuri Broom-style bonsai, also sometimes known as *Hokidachi*

Humidity The water content in the atmosphere, expressed as a percentage.

Humus Partially decayed organic material which is often used in soil mixtures for potting bonsai

Kengai Cascade-style bonsai, normally with the trunk angled down below the pot by 45 degrees or more

Ibigawa Japanese rock formed by the amalgamation of various types of rock through volcanic activity

Ikadabuki Raft-style bonsai, emulating a tree that has fallen with the trunk lying on the ground in a horizontal position, subsequently re-rooting and with the branches developing into the trunks

Inarching Grafting technique used for introducing a new branch into the trunk of a tree

Inorganic Chemical compound not containing carbon; horticulturally manufactured fertilizers, treatments and growing mediums

Chinese elm (Ulmus parvifolia)

Internode Distance between leaf nodes on shoots

Ishizuki Generally, a bonsai with roots growing in, on or over a piece of rock

Jin Branch or trunk apex with its bark removed exposing shaped, bleached and preserved heartwood for artistic effect

Juvenile foliage Leaves produced during rapid stages of growth as distinct from adult foliage

Kanuma Japanese granular acidic subsoil, suitable for ericaceous plants such as azaleas

Kiryu Japanese granular alkaline subsoil, suitable for pines and junipers

Knob cutters Japanese cutting tool similar to side cutters but with double concave cutting edges, sometimes known as wen cutters

Jinning tool A tool somewhat similar to electrician's pliers that is used for creating Jin

Lateral Side shoots originating from branch or trunk

Lava Wingless grub that is the second stage of an insect lifecycle

Leader Upper part of main stem

Leaf mould Partly decayed dead leaves used in compost

Leaf scorch Damage to foliage caused by the action of strong wind or sun

Lime Calcium as a soil component

Lime sulphur Strong-smelling compound used to bleach and preserve Jin and sharimiki (shari)

Loam A rich, fertile soil originating from pastureland and used in potting composts (soil mixes)

Mame Miniature bonsai, normally up to about 12.5cm (6in) high

Japanese white pine (Pinus parviflora)

Microclimate Local climatic conditions within the immediate vicinity of a plant

Misting Fine watering of plants using an atomizing spray

Moyogi Informal upright style, usually with a slightly curved, interesting trunk but not one that is over-exaggerated. One of the most common styles of bonsai

Needle A very narrow leaf such as that on a pine or larch

Nitrogen One of the most essential elements of plant nutrition. Responsible for the green vegetative growth in stems and leaves and identified by the letter N

Node The position on a shoot from which leaves or new shoots appear

NPK An abbreviation used to denote the proportions of the three main elements in fertilizer, which are are nitrogen (N), phosphorous (P) and potassium (K)

Old wood Any part of a plant that originated during the previous season's growth

Organic Chemical compound which contains carbon; horticulturally a compound or growing medium that is not manufactured or synthetic

Peat Partially decayed organic matter, such as sphagnum moss, that is found in bogs or marshy ground. Used as a moisture-retaining ingredient in many potting mixes

Penjing Chinese version of bonsai. The meaning is the same as the Japanese "plant in a container"

Petiole The stalk of a leaf

pH Unit of measurement describing the acid or alkaline level in soil

Phosphorous One of the most essential elements of plant nutrition. Responsible for encouraging root development and the ripening of shoots, fruit and seeds and identified by the letter P

Photosynthesis The production of food substances by leaves using sunlight, water and carbon dioxide

Pinching out Removing shoots or foliage with the fingers

Potassium One of the most essential elements of plant nutrition. Responsible for encouraging new strong growth and development of flower buds and fruit formation, and identified by the letter K

Pot-bound The condition of a plant that has been grown in a pot when the roots have completely filled the space inside. This will eliminate all the air space and may result in the premature death of the plant

Prostrate A plant that has a habit of growing along the ground as opposed to growing upright

Pruning Removing leaves, shoots or branches to stimulate new growth within a plant

Raffia Natural fibre that is wrapped around a trunk or branches prior to wiring. The raffia protects the bark from wire damage and assists regeneration of tissues following bending of trunk or branch

Ramification The division of branches into a dense formation of shoots and twigs. Normally achieved by constant pinching of shoot tips

Repotting The process of removing a pot-grown plant from its pot at regular intervals and replanting with fresh soil to encourage new root growth

Root Part of plant used to absorb water and nutrients from within the growing medium

Root-ball Mass of soil and roots seen when a plant is lifted from the ground or removed from its pot

Rootstock The main stem and root system when used as the basis for a new plant for propagation by grafting

Root grafting Technique for attaching new roots to a tree

Root pruning Reduction of root mass used for encouraging new healthy, compact root growth

Root burn Damage to roots normally caused by a fertilizer overdose or by applying fertilizer too soon following repotting and root pruning

Saikei Miniature landscape of rocks and plants grown in a shallow container

Sapwood Living tissues forming the wood layers beneath the bark

Scion Small section of a plant that is used to propagate a new plant by grafting. This will retain the characteristics of the parent plant in the new plant created

Seedling Early stages of plant grown from seed

Semi hardwood Half-ripe shoots used for cuttings

Shakan Slanting-trunk-style bonsai

Sharimiki (or shari) Part of trunk that has had the bark removed for special artistic effect

Japanese maple (Acer palmatum)

Shohin Small bonsai usually measuring from 12.5cm (6in) up to about 25cm (12in)

Sieve Screening device for separating soil particles of different sizes

Slow release Normally used to refer to a fertilizer that releases nutrients over an extended period

Softwood Immature shoots used for cuttings

Sokan Bonsai style with twin trunks in which the trunks must be visibly connected at the buttress

Soju Twin-tree bonsai style made up of two separate trees as distinct from twin trunk or *Sokan*

Species Subordinate classification to genus differing from genus in detail only

Sphagnum moss Type of moss common in bogs and marshy land, used in bonsai for air layering and root formation

Stratification The overwintering of hardy plant seeds outdoors or in a refrigerator to break seed dormancy and thereby induce germination

Systemic A fungicide or insecticide that enters the sap of a plant to prevent infestation by disease or insects

Tap root Main root which normally acts to anchor a tree or plant in the ground

Tender Trees that are unable to tolerate low temperatures and will require winter protection. Tenderness is measured relative to the local climate in which the plant is grown

Training pot Any container that is suitable to enable the tree to form strong, vigorous growth during the initial styling and training period. This could be a wooden box, plastic washing bowl or flowerpot etc with suitably large drainage holes

Transpiration Natural water loss from the leaves and stems

Tufa Type of sedimentary limestone often used for rock plantings because of its porous, moisture-retaining nature

Turntable Useful, rotating platform widely used by bonsai growers for displaying trees and for practical purposes whilst repotting and styling

Variety Sub-division of species displaying variations from the naturally occurring parent plant

Viability Ability of seeds to germinate

Wire Usually aluminium, anodized aluminium or copper; used extensively for bonsai shaping

Wiring The practice of applying wire to the trunk or branches of bonsai during the styling and training process

Woody A plant stem that has hardened, will not die and has taken on the appearance of an old trunk

Wound sealer Protective paste used to cover cuts following pruning

Yose-uye Group or forest planting

Suppliers

UNITED KINGDOM

Bryan Albright Bonsai Pots
Tel: 01263 587587
www.bonsai.free-online.co.uk

Bushukan Bonsai
Ricbra
Lower Road
Hockley
Essex SS5 5HL
Tel: 01702 201029
www.bushukan-bonsai.com

Dai-Ichi Bonsai, Hillier Garden Centre
Priors Court Road
Hermitage, Newbury
Berkshire RG18 9TG
Tel: 01635 200667
www.dai-ichibonsai.com

Erin Pottery and Bonsai
41 Savoy Road
Brislington
Bristol BS4 3SZ
www.erinpottery.com

Glenbrook Bonsai Nursery
Tickenham, Clevedon
North Somerset BS21 6SE
Tel: 01275 858596
www.glenbrookbonsai.co.uk

Green Lawns Bonsai
Hadleigh Road
Boxford, Nr Sudbury
Suffolk CO10 5JH
Tel: 01787 210501
www.greenlawns.co.uk

Greenwood Bonsai Studio
Ollerton Road, Arnold
Nottingham NG5 8PR
Tel: 0115 920 5757
www.bonsai.co.uk

John Hanby Bonsai School
Newstead Lane, Havercroft
Wakefield
West Yorkshire WF4 2HW
Tel: 01977 610040
www.johnhanbybonsai.co.uk

A. Harriman – Bonsai Pottery
58 Station Road,
Misterton
Nr Doncaster
South Yorkshire DN10 4DE
Tel: 01437 890434
www.chinamist.co.uk

Herons Bonsai Ltd
Wire Mill Lane
Newchapel
Nr Lingfield
Surrey RH7 6HJ
Tel: 01342 832657
www.herons.co.uk

Kaizen Bonsai
Tel: 0800 4580672
www.kaizenbonsai.com

Observatory Bonsai
Cardiff
Tel: 02920 484892 or 07980 897264
www.observatorybonsai.co.uk

John Pitt Bonsai Ceramics
Etwall
Derbyshire
Tel: 01283 733479
john@johnpittbonsaiceramics.co.uk
http://johnpittbonsaiceramics.co.uk/
Visitors by appointment only.

Root grafting an Acer buergerianum

Formal upright bonsai

Tokonoma Bonsai Nursery
London Road
Shenley
Radlett
Hertfordshire WD7 9EN
Tel: 01923 858587
or 01923 855670
www.tokonomabonsai.co.uk

Walsall Studio Ceramics
Tantara Street
Walsall
West Midlands WS1 2HU
Tel: 01922 645707
www.walsall-studio-ceramics.com

Kevin Willson Yamadori Bonsai
15 Oxley Hill
Tolleshunt
Darcy
Maldon
Essex CN9 8ES
Tel: 01621 815285
www.kevinwillsonbonsai.com

Windybank Bonsai
60 Woodmansterne Lane
Carshalton
Surrey SM5 4BJ
Tel: 020 8669 8847
www.windybankbonsai.co.uk

EUROPE

Salvatori Liporace
Studio Botanico
Via Rubens 9-20148
Milan, Italy
Tel: 02 4045565
www.liporace.it

Pius Notter Bonsai Arboretum
Boswil
Lucerne, Switzerland
mail@swiss-bonsai.ch

Ginkgo Bonsai Centre
Heireg 190
9270 Laarne, Belgium
Tel: 9 355 1485
www.

Bonsai Vaerkstedet
Bonsai & Satsuki Centre
V/Hans Jurgen Nielsen
Strynovej 36
6710 Esberg V, Denmark
Tel: 7515 6734

NORTH AMERICA

PFM Bonsai Studio
7 Western Avenue
West Charlton
New York
Tel: (518) 882-1039
www.pfmbonsai.com

Rosade Bonsai Studio
6912 Ely Road
Solebury
New Hope
PA 18938-9634
Tel: (215) 862-5925
www.rosadebonsai.com

Shikoku Bonsai
Vancouver
British Columbia
Canada
Tel: (604) 886-3915

AUSTRALIA

Bonsai Emporium
4433 West Swan Road
West Swan
Western Australia
Tel: 9374 0555

Bonsai Kingdom
10 Haywards Road
Gosnells, Western Australia
Tel: 9398 8311

Bonsai-n-Bamboo
848 Forest Road
Jandakot, Western Australia
Tel: 9414 9966

Bonsai Palace
Stock Road Markets
Bibra Lake
Western Australia
Tel: 0419 047 244

Lee's Bonsai World
180 Grand Promenade
Bedford
Western Australia
Tel: 9370 5915

NEW ZEALAND

Bonsai Boutique
PO Box 9113
Tauranga
Tel: 7 578 4854
www.home.clear.net.nz/pages/bonsai-boutique

Bonsai New Zealand Ltd
147 Seabrook Avenue
New Lyn
Auckland
Tel: 9 827 3439
www.bonsai.co.nz

Pruning

Catlins Natural
Balclutha
Tel: 3 418 1798
www.catlinesnatural.co.nz

Cedar Lodge Nurseries Ltd
63 Egmont Road
R.D.2
New Plymouth
Tel: 6 755 0369
http://www.conifers.co.nz

EfilDoog
Akatarawa Valley Road
Upper Hutt
Tel: 4 526 7924
www.efildoog-nz.com/index.htm

Joy's Bonsai Studio
6 Torquay Street
Abbotsford
Dunedin
Tel: 3 488 4592
joys-bonsai@clear.net.nz
www.home.clear.net.nz/pages/joys-bonsai

Vanz Bonsai & Pottery
27 Raxworthy Street
Ilam
Christchurch
Tel: 3 358 2591
vanzsa@xtra.co.nz

SOUTH AFRICA

Dunmau Bonsai
130 Major Road
Clayville
East Olifantsfontein
Gauteng
Tel: 11 3162910
wiles@icon.co.za

Imithi Bonsai
85B Longwy Road
Lorraine
Port Elizabeth
Eastern Cape
Tel: 41 3794789

Misty Moon Bonsai
204 Kay Ridge Road
Assegay
Kwa-Zulu Natal
Tel: 31 7681198
mistymoon@mweb.co.za

Bonsai Collections

UNITED KINGDOM

Ken and Ann Norman Bonsai
Collection (Norman Bonsai)
Leonardslee Gardens
West Sussex RH13 6PP
Tel: 01273 506476 or 01403 891457
www.hortic.com/normanbonsai

National Bonsai Collection
Birmingham Botanical Gardens and
Glasshouse (BBGG)
Westbourne Road
Edgbaston
Birmingham B15 3TR
Tel: 0121 454 1860
www.nationalbonsaicollection.org

Royal Horticultural Society Garden at
Wisley, Bonsai Collection
Woking
Surrey GU23 6QB
Tel: 01483 224234
www.rhs.org.uk

EUROPE

Belgium Bonsai Museum
Ginkgo Bonsai Centre
Antwerpsesteenweg 148-9080
Lochristi, Nr Ghent
Belgium
Tel: 9 355 1485

Acer palmatum 'Ukon'

Bonsai Centrum
Mannheimerstr. 401
9123 Heidelberg-Wieblingen
Germany
Tel: 06221 84910
www.bonsai-centrum.de

NORTH AMERICA

Brooklyn Botanic Garden
Bonsai Collection
1000 Washington Avenue
Brooklyn, NY 11225-1099
Tel: (718) 623-7200
www.bbg.org

International Bonsai Arboretum
William N Valavanis
1070 Martin Road
West Henrietta
Rochester, NY 14692-3894
Tel: (585)334-2595
wnv@internationalbonsai.com

Montreal Botanical Garden Bonsai
Collection
4101 Sherbrooke East
Montreal
Quebec
Tel: (514) 872-1400
www.ville.montreal.qc.ca/jardin/
vedettes/bonsai.htm

National Bonsai Foundation
National Bonsai and Penjing Museum
US National Arboretum
3501 New York Avenue
North East Washington DC
www.bonsai-nbf.org

North Carolina Arboretum
100 Frederick Law Olmstead Way
Asheville
North Carolina 28806
Tel: (828) 665-2492
www.ncarboretum.org

Pacific Rim Bonsai Collection
33633 Weyerhaeuser Way South
Federal Way
Washington 98003
Tel: (253) 924-5206

Clump-style Japanese maple (Acer palmatum)

Southern California Bonsai Collection
Huntingdon Library
1151 Oxford Road
San Marino
CA 91108
Tel: (625) 405-2100
www.huntingdon.org

AUSTRALIA

Auburn Japanese Gardens
Chiswick and Chisholm Roads
Auburn
New South Wales
Tel: (612) 9871 5630
shellan@bigpond.com.au

The Bonsai House
The Brisbane Botanic Gardens
Mount Coot-tha Road
Toowang
Brisbane
Queensland 4066

NEW ZEALAND

Bonsaiville
Mount Albert
Auckland
Tel: 9 629 3662
www.bonsaiville.co.nz

North Canterbury Bonsai
Christchurch
Tel: 3 355 5411

Organizations

UNITED KINGDOM

Association of British Bonsai Artists
(ABBA)
Tel: 01803 872856
enquiries@bonsaiartists.co.uk
www.bonsaiartists.co.uk

Federation of British Bonsai Societies
(FOBBS)
Contact: Reg Bolton
Tel: 01793 822470
reg.bolton@ic24.net
www.fobbs.info

Japanese Garden Society
www.jgs.org.uk
Arranges events and meetings
throughout the UK.

EUROPE

European Bonsai Association (EBA)
Contact: Reg Bolton
Tel: 01793 822470
reg.bolton@ic24.net
www.ebabonsai.com

NORTH AMERICA

American Bonsai Society
PO Box 351604
Toledo
OH 43635-1604
www.absbonsai.org

North American Bonsai Federation
(NABF)
www.bonsai-wbff.org

Toronto Bonsai Society
PO Box 155
Toronto
Ontario M3C 2E8
www.torontobonsai.org

AUSTRALIA

Australian Associated Bonsai Clubs
(AABC)
http://godzilla.zeta.org.au

Bonsai Northwest Inc.
135 Stephen Yarraville
Victoria
www.bonsainorthwest.com.au

Bonsai Society of Australia Inc.
West Pennant Hills Community Centre
42 Hill Road
West Pennant Hills
New South Wales
www.bonsai.asn.au

Suiseki Australia
Don Moore Centre
North Rocks Road
North Rocks
New South Wales
shellan@bigpond.com.au

Waverley Garden Club, Bonsai Group
St Johns Uniting Church Hall
Virginia Street
Mount Waverley
Victoria 3149
Tel: 9544 5039

NEW ZEALAND

New Zealand Bonsai Association
16 Elder Street
Dunedin
Tel: 7 323 7560
www.bonsaiTALK.com

European olive (Olea europaea)

SOUTH AFRICA

South African Bonsai Association
www.saba.org.za

INTERNATIONAL

Bonsai Clubs International
www.bonsai-bci.com

International Bonsai Magazine
www.international bonsai.com

World Bonsai Friendship Federation
(WBFF)
www.bonsai-wbff.org

An outdoor bonsai display

Index

A

accent planting 166–7
accessories 164–5, 180
  pots 158–9
  stands 160–1
Acer 16, 74, 76, 80, 185
  A. buergerianum 41, 42, 45, 46, 53, 134, 204
    grafting 65
    pruning 74
  A. palmatum 8, 16, 21, 24, 25, 30, 38, 46, 49, 62, 64, 176, 179, 180, 187, 190, 191, 194, 195, 200, 204, 240
    air layering and repotting 68–9
    pruning 73
  A. p. 'Deshojo' 22, 23, 36, 48, 50, 73, 77, 186, 187, 198, 203, 204
  A. p. 'Kamagata' 204
  A. p. 'Kiyohime' 41, 168, 206
  A. p. 'Nomura' 33
  A. p. 'Shindeshojo' 206
  A. p. 'Ukon' 8, 28, 76
Acorus gramineus 166
air layering 66–7
  repotting 68–9
akadama 55, 62, 71
Albright, Bryan 30, 38, 46, 49, 50
aluminium wire 55, 57
aphids 236–7
Aralia elegantissima 18, 19, 144–5, 206
  bonsai 144–5
Aruncus aethusifolius 166, 167
Aspinall, Derek 28, 36, 37, 38, 41, 48, 50
associations 169
Astilbe 166
  A. x *crispa* 'Lilliput' 167

B

backgrounds 27, 175, 176, 179–80
bamboos 166
barberry *see Berberis*
beech *see Fagus*
benches 24, 155, 172
  outdoors 176
Berberis thunbergii 206
big-leafed podocarp *see Podocarpus macrophyllus*
bird plum cherry *see Sageretia theezans*
black spruce *see Picea mariana 'Nana'*
blackthorn *see Prunus spinosa*
blue Atlas cedar *see Cedrus libani* subsp. *atlantica* 'Glauca'
bonsai 7, 8–9
  accent planting 166–7
  aesthetics 22–3
  buying 24–5
  history 10–13
  inspiration 14–15
  proportions 22–3
  shows 182–3
  size 20–1
  suitable plants 16–19
Bonsai Kai 157, 182, 183
Bougainvillea spectabilis (bougainvillea) 18, 206
box *see Buxus sempervirens*
box-leaved holly *see Ilex crenata*
branch cutters 54, 57, 72, 78

branches 14–15, 22, 23
  pruning 72–3
broadleaf trees 16, 74, 76, 82, 158, 234
  propagating 62
  pruning 72–3, 74
broom (*hokidachi*) 41, 44, 48, 140–1
  Acer palmatum 49
  Olea europaea 44
  Zelkova serrata 41
brushes 57
Buddhism 10, 168
buds 76
bunjin (literati) 51, 126–7
bush clover *see Lespedeza bicolor*
Buxus sempervirens (box) 162, 207
buying plants 18, 24–5

C

cambium 64, 66
candles 75, 189
care 225
  seasonal 240–3
Carpinus 16
  C. betulus 207
  C. laxiflora 38, 73, 185, 190, 191, 195, 199, 207
cascade (*kengai*) 102–3
Cassell's Encyclopedia of Gardening 12
caterpillars 237
cedar of Lebanon *see Cedrus libani*
Cedrus (cedar) 16
  C. deodara 14, 128, 207
  C. libani 207
  C. l. subsp. *atlantica* 208
  C. l. subsp. *atlantica* 'Glauca' 80, 92, 208
Celtis bungeana 208
central heating 170
Cercis siliquastrum 16, 208
Chaenomeles japonica 209
Chamaecyparis obtusa 209
Chamaecyparis pisifera 23, 28, 209
Chelsea Flower Show 172, 182
cherry plum *see Prunus cerasifera*
cherry *see Prunus*
China 10, 12, 168
Chinese banyan *see Ficus microcarpa*
Chinese elm *see Ulmus parvifolia*
Chinese juniper *see Juniperus chinensis*
Chinese wisteria *see Wisteria sinensis*
chisels 57
chokkan (formal upright) 33, 92–3
chopsticks 53, 56, 60, 62, 88
Chrysanthemum 10, 12, 209
  autumn 195–6
chumono 20, 21

clubs 9, 169
clump (*kabubuki* or *kabudachi*) 136–9
  Acer palmatum 30, 46
  Acer palmatum 'Kiyohime' 41
coco brushes 57, 88
cold frames 18
collecting garden plants 58–9
collections 12, 250–1
common beech *see Fagus sylvatica*
common juniper *see Juniperus communis*
common oak *see Quercus robur*
common olive *see Olea europaea*
conifers 74, 76, 78, 82, 106, 126, 234
  propagating 62
  pruning 73, 75
Connolly, Joey 28
containers 9, 10, 156–9, 174
copper wire 55
Cotoneaster 17, 25
  C. horizontalis 102, 210
  C. x *suecicus* 'Coral Beauty' 210
  slab planting 163
crab apple *see Malus*
Crassula arborescens 18, 19, 210
  bonsai 146–7
Crataegus 16, 114
  C. monogyna 210–11
Cryptomeria japonica 15, 17, 37, 211, 241
  pinching out 75
  pruning 75
curtain fig *see Ficus microcarpa*
cutters 54–5, 57, 72
Cyclamen 166, 167
cypress *see Chamaecyparis*

D

daisies 166
damping off 238
dandelions 166
deciduous trees *see* broad-leaf trees
defoliating 74, 76–7
diseases 225, 238–9
display 27, 155, 225
  backgrounds 25, 175, 176, 179–80
  grouping 175
  indoors 170–4
  outdoors 176–81
driftwood (*sharimiki*) 33, 128–31
  Larix leptolepsis 33
Duffett, Gordon 30, 33, 41, 45
dwarf Japanese maple *see Acer palmatum* 'Kamagata'
dwarf Japanese maple *see Acer palmatum* 'Kiyohime'
dwarf Scots pine *see Pinus sylvestris*

E

edible olive *see Olea europaea*

Chinese juniper (Juniperus chinensis)

*Japanese maple (*Acer palmatum*)*

Edo period 168–9
electrical tools 57
elm *see Ulmus*
Engelke-Tomlinson, Petra 37
English elm *see Ulmus procera*
English oak *see Quercus robur*
environmental conditions 226–7
equipment 53, 54–7
Equisetum 166
European beech *see Fagus
    sylvatica*
European hornbeam *see Carpinus
    betulus*
European larch *see Larix decidua*
European olive *see Olea europaea*
exhibitions 225
exposed root (*neagari*) 134–5

F
Fagus (beech) 16, 25, 59
    F. crenata 33, 198, 199, 211
    F. sylvatica 28, 136, 156, 211
    F. s. 'Lanciniata' 14
    F. s. 'Purpurea' 110
feeding 230–1
    autumn 197
    summer 193
fences 176, 180
fertilizers 71, 88, 230–1
Ficus (fig)
    cuttings 63
    F. benjamina 18, 212, 226
    F. b. 'Variegata' 172, 212
    F. b. 'Wiandii' 19, 143, 148–9
    bonsai 148–9
    F. microcarpa 18, 212
    F. microphylla 18
finger aralia *see Aralia
    elegantissima*
firethorn *see Pyracantha*
flexibility 80
flowerpots 62
flowers 16, 60, 72, 166, 185
    spring 187–8
formal upright (*chokkan*) 92–3
    Fagus crenata 33
    pruning 78

Frankenia thymifolia 165, 167
fruit 16, 60, 185
Fuchsia 18, 191, 212
    summer 192–3
fukinagashi (windswept) 114–15
fungi 62

G
garden plants 58–9
gardenias 18
gentians 166
Gingko biloba 212
glazing 157
glossy-leaved fig *see Ficus
    microcarpa*
gongshi 168
grafting 64–5
grasses 166
gravel 164, 165
greenhouses 18, 61
grit 71, 165
ground layering 66
group or forest (*yose-uye*) 110–13
    Carpinus laxiflora 38
    Cryptomeria japonica 37
    Zelkova serrata 44, 49

H
hackberry *see Celtis bungeana*
Hakonechloa macra 166
    H. m. 'Alboaurea' 167
Hamamelis (hazel)
    H. x intermedia 213
    winter 201
han-kengai (semi-cascade) 51,
    100–1
hardwood cuttings 62
hawthorn *see Crataegus*
heartwood 66, 73
heavenly bamboo *see Nandina
    domestica*
hedges 59
hedging honeysuckle *see Lonicera
    nitida*
Heian period 11
Himalayan cedar *see Cedrus
    deodara*

Hinoki cypress *see Chamaecyparis
    obtusa*
hokidachi (broom) 41, 44, 48,
    140–1
holly *see Ilex*
honeysuckle *see Lonicera*
hornbeam *see Carpinus*
houseplants 18
humidity 18, 61, 62, 63, 143,
    170–1

I
ibigawa 168, 169
ikadabuki (raft) 116–19
Ilex crenata 213
Ilex serrata 194, 195, 213
Imperata cylindrica 166
inarch grafting 64
Indian laurel *see Ficus microcarpa*
indoor bonsai 16, 18–19, 24, 143,
    226, 229
    Aralia elegantissima 144–5
    Crassula arborescens 146–7
    Ficus benjamina 'Wiandii' 148–9
    Myrtus communis 150–1
    Sagaretia theezans 152–3
indoor displays 170–5
informal upright (*moyogi*) 94–7
    Acer buergerianum 42, 45
    Acer palmatum 38
    Acer p. 'Deshojo' 48, 50
    Acer p. 'Nomura' 33
    Chamaecyparis pisifera 28
    Fagus sylvatica 28
    Larix leptolepsis 50
    Malus cerasifera 46
    Pinus parviflora 42
    Pinus pentaphylla 36
    Pinus sylvestris 30
    Pinus thunbergii 38
    Rhododendron indicum 'Komei'
        42, 45
    Ulmus procera 30
insects 61
ishizuki (root-in-rock planting)
    120–1

J
jade plant *see Crassula
    arborescens*
Japan 10, 12
Japan Society of London 12
Japanese beech *see Fagus crenata*
Japanese black pine *see Pinus
    thunbergii*
Japanese crab *see Malus
    floribunda*
Japanese grey bark elm *see Zelkova
    serrata*
Japanese holly *see Ilex crenata*
Japanese hornbeam *see Carpinus
    laxiflora*
Japanese larch *see Larix kaempferi*
Japanese maple *see Acer
    palmatum*
Japanese quince *see Chaenomeles
    japonica*
Japanese red cedar *see
    Cryptomeria japonica*
Japanese white pine *see Pinus
    parviflora*
Japanese winterberry *see Ilex
    serrata*
Japanese wisteria *see Wisteria
    floribunda*
Jasminum nudiflorum 213
jin 22, 55, 73, 82–3, 84
jinning pliers 55, 56
Judas tree *see Cercis siliquastrum*
Juniperus (juniper) 16, 25, 59,
    74, 82, 84, 114, 185, 186,
    194, 197
    cuttings 63
    J. chinensis 17, 62, 72, 83,
        85, 114, 116, 169, 181,
        189, 214, 232
    air layering 67
    pruning 91
    root pruning 87
    sharimiki 85
    J. communis 214
    J. davurica 17

Elm and rhododendron styled into different bonsai sizes

J. horizontalis 'Green Carpet' 100
J. procumbens 17, 214
J. p. 'Nana' 120
J. rigida 16, 214
J. squamata 17

K

kabubuki or kabudachi (clump)
   136–9
Kamakura period 11, 168
kanuma 71
Kasuga Shrine 11
kengai (cascade) 102–3
key features 23
Kirishima azalea see
   Rhododendron obtusum
   'Amoenum'
kiryu 71
knives 62, 64, 66, 86
knob cutters 54, 57
Korea 10, 12
Korean hornbeam see Carpinus
   laxiflora
kumquats 191

L

labels 164–5
lady's ear drops see Fuchsia
lanterns 164, 180
Larix (larch) 16, 25, 189, 243
   L. decidua 22, 23, 51, 60,
      106, 214
   L. kaempferi 9, 33, 50, 60, 216
   pruning 78, 79
leaf shears 57
leaf-cutter bees 237
leaves 60, 74, 197
   defoliating 76–7
Leonardslee Gardens, West Sussex,
   England 177
Lespedeza bicolor 216
lichens 166
lifting plants 58
light 143, 155, 170, 174, 176
lightning strike 84
Ligustrum 59
literati (bunjin) 126–7
   Larix decidua 51
   pruning 78
Lonicera 59
   L. nitida 216
   L. pileata 216
love tree see Cercis siliquastrum

M

maidenhair tree see Ginkgo biloba
maintenance 18, 225, 232–5
   tools 55, 56
Malay banyan see Ficus microcarpa
Malus 16, 188
   autumn 196–7
   M. cerasifera 24, 46, 197
   M. floribunda 186, 188, 216
   mame 20, 21
maples see Acer
matting 27, 164
Maule's quince see Chaenomeles
   japonica
May see Crataegus
Meiji period 169

Close pruning of a Cryptomeria japonica

mildew 238
Miscanthus 166
money plant see Crassula
   arborescens
Morus alba 217
moss 98, 124, 165, 166
mould 239
mountain pine see Pinus mugo
moyogi (informal upright) 28, 30,
   33, 36, 38, 42, 45, 46, 48, 50,
   94–7
Muramachi period 168
mycorrhiza 86
Myrtis communis (myrtle) 18, 19,
   150–1, 217
   bonsai 150–1

N

Nagasaki crab apple see Malus
   cerasifera
Nandina domestica 18, 34, 217
needle juniper see Juniperus rigida
needles 60
   pruning 74
negari (exposed root) 134–5
nejkan (twisted trunk) 132–3
nettle tree see Celtis bungeana

O

O'Neil, Denis 28
oak see Quercus
Olea europaea (olive) 44, 191, 217
Ophiopogon planiscarpus
   'Nigrescens' 166, 167
Oriental hornbeam see Carpinus
   laxiflora
outdoor bonsai 16–18, 24, 200,
   227, 228
outdoor displays 176–81

P

Parthenocissus 182
peach leaf curl 268
pedunculate oak see Quercus robur
Penisetum 166
penjing 10, 168, 175

pests 61, 225, 236–7
Picea 74
   P. mariana 217
   P. m. 'Nana' 34
pinching out 75, 76
Pinus (pine) 14, 16, 71, 80, 82,
   84, 114, 126, 185, 186, 189,
   194, 197
   P. mugo 84, 132
   P. m. 'Pumilio' 122
   P. parviflora 22, 27, 42, 81, 86,
      178, 180, 181, 218
   P. sylvestris 14, 15, 30, 96,
      126, 218
   P. s. 'Jeremy' 94
   P. thunbergii 23, 38, 168, 175,
      218, 226
plants 9, 16, 203
   accent planting 166–7
plastic mesh 56
pliers 54, 55, 56, 84
plum see Prunus
Podocarpus 174
   P. macrophyllus 218
pomegranate 16
pomegranate see Punica granatum
pots 9, 10, 20, 27, 60, 155,
   156–9, 225
   maintenance 232
   preparing 87
Potter, Ken 44
potting 88
privet see Ligustrum
procumbent juniper see Juniperus
   procumbens
propagation
   air layering 66–9
   cuttings 62–3
   grafting 64–5
   seed 60–1
pruners see secateurs
pruning 58, 72–5
   annual pruning 74
   autumn 197
   root pruning 18, 86–7
   shaping by 78–9

spring 189
summer 193
tools 54
winter 200
Prunus 188
   P. cerasifera 219
   P. incisa 'Kojo-no-mai' 187
   P. spinosa 219
   P. yedoensis 219
Punica granatum 18, 219
Pyracantha 219

Q

Quercus (oak) 82
   Q. robur 61, 220

R

raffia 80
raft (ikadabuki) 116–19
rakes 56, 88
refining techniques 233
repotting 18, 55, 87–9
   Acer palmatum 68–9
   spring 189
   summer 193
   winter 200
Rhododendron 16, 98, 191–2
   summer 190–1
   R. indica 220
   R. i. 'Komei' 42, 45, 58, 59
   R. obtusa 220
   R. o. 'Amoenum' 37
   R. racemosum 'Ginny Gee' 104
rock landscape
   Ulmus parvifolia 34
rock plantings 10
rocks 162–3
root grafting 64
root hooks 56, 86
root pruning 18, 86–7
   spring 189
   summer 193
   winter 200
root shears 56
root systems 58, 62, 66, 68, 69,
   70, 86, 91
root-in-rock planting (ishizuki)
   120–1
   Picea mariana 'Nana' 34
root-over-rock (sekijoju) 122–5
   Acer buergerianum 41, 46
   Acer palmatum 'Deshojo' 36
rooting powder 62, 64, 66
Royal Horticultural Society 24, 25,
   182, 183, 162
rust 238

S

sacred bamboo see Nandina
   domestica
Sageretia theezans 18, 19, 152–3,
   164, 171, 220
   bonsai 152–3
Saigyo Momogatari Emaki 11
saikei, Nandina domestica 34
sambon-yose (triple trunk) 106–9
Samurai 168, 169
sandstone 162
Satsuki azalea see Rhododendron
   indica 'Komei'

Sawara cypress *see Chamaecyparis pisifera*
saws 57
scale insects 236
scissors 53, 54, 56, 57, 62, 72, 78, 86
Scots pine *see Pinus sylvetris*
seasons 185
secateurs 54, 72
seed 60–1
seed trays 60–1, 62
sekijoju (root-over-rock) 36, 41, 46, 122–5
semi-cascade (*han-kengai*) 100–1
  Ulmus parvifolia 51
Serissa foetida 18, 172, 175, 222
shakan (slanting) 37, 98–9
shaping 18
  pruning 78–9
  wiring 80–1
sharimiki (driftwood) 33, 128–31
  creating 84–5
shohin 20, 21
shoots
  pinching 75
  pruning 73, 74
shows 172, 182–3, 225
shrubby honeysuckle *see Lonicera pileata*
shrubs 9, 16–19
side cutters 54, 57
sieves 57, 88
silverbells *see Styrax japonicus*
Sisyrinchium 166
sizes 20–1
slabs 162–3
slanting (*shakan*) 98–9
  Rhododendron obtusa 'Amoenum' 37
slate 162, 164, 169
sloe *see Prunus spinosa*
slugs and snails 61, 237
snowbell *see Styrax japonicus*
societies 9, 12, 169
softwood cuttings 62
soil 9, 18, 60, 62, 66, 70–1
sokan (twin trunk) 28, 104–5
spatulas 56
specialist tools 55, 56–7
sphagnum moss 66, 68, 70
spraying 18, 170–1, 239
spring 59, 62, 66, 185, 186–8
  care 186, 240–1
  key tasks 189
spruce *see Picea*
stands 27, 155, 160–1, 172
  outdoors 176
stones 164, 166
  suiseki 168–9
storing plants 58
styles 9, 91
  broom (*hokidachi*) 41, 44, 48, 140–1
  cascade (*kengai*) 102–3
  clump (*kabubuki*/*kabudachi*) 136–9
  driftwood (*sharimiki*) 33, 128–31
  exposed root (*neagari*) 134–5
  formal upright (*chokkan*) 92–3
  group or forest (*yose-uye*) 37, 38, 44, 49, 110–13

informal upright (*moyogi*) 28, 30, 33, 36, 38, 42, 45, 46, 48, 50, 94–7
literati (*bunjin*) 51, 126–7
raft (*ikadabuki*) 116–19
root-in-rock planting (*ishizuki*) 120–1
root-over-rock planting (*sekijoju*) 36, 41, 46, 122–5
semi-cascade (*han-kengai*) 51, 100–1
slanting (*shakan*) 37, 98–9
triple trunk (*sambon-yose*) 106–9
twin trunk (*sokan*) 28, 104–5
twisted trunk (*nejkan*) 132–3
windswept (*fukinagashi*) 114–15
styling a young plant 59
Styrax japonicus 222
Suiko, Empress Regent 168
suiseki 168–9
summer 62, 66, 68, 82, 84, 190–2
  care 190, 241–2
  key tasks 193
suppliers 12, 248–9

T
tables 172
Taxus baccata 222
techniques 53
temple juniper *see Juniperus rigida*
Theophrastus 166
thread grafting 64
Threadgold, Susan 51
three-lobed maple *see Acer buergerianum*
tokonoma 11, 172–3
Tokyo cherry *see Prunus yedoensis*
tools 553, 4–7
  repotting 88
  root pruning 86
top-dressings 70, 165
training pots 68
tray landscapes 10

tree of a thousand stars *see Serissa foetida*
trees 9, 14–15, 16–19
  maintenance 232–3
trident maple *see Acer buergerianum*
triple trunk (*sambon-yose*) 106–9
trunks 22, 23, 64, 65
turntables 55
tweezers 56, 62
twin trunk (*sokan*) 104–5
  Acer palmatum 'Ukon' 28
  pruning 79
twisted trunk (*nejkan*) 132–3

U
Ulmus 16, 140
  U. glabra 222
  U. parvifolia 7, 24, 25, 34, 51, 155, 170, 171, 223
  U. procera 30, 165, 223

V
variegated weeping fig *see Ficus benjamina* 'Variegata'
verticillium wilt 238
vine pruners 56, 73
vine weevils 236

violets 166
Virginia creeper *see Parthenocissus*

W
walls 176, 180
watering 88, 228–9
  autumn 197
  spring 189
  summer 193
  winter 200
weeping fig *see Ficus benjamina*
wen cutters 54
white mulberry *see Morus alba*
wild flowers 166
wind chimes 180
Windsor Castle 12
windswept (*fukinagashi*) 114–15
winter 68, 198–201
  care 198–200, 243
  key tasks 200
winter jasmine *see Jasminum nudiflorum*
wire 24, 54, 55, 70
wire cutters 54–5, 57
wiring 80–1
  autumn 197
  spring 189
  summer 193
  tools 54–5
  winter 200
Wisteria 16
  spring 188–9
  W. floribunda 223
  W. sinensis 223
witch hazel *see Hamamelis* x *intermedia*
wood gouges 57
wound sealer 72, 78–9
wych elm *see Ulmus glabra*

Y
yew *see Taxus baccata*
Yew Tree Potters 41
yose-uye (group or forest) 37, 38, 44, 49, 110–13

Z
Zelkova serrata 41, 44, 49, 164, 194, 195, 223
Zen 168

*English elm (*Ulmus procera*)*

*Common beech (*Fagus sylvatica*)*

Plant Hardiness

Each of the plants in this book has been given a plant hardiness rating (for European readers) and a zone range (for readers in the United States):-

HARDINESS RATINGS
Frost tender Plant may be damaged by temperatures below 5°C (41°F).
Half hardy Plant can withstand temperatures down to 0°C (32°F).

Frost hardy Plant can withstand temperatures down to -5°C (23°F).
Fully hardy Plant can withstand temperatures down to -15°C (5°F).

PLANT HARDINESS ZONES
Plant entries in this book have been given zone numbers, and these zones relate to their hardiness. The zonal system used, shown below, was developed by the Agricultural Research Service of the U. S. Department of Agriculture. According to this system, there are 11 zones, based on the average annual minimum temperature in a particular geographical zone. When a range of zones is given for a plant, the smaller number indicates the northernmost zone in which a plant can survive the winter, and the higher number gives the most southerly area in which it will perform consistently.

As with any system, this one is not hard and fast. It is simply a rough indicator, as many factors other than temperature also play an important part where hardiness is concerned. These factors include altitude, wind exposure, proximity to water, soil type, the presence of snow or existence of shade, night temperature, and the amount of water received by a plant. Factors such as these can easily alter a plant's hardiness by as much as two zones.

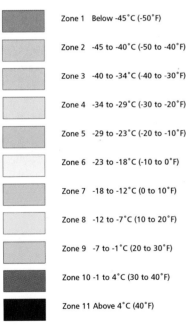

Zone 1 Below -45°C (-50°F)

Zone 2 -45 to -40°C (-50 to -40°F)

Zone 3 -40 to -34°C (-40 to -30°F)

Zone 4 -34 to -29°C (-30 to -20°F)

Zone 5 -29 to -23°C (-20 to -10°F)

Zone 6 -23 to -18°C (-10 to 0°F)

Zone 7 -18 to -12°C (0 to 10°F)

Zone 8 -12 to -7°C (10 to 20°F)

Zone 9 -7 to -1°C (20 to 30°F)

Zone 10 -1 to 4°C (30 to 40°F)

Zone 11 Above 4°C (40°F)

Acknowledgements

Author's acknowledgements
I would like to thank my wife Ann for her very valuable help with the preparation of materials, proofreading and IT input; Robin and Jane Loder for the use of the facilities provided at Leonardslee Gardens, West Sussex, England; members of Bonsai Kai for allowing photography of their trees; Neil Sutherland for the majority of the photographs and for entering into the spirit of the project.

Publisher's acknowledgements
Most of the photographs in this book were taken by Neil Sutherland. Other images were taken by Peter Anderson, John Freeman and Steve Wooster.

Unless listed below photographs are © Anness Publishing Ltd.
t=top; b=bottom; c=centre; r=right; l=left
Garden World Images: 220bl, 238tr, 239tl; **Ken Norman**: 44t, 97, 190br, 195b, 196t, 196b, 243bc; **Science Photo Library**: 24b, 178b, 180bl, 181bl, 186tr.

All materials, plants and trees supplied by Ken Norman except where quoted: 24b, 157br, 162bl, 182tr, 182bl, 183t, 183b courtesy **Bonsai Kai**; 25b, 158t courtesy **Peter Christian-Lau**; 14br, 14bl, 15t, 15b courtesy **Leonardsleee Gardens**. Stands 169cl, 169bc, 169br by **Paul Smith**; 169tr by **Ian Smith**.